COME AND SEE
*An Insight into the Religious Thought
of Teilhard de Chardin*

COME AND SEE
An Insight into the Religious Thought of Teilhard de Chardin

Rev. Frances MacLellan,
M.A., M.Div., D.D.

Lancelot Press
Hantsport, N.S.

ISBN 0-88999-247-9

Published 1984

All rights reserved. No part of this book may be reproduced in any form without written permission of the publishers except brief quotations embodied in critical articles or reviews.

LANCELOT PRESS LIMITED, Hantsport, N.S.
Office and plant situated on Highway No. 1, ½ mile east of Hantsport.

CONTENTS

Dedication 6
Foreword 7
Acknowledgements 9
The Prologue: An Invitation 13
The Mid-Twentieth Century Universe 17
The Truth for Teilhard: A Summary of his Thought 34
The One and Only Foundation: The Cosmic Christ 54
The Seamless Robe: Creation, Incarnation,
    and Redemption 70
We See Jesus 90
His Garment of Flesh: The Church 131
A New Formula for Holiness
    Part 1: The Christian Life 154
A New Formula for Holiness
    Part 2: Especially for Sufferers 179
A Viewpoint from which Everything is Bathed in Light
    Part 1: Looking at Theology 201
A Viewpoint from which Everything is Bathed in Light
    Part 2: Looking at Church Life 215
Appendix: The Smiling Scientist 224
Bibliography 257

To the greater glory of God

FOREWORD

"Then felt I like some watcher of the skies
When a new planet swims into his ken;
Or like stout Cortez, when, with eagle eyes
He stared at the Pacific — and all his men
Looked at each other with a wild surmise —
Silent, upon a peak in Darien."

Only these words of the poet Keats about his feeling on first looking into Chapman's Homer express how I, a minister of the Christian Church, felt when, in 1965, I read my first book by Teilhard de Chardin, *The Phenomenon of Man*.

Although there were more pages in it I did not understand than I did, what I read so excited me, so deepened my faith and widened my vision of the greatness of God and his work, that I burned to have others share my experience.

It did not take me long to discover, however, that when I recommended Teilhard even to my colleagues, the majority confessed they found him too hard going. What chance of catching the vision was there then for those others about whom I was even more concerned, the searching people of my congregations and theirs? Only if I could help them understand what Teilhard was saying about the Christian faith.

However, for seven years the responsibilities of three multi-point pastoral charges and my home took all my time and energy. It was not until 1972 that I was able to take a two-year study leave to start the work in the libraries, lecture halls and quiet of college rooms at Oxford and Cambridge.

The task I had was a big one, for not only did I have to read all the then-translated works of Teilhard, but also —

because my scientific education had been terminated with freshman courses in chemistry and psychology in the mid-thirties — I had to try to update myself in these areas in order to be sure Teilhard's ideas were credible.

All that I discovered confirmed and strengthened my first impression. Here was a message desperately needed by those who were seeking for the meaning of life in this latter part of the twentieth century. Especially was it needed by the people for whom my heart had been growing increasingly heavy over the past ten years — the faithful, increasing by few, of the little congregations I had been serving. In their hearts these people were convinced that the faith of their fathers was the very Word of Life; yet, in a world so drastically changed since their parents' day, that faith no longer seemed intellectually tenable. Because of what their hearts told them they were holding doggedly on, supporting their churches in order to commend to the world what every new change seemed to prove to be irrelevant. No wonder for many the light and joy had gone out of their religion.

Because I know from experience that the vision Teilhard introduces can restore that light and joy, I have written my exposition of his thoughts, for ministers with responsibility for teaching and preaching, for those to whom we minister, and for all seekers after faith and hope. Especially have I written for all who, fearing that the changes of the last half of this century are eroding all they know to be most noble and necessary, are afraid to move into anything new and different.

There have, indeed, been changes, not only before this book was written but since. Since these are not part of the background which helped to form Teilhard's thought [as he died in 1955], I have not attempted to up-date the first chapter which is deliberately entitled "The *Mid*-Twentieth Century Universe," to warn those who are knowledgeable of later developments that these will not be found here.

For those who may wish to know about Teilhard the man, and his credentials, the last chapter deals with these and can be read any time without interrupting the development of the thought.

ACKNOWLEDGEMENTS

Mark Twain is reported to have said that all ideas are secondhand and while it takes thousands to bring them to fruition, only the last will get the credit. I am deeply conscious that this is the case here; I am indebted to all I have encountered in the whole of my life.

However, there are those who should be named, who have contributed consciously to this effort. First there is Dr. Antony Dyson, sometime principal of Ripon Hall, Oxford, without whose help and encouragement I could not have embarked on this project, a very busy man who has a deep and broad acquaintance with the works of Teilhard. He kindly read the early chapters of my work but is in no way responsible for anything found therein.

Because I am no scientist, I was very grateful to have the second chapter dealing with the subject read by knowledgeable people. These were Mr. Simon Spencer, who in 1973, when I was reading in Oxford, was working in the Department of Zoology, Oxford University; Mrs. Jane Mathison, Senior Lecturer in Zoology, North East London Polytechnic, and Dr. K.A. Joysey, Director and Strickland Curator of the University Museum of Zoology, Cambridge, all of England.

It has been very helpful to have a group of lay people in the church read, comment on and suggest improvements for my manuscript. I am indebted for these to Mrs. Ruth Bonang, Mrs. Gail Scott, the late Miss Dorothy Phillips, and especially Miss Evelyn Blois who gave me wise guidance in many areas, especially in the suggestion of acknowledging in the title the very limited and personal nature of this study.

No writer can get along without a typist, and for her work and patience I am extremely grateful to Miss Lillian

Mellish, also to her stand-in, Mrs. Shirley MacLean and to an unnamed Trinidadian who not only managed to switch from oil to theology, but dealt efficiently with hearing that theology by dictaphone in a Canadian accent! Finally, I acknowledge my debt to the Halifax Regional Library reference staff and especially their coordinator, reference services, Miss Ellen Webster.

Nothing I have been able to do would have been possible without the generosity of The United Church of Canada which not only set me free from pastoral duties for the two years I spent on research and writing in England, but also provided some financial help for my stay there. To my church I say a sincere "thank you."

And now seven years later, I have other people still to thank. First and foremost is the Second Mile Society whose generous award to me has made possible the publication of this book.

Once again I am indebted beyond measure to librarians. To those already named I would add the Killam and MacDonald Libraries of Dalhousie, St. Mary's University Library, and Library of King's College and especially the Library of the Atlantic School of Theology who gave me not only service but encouragement through the chief librarian, Mrs. Alice Harrison. In addition to these, friends in England have done searching and checking for me not possible here. The Hartnells of Wellingborough and the staff of the Teilhard Centre for the Future of Man have been so very helpful.

Nothing could have happened to the manuscript, however had I not had again the assistance of Mrs. Shirley MacLean who treated the work as if it were her own precious project and toiled away far beyond the call of duty.

What follows is surely not the work of any one person but a great company, most unnamed. The strengths are theirs, the weaknesses mine.

The author and publisher acknowledge with thanks the following, in permitting the use of copyright material:

Hugh Barbour for *In The Field With Teilhard de Chardin* by George Barbour; Collins Publishers, for *The Works of Teilhard, The Biology of Ultimate Concern* by Theodosius Dobzhansky; "Pierre Teilhard de Chardin as Scientist" in

Letters To Two Friends by T. Dobzhansky, *Teilhard de Chardin, A Guide To His Thought* by Emile Rideau, *Memories of Teilhard de Chardin* by Helmut de Terra, *God And The Unconscious* by Victor White, *Teilhard de Chardin, Album*, by Jeanne Mortier and Marie-Louise Aboux, *The Humanity of God* by Karl Barth, *Teilhard de Chardin, A Biography* by Robert Speight, *Teilhard de Chardin, Scientist and Seer*, by Charles Raven, *The Spirituality of Teilhard de Chardin* by Thomas Corbishly; *The Encyclopaedia Britannica* for material from "Geology," 14th edition (1972); Neville Braybrooke for *Teilhard de Chardin, Pilgrim Of The Future* by Neville Braybrooke; A.D. Peters & Co. Ltd. for *Roots of Coincidence* by Arthur Koestler; George Allen & Unwin for *Physics and Beyond* by W. Heisenburg and *The Meaning Of The Twentieth Century* by Kenneth Boulding; Clarendon Press for *Concordant Discord* by R.C. Zaehner; Geoffrey Bles Publisher for *George MacDonald, An Anthology* by C.S. Lewis published by Collins; The Crossroads Publishing Company for *Letters From Paris* by Teilhard de Chardin; Burns and Oates Ltd, for *The Faith Of Teilhard de Chardin* by Henri de Lubac and *Inspiration In The Bible* by Karl Rahner; Cambridge University Press for *The Mysterious Universe* by Sir James Jeans, *Science And The Modern World* by A.N. Whitehead, *Creative Aspects of Natural Law* by R.A. Fisher, *The Nature Of The Physical World* by Thomas Eddington, *Biology And The Soul* by John Hick; Darton Longman & Todd Ltd., for *Teilhard Reassessed* by Hanson (1970); Faber and Faber Ltd. for *The Confidential Clerk* by T.S. Eliot; Brooks/Cole Publishing Co., *The Human Dilemma* by Rollo May; The Catholic University of America for an extract from the *New Catholic Encyclopedia* Vol. 13; Chatto & Windus, the Hogarth Press for *The Sixth Sense* by Rosalind Heywood; Hodder & Stoughton for *The Soldier's Armoury*, June 30th 1973; the Linnaen Society of London for an extract from *Proceedings* Vol. 167, pt. 1; Thomas Nelson and Sons for *Inspiration In The Bible* by Karl Rahner; Littlefield Adams & Co. for *Out Of My Later years* by Albert Einstein; Lutterworth Press for *Concerning Teilhard and Other Writings On Religion And Science* by Bernard Towers; Methuen & Co., Ltd. for *The Future of Man* by Peter

Medawar and *Science, Men and Morals* by W.H. Thorpe; Oxford University Press for *Science and The Christian Experiment* by Arthur Peacocke and *Science and The Christian Belief* by C.A. Coulson; The Open University Press for *Unit 4 S100 Science Foundation Course*; Mrs. Elizabeth Partridge for *The Chaplet of Grace* by Basil G. Partridge; Bodley Head for *The Sword In The Stone* by T.H. White; Mr. Norman Hart ed. *Reform* for *Editorial*, Nov. 1972; The Teilhard Review for "The World Vision of Teilhard de Chardin" by F.G. Elliott, "Teilhard and Monot" by T. Dobzhansky, "Theological Methods in an Evolutionary World" by Karl Schmitz-Moorman, The Oklahoma Geological Survey for *Oklahoma Geology Notes* by Arthur J. Meyers and J.L. Kulp; SCM Press Ltd. for *Basic Questions In Theology* by W. Pannenburg, (also Westminster Press) University Press of America Inc. for *The Foundations of Metaphysics in Science* (1938) by Errol Harris; Burnes & Oatest Ltd., for *Teilhard de Chardin* by Claude Cuenot.

Burnes & Oatest Ltd., for *Teilhard de Chardin* by Claude Cuenot.

THE PROLOGUE AND INVITATION

On Easter evening, April 10th, 1955, there died in New York City one of our century's most original and influential thinkers, Pierre Teilhard de Chardin.* Although his church had refused him permission to publish anything, his speeches and letters, private papers, and most of all his wide personal contacts profoundly influenced the thinking of his time, especially the thinking of the young.

Indeed, it was because of this appeal to youth that he had had to live all his adult life in China, exiled from his beloved homeland, France. The church authorities feared that he would lead the young astray through the ideas he had worked out as he wrestled to reconcile his beloved science and his equally beloved religion.

Many times his superiors warned him to confine himself to the science in which he had earned considerable fame, and to leave religion alone. But he insisted on being both scientist and theologian; and his refusal to keep the two disciplines in thought-tight compartments enabled him to carry out what he saw as his real ministry, to help back to faith people who had discarded Christianity because they felt they could no longer hold it with intellectual honesty.

Among the many he so helped were the sculptor, Lucille Swan and a Jewish friend of hers. Both of them he returned to the faith of their forebears. Another was the scientist Max

---

* Teilhard is pronounced TA-Yar. This is his surname; de Chardin, pronounced [Shar-den] designates the branch of the Teilhard family and is never used alone as his name.

13

Begouen who later wrote down how he had felt after Teilhard spent an evening with him explaining his conception of the Christian faith. "I came to life like Lazarus coming out of the tomb . . . It was a dazzling experience which soon changed my life from top to bottom." (*Frontier*, Vol. III Autumn, Editorial)

It is not surprising that the Jesuit, Teilhard, had this touch. He admitted that he felt much more at home in the clothes he wore on field trips in Asia and Africa as a paleonologist than in the clothing which priests invariably wore at that time. And because his work took him more into the company of scientists than of clerics, he early felt himself to be called to be 'an apostle to the "Gentiles"' as he called his co-workers and friends in the skeptical scientific community.

For many of these, and the countless more who came to know his ideas through the books which came on the market after his death, first in their original French and then in translation into at least fifteen languages including Russian, "He was one who opened doors," says Begouen.

Especially to those who are groping for the door of a faith by which to live because they find themselves unable to enter the one they grew up with, I call, with Teilhard, "Come and See."

Come and see a new way of looking at the truth you have been taught in the light of what you have learned as worked out by a brilliant and original thinker who knew from experience the dilemma in which you may be dwelling.

His ideas may not give you answers, for, as the editor of *FRONTIER* puts it, Teilhard "was not one who brought things to a conclusion." But he will offer you new ideas and concepts with which to do your own thinking from a new direction. This is what he wanted to do. He once said that he would feel that he had succeeded only when he was superceded.

Because Teilhard's style has proved difficult for many to read and has closed his open door to them, and because his religious ideas are scattered through the many volumes occupied by his papers and letters, I have been so bold as to try to make these ideas easier to follow by passing them through my own very ordinary mind. I have also included in my thinking ideas and illustrations Teilhard's writings have started in me.

AN INVITATION

"This is not a thesis, but a . . . summons . . . The summons of a traveller who has left the road and so by chance has arrived at a viewpoint from which everything is bathed in light, and calls out to his companions, "Come and see!"

Teilhard de Chardin
ACTIVATION OF ENERGY, last word as
in De Lubac, CORRESPONDENCE

Jesus said, "I go to prepare a place for you."
John 14:2
"And they said to him, "Rabbi (which means 'Teacher') where are you staying" He said to them, Come and see."
John 1: 38-39

Chapter 1
THE MID-TWENTIETH CENTURY UNIVERSE

"Take the world, honestly, as we see it today in the light of reason; not the four-thousand-year-old world, surrounded by its eight or nine spheres *for which the theology of our textbooks was written*, but the universe which we can see organically emerging from a boundless time and space,"[1]

Teilhard de Chardin was a scientist and the particular contribution which he had to make came out of a lifetime of struggle to enable him to hold both his science and his faith. In order to understand him one needs at least some knowledge of the findings of modern science as Teilhard knew it in the mid-twentieth century.

If one has kept up with the developments in science in the last fifty years, this chapter will undoubtedly not be necessary. Indeed there have been remarkable developments and advances in the ten years since this chapter was written.

However if one comes to Teilhard as I came to him ten years ago, with the background of a very elementary scientific education received nearly a half-century before, considerable up-dating is required. Indeed I spent almost half my year of research in preparation for this book reading popular books of science from various areas, for, as Teilhard's life shows, he was versed in more than one science. I have tried to glean from this reading those details which have helped me in my understanding of what Teilhard has to say.

Some of the information which follows has come to light only since Teilhard's day. It is impossible for one like me to sort out which this is. However, I believe that does not matter; it is the opinion of the noted geneticist Dobzhansky that, though what Teilhard said is scientifically dated, since he lived in quasi-isolation and quasi-exile for more than a quarter of a century "present day views . . . happen to be even more favourable for the Teilhardian synthesis than were the views that he himself accepted."[2]

New Knowledge Of The Size And Stuff Of The Universe

In little over a century there has been an explosion in scientific knowledge not unequal in size to that of the atom bomb. This has affected our view of the universe. Instead of living, as people until fairly recently believed they did, in a fairly cosy universe of which, even though it was no longer thought to be the center, earth was at least a considerable part, we now know that our planet is only one member of a galaxy of one hundred thousand million stars. This galaxy is, in turn, only one of the millions in the universe. (Four million of those are now detectable from earth.) The universe is so enormous that distances in it can be measured only in light-years — the distance light travels in one year at three hundred thousand kilometers per second — i.e., almost ten million million kilometers. The moon, that now familiar body, is 1.25 light-seconds from earth. Since our television viewing has given us some idea how long it takes people to cover that distance, we can begin to appreciate the distances involved. This galaxy, a flattened disc of gas, dust and stars — our neighbourhood — is eighty thousand light-years across. In other words, the universe we live in has grown beyond all recognition.

On the other hand, our knowledge of the stuff of this universe has also altered, at least as drastically. Not so long ago we thought that the atom, earth's basic building block, was a tiny solid particle. Now we know that even its solidity is not solid at all. And as far as anything solid is concerned, Eddington, late professor of astronomy at Cambridge, writing in his introduction to "The Nature of the Physical Universe", makes plain what an illusion this is in his lively description of the desk on which he is writing. It really consists, he says, almost entirely of empty space sprinkled with unimaginable tiny specks, electrons whirling about their nuclei but separated from them by distances a hundred thousand times their own size.[3]

Not just seemingly solid desks, but all forms of matter have been found to be just as insubstantial. The ninety-odd elements of chemistry, called elements because they are the foundation stones of all material things, have been found to be made out of the same insubstantial building blocks in different combinations, "parcels of compressed energy packed and patterned according to certain mathematical formulae".

Energy is fundamental to the universe; light, heat and radiowaves are energy; it is the energy of sunlight that allows plants to grow, and humans to live. It is the energy of our food that we use in work, in thinking, in seeing. It is the flow of energy through the earth from the sun and then back into space that organizes and upholds life on earth.

In order to measure, study, and compare building blocks of the universe, scientists have to resort to using space-time. That means, as it does when they are dealing with the vastness of the universe, their measure will be the lenght of time taken to cover a given space. In this instance, however, they are dealing not with the unimaginably large but with the unimaginably small, with the "quantum". And "unimaginably" is the right word.

Heisenburg, great research physicist, warns that to conjure up a picture of these elementary particles or to think of them in visual terms is wholly to misrepresent them.[4] Having referred to this in his book *The Roots of Coincidence*", Koestler remarks, "Modern physics seems to obey the Second Commandment, 'Thou shalt not make unto thee any graven image' — either of gods or of protons."[5]

Thus that science which deals with the physical universe speaks now largely only in mathematical formulae about things which are invisible, and which can only be known as they are experienced. Nor can they ever speak of these invisible components of the universe in one way alone, for the "specks"

19

which Eddington pictures in the vast empty space of his desk have turned out to be not things but processes which can't be looked at in one way. They behave as unsubstantial waves or as massive particles.[6]

Yet we do experience solidity in our contact with material things. We stub our toes against very solid furniture. This solidity, however, when examined by physicists, turns out to be due to something equally intangible — forces. There is the very familiar, though invisible force of gravity which, as Newton discovered, both draws the falling apple to the ground and keeps the planets swinging in their orbits. And though this discovery was made nearly three hundred years ago, a note with Newton's papers in the British Museum states that it is a process still fundamentally as mysterious as it was then. We know that it affects all bodies and that it acts to draw them together, center to center, as if all their mass were concentrated in their center. Einstein has shown that it is a property, not of bodies themselves, but of the space these bodies occupy, and yet, at the same time, that those bodies affect the properties of that space.

There are other forces present within the center of the atom. "Within the nucleus of the atom there is a repulsive force ... which is a million, million, million, million, million, million times greater than the gravitational pull ... therefore there must be a very strong attractive force within the atom. ... It must act on both protons and neutrons as nuclei are stable."[7]

This is the force with which we have become familiar from the energy released in nuclear fission, in the form of nuclear heat, or atomic explosion, depending on the conditions, and it is human beings who decide the conditions.

Possible Sources Of The Stuff Of The Universe

Where did these building blocks come from, these dwelling-places of such enormous energy? It seems from present knowledge that they were born from hydrogen, the lightest and most abundant element in the universe, under the influence of these forces of attraction and repulsion.

By gravitation hydrogen was drawn into spirals. In their center through gravitational contraction heating took place to temperature ranges through which the atomic fuel was transformed into heavier elements. The reactions at the same time released light, and a star was born. After a time, as the process continued, the forces of repulsion caused the star to explode, releasing a stockpile of elements. These in turn formed the starting point of new stars and the process went on under varying conditions to produce elements of progressively higher atomic weights. Thus, in the birth and death of stars, all the known elements, the chemically indivisible substances that are the basic materials of the solar system, were born, beginning over five thousand million years ago.

Everything, from rocks to plants, from water to people, is composed of these same basic elements. As F. G. Elliot, a bio-chemist who has done research on the electro-chemistry of proteins, puts it, "Between the atoms of carbon that are found in the carbon anhydride of the atmosphere, in the carbonate of minerals, in a molecule of sugar or protein and the tissues of our organism, there is no real difference. The only distinguishing feature is to be found not in the atom, but in its surroundings, that is, in the other atoms round about, which form a complex in which it is held, just as a letter becomes quite different depending on the word in which it is used."[8]

The Importance of Organization In The Universe

Here we see another interesting thing about our universe. What distinguishes one material from another is not its basic components, but its organization. It is the forces of attraction and repulsion which are found in all the universe which, under differing circumstances, form the variety of the basic elements and organize them in turn into all the forms which we know and experience.

An absolutely fascinating exhibit which shows some of this at work is to be seen in "The Story of Earth", a permanent exhibit in the Geological Museum in London. Here in pictures, movies, slides, models, we see and hear how the scientists conceive the birth of our planet and all that is on it. It is an exhausting experience to go through it. There is so much motion, so much intricate detail. There is also a marvellous, incredible continuity flowing through it all. One is carried from exhibit to exhibit so logically and smoothly that one can really appreciate the remark of Sir James Jeans, "The universe looks more like a great thought than like a great machine."[9]

Another analogy which comes to mind is that of a river flowing inexorably. Certainly this is how Sir Alistair Hardy, the zoologist, pictures the story of life in his book, *The Living Stream*, which deals with biological evolution.

Unfortunately there are still some Christians who gibe at the term "evolution" and defend their position by pointing out that it is still only a theory. However, as Dr. John Habgood, scientist and bishop of the Church of England points out in his article on Darwin, "There is a stage in the development of some major scientific theories when they cease to be regarded as theories, and become unquestioned assumptions underlying a whole branch of science. This is now the status of the theory of evolution. Without it modern biology would be a shambles."[10] Perhaps we don't care about what would happen to modern biology; we are too concerned about what we feel is the shambles "evolution" has been making of religion when it has been charged with asserting that human beings are little more than "naked apes," that things have become what they are through mere chance, that what has governed survival in a ruthlessly destructive world is sheer brutality and aggressiveness, concepts that strike a blow at the fundamentals of the Christian faith. To people who have such fears, Habgood speaks further, " . . . despite the difficulties [evolution] is a potentially valuable source of theological insight and no real alternative is thinkable, either scientifically or theologically."[11]

When a man of stature in both the world of science and religion thus states that we have to live with the concept of evolution, it would be well for us to become better acquainted with it than we are. First of all, we should be aware that, since Darwin wrote *The Origin of Species*, which brought to the public that of which many scientists were aware, there have been many modifications of his theory and further discoveries which have made the idea of evolution less threatening to religion than many felt it to be.

Certainly it is based on the assumption that everything that lives has been "born," — that is, has its antecedents in the universe. It asserts that every living thing is related to every other and that the various species there are have developed from earlier forms, mainly in response to the challenge of their environment. As far as defining what evolution is, Dobzhansky says, "There is no satisfactory definition of evolution. 'Sustained change' comes probably as close as possible at present."[12]

Although the word "evolution" usually means biological evolution, we have already reviewed a process of change in the formation of the stuff of the universe from primordial hydrogen. There is also the sustained change from atom to molecule, to cell, to organism as the building blocks of the universe come together in more and more complex forms. One of these complex forms, the molecule DNA, we now know as the blueprint of life. DNA is the molecular basis of the genetic code. The molecule contains coded information on the nature of the organism, which, when replicated, can provide the blueprint for the construction of a new identical organism. Thus with the advent of the DNA molecule, life became capable of self-replication; that is, of reproduction. When this molecule emerged first, the stream of change had arrived at one of those threshhold moments when out of a certain degree of organization something entirely new was born. Let us now look at this matter of newness.

The Emergence Of The New, Including Man

A molecule is composed of atoms, but when atoms come together to form molecules they are no longer just a collection of individual atoms but an entity with new properties. What these properties are depends on the organization within the molecule which, in turn, depends on a number of other things, not least of all the environment. So it is also as molecules come together to form cells, and as cells do the same to form organisms. For instance, in that organism which we call the human body, the cells form organs. Each one of these not only has its own specific function, but also a life that is also so individual that it can be separated from the body and, under rather special conditions, can sometimes be transplanted from one individual to another. Yet the parts together constitute a whole, with properties distinctly different from, and greater than, just the sum of the parts.

Now "Man is the summit of *complexity*. For if it is true that the earth contains a larger number of atoms than man (10^{23}) a single man contains more different kinds of molecules than the whole terrestrial globe with all its minerals, and he is indisputably a more varied and unified complex."[13]

Within humans the most complex and highly organized part is that which is also the seat of their 'dominion' over all the rest — the brain — which has 7,000,000,000 nerve cells. The outer cover, the cerebral cortex alone, has forty thousand neurons per one seven-hundredth of a square inch, and each neuron has several hundred synaptic connections with other neurons.

It has, of course, been the size and structure of the skull which houses the brain which have enabled those attempting to trace the development of the human species to do their work. Brains, like all living tissue, soon disintegrate, but bone, given favourable conditions, endures. How long any one bone has endured we have now found out how to measure. Using radiocarbon dating, it is possible to date bone back to about 70,000 B.C., and using potassium argon dating on rocks associated with bones, it is possible to date back 500,000 million years.

What surely highlights the fact that our era is one of explosive scientific knowledge is that the sequence of discoveries which have led to the present state of knowledge of our beginnings is barely one hundred and fifty years old. In 1830 the discovery by a clergyman of flint tools and human remains in Devon led the discoverer to the conclusion that our species is as old as the fossil animals there.

At present it is estimated that humans as we know them emerged some 2,500,000 years ago. Behind them, of course, at dizzying distances in time were those furnaces of primordial hydrogen, but much, much nearer the branch of life called the mammals, a small branch of which were small insect-eating mammals. Tree shrews represent a survival of these. An offshoot of this branch was the primates, distinguished by large brains, grasping hands, and fingers with nails rather than claws. Monkeys are survivors of this group. At an early stage in the evolution of the primates (seventy million years ago) the demands of life in the trees resulted in a heightening of the senses of sight, and hearing, and touch took the place of smell as the leading sense. In connection with this development the cerebrum became enlarged. As the layer of specialized nerve cells forming the cortex or cover continued to increase in area, it became enfolded forming a complex pattern of convolutions and fissures.[14]

It was during this last period of development that the branch of hominids came off the primate branch (where humans and apes parted company, at least some five million years ago). One of the branches of this branch was Peking Man, in whose placement in the scheme of things Teilhard played a part. Other types of hominids, such as those whose fossil skulls and bones have been found in various parts of the world, were along this branch as well. And one of these branches was *Homo Sapiens*, the complexity of whose brain was earlier described. This is the sole survivor of the hominids.

The Importance Of Adaptation To Environment

During that account of the development of the brain you will notice the mention of "adaptation to life in the trees." Increasingly since Darwin's day scientists have become more and more aware of the part played by changing environment in the evolutionary process. There is, even now, a school of thought which thinks that behaviour plays its part as well.

Since Darwin's day there has been a re-discovery of the part played by mutations — those sudden departures from the parent type in species — in providing the raw material for evolution. In this realm we begin to come into contact with the terms "random" and "chance" for, as Dobzhansky points out, "Mutation is unpredictable except in a statistical sense . . . A gene can mutate in many ways but not in an infinite number of ways. Its mutational repertory is set by its structure, which in turn is the product of evolutionary history . . . The chance in mutation is blind, but it is neither 'pure' nor 'absolutely free'. The biological meaning of chance is that mutations happen regardless of whether they will be useful when they occur or ever."[15] The mention of the word "gene" here reminds us also that since Darwin's day there has developed the science of genetics.

The complexity of the process by which any human being comes into the world and the content of this word "random" are made clear by this description of "the genetic process by which each of us has been uniquely formed . . . Behind each of us there lies an astronomical number of other possible arrangements of the same genetic material . . . father's contribution — 300-600 million sperms — each one . . . unique . . . Only one of these . . . can win the race to the ovum . . . A single sperm, unsupported by its millions of companions, would not be able to make its way across the mucous area at the entry to the uterus, up the Fallopian tube, and through the membrane protecting the egg . . . Each sperm produces only a minute quantity of the enzyme which digests the material to be penetrated . . . hundreds of millions perish in enabling one of their number to continue in the life of the new organism . . . the sperm carries only half the total complement of human chromosomes . . . Each . . . egg(s) contains its own unique arrangement of chromosomes . . . out of this astronomical number of different potential individuals, exhibiting the kinds of differences that can occur between children of the same parents . . . a single individual comes into being . . . Thus the process includes . . . elements of randomness . . . not unpredictable in principle . . . but only . . . in fact . . . outside the scope of human predictability . . . the processes involved are so complex that their outcome is unpredictable in practice and in that sense random from the human point of view."[16]

What Is Really Meant By "Natural Selection"

Important in the process of evolution is "natural selection", once conjured up by as a bogey when seen as the poet described it as "nature red in tooth and claw." However, Dobzhansky speaks of it as an "anti-chance agent", describing its action as "a cybernetic device which transfers to the living species 'information' about the state of its environment."[17]

The Bible verse, "Many are called but few are chosen" would be a good text here. Certainly if every individual born into the world were to survive, life would long ago have buried itself in its own produce. On the human level alone one has only to look at a few generations of one's family tree to see what two individuals can start. The term which Darwin used to describe the law governing natural selection, "survival of the fittest", when it has been interpreted as exalting aggressiveness and brute force, has been seen as negating the value of every Christian virtue. But scientists have long since discovered that better than "fittest" would be "most adaptable." Those individuals and species survive which are most ready for change when change would be advantageous.

So, by these complex and marvellous processes, our species and each individual in it comes into being, the most complex of all living things. Looking back over that history of living things directly preceding us, in which we deal with branches of branches of branches, it must be plain that what has often been called the "tree of life" would more aptly be called a "bush". And the topmost shoot of this bush is the human who "... is not the center of the universe as was naively believed in the past, but something much more beautiful — Man the ascending arrow of the great biological synthesis. Man is the last born, the keenest, the most complex, the most subtle of the successive layers of life."[18] It is with these words from *The Phenomenon of Man* in his own translation that the eminent geneticist Dobzhansky chooses to conclude his book, *Mankind Evolving.*[18]

What conclusion can we draw from this wonderful process whose workings I have been able only to hint at in these pages? W. Russell Hindermarsh, an atomic physicist, commenting on the intricacies of the atom and the world of forces, writes, "... what as Christians we can certainly assert is that this marvellous world with its beauty born of symnetry and its intricacy born of simplicity... is the world which God created and to which he gave this inner cohesion and integrity."[19]

Modern Biology and Religion

John Hick, commenting on the marvels of the phenomenon of life and of the way in which each of us becomes a unique self, writes: "Our dependent status is ultimately traceable by religious thought back to the dependence of the entire natural order upon the creative will of God."[20]

Thus, despite very widespread popular opinion, Towers, British anatomist, insists, "There is nothing in modern biology which can be construed as essentially anti-religious in the way materialist philosophy must be."[21]

Now the strange part is that religion has never tried to explain itself except in terms of philosophy. Teilhard pled in vain with his church to do what he had had to do to satisfy his own need for integrity — re-interpret it in scientific terms. This does not mean that this is the only way it should be done, though it may well be for many during a period which is so scientifically oriented.

Certainly it does not mean that we must throw out anything of the faith or anything in the Bible because it cannot be scientifically "explained." What it does mean is that we come to terms with the truth that science — particularly physics right now — has come to realize, that to speak about the invisible and the non-material it is necessary still to speak in terms that are familiar to us. Far too many of the figures of speech of religion are couched in language which belong to a way of life long since gone — the world of slavery, of feudal lords, of kings and princes, nomads and primitive tillers of the soil. Our world now thinks in terms of the scientific advances outlined here, not least of all of a world in evolution.

At the moment religion is especially aware of the importance of people. "In scientific circles there is no longer any doubt as to whether or not man is a product of an evolutionary process" says Towers; "But there is a great deal of doubt as to ... whether it shows 'direction' ... whether or not there can be detected any 'meaning' in the evolutionary process."[22]

The area of meaning is the realm of religion. For a very long time science denied categorically that there was any place at all for such concepts as meaning or value in its discipline. Now it is not quite so sure. Teilhard became convinced from a lifetime in the world of science and of the study of the evolutionary process that there is in it both direction and meaning.

A Twentieth Century Time-Scale

Just before we look at these ideas, so that we can get our conception of time in line with Teilhard's, I would direct your attention to the following "Scale of Time," taken from the 1973 edition of the *Encyclopedia Britannica*, and a popular interpretation of this that follows. Because we are bounded in our thought by the familiar threescore years and ten, even though it has now been stretched to several more than this by modern advances in medicine, we still think in very small numbers compared with those which comprise the age of our species, let alone our earth.

Geologic Column And Scale Of Time[23]

(Ages increase from top downwards, as in a sequence of sedimentary rock.)

System and Period	Series and Epoch	Distinctive Records of Life	Began (Millions of Years Ago)
		CENOZOIC ERA	
Quaternary	Recent (last 11,00 years)		
	Pleistocene	Early man	2+
	Pliocene	Large carnivores	10
	Miocene	Whales, apes, grazing forms	27
Tertiary	Oligocene	Large browsing mammals	38
	Eocene	Rise of flowering plants	55
	Paleocene	First Placental mammals	65-70

Geologic Column And Scale Of Time (Cont'd.)

System and Period	Series and Epoch	Distinctive Records of Life	Began (Millions of Years Ago)
		PRECAMBRIAN TIME	
		Plants and animals with soft tissues, few fossils	Samples of isotopic dates
No known basis for systematic division			1,500* 1,900+ 3,200# 3,490@

*Schist from Clark County, Nevada.
+Gunflint chert from Canada.
#Basement rocks from Minnesota.
@Basement rocks from the Congo region.

Perhaps even more illuminating then the foregoing chart in this matter of time is a scheme published in *Oklahoma Geology Notes* in 1963. The geologic times scale, for purposes or comparison, is worked out in terms of a 365-day year. "The conversion factor used was one day equals approximately 12,329 million years."

There are discrepancies between the dates given for some of the periods between the Oklahoma chart of 1963 and the Britannica chart of ten years later. This is not surprising. There *is* no universal agreement on the exact dating of these geologic ages. Each new theory and find moves them one way or another. However, this will not really affect the use of this teaching aid in giving us an idea of the relations involved.

Geologic Column And Scale Of Time (Cont'd.)

System and Period	Series and Epoch	Distinctive Records of Life	Began (Millions of Years Ago)
		MESOZOIC ERA	
Cretaceous		Extinction of dinosaurs: appearance of floras with modern aspects	130

System and Period	Series and Epoch	Distinctive Records of Life	Began (Millions of Years Ago)
Jurassic		Dinosaurs' zenith, primitive birds, first small mammals	180
Triassic		Appearance of dinosaurs	225

PALEOZOIC ERA

System and Period	Series and Epoch	Distinctive Records of Life	Began (Millions of Years Ago)
Permian		Conifers abundant, reptiles developed	260
Carboniferous	Upper (Pennsylvanian)	First reptiles, great coal forests	300
	Lower (Mississippian)	Sharks abundant	340
Devonian		Amphibians appeared, fishes abundant	405
Silurian		Earliest land plants and animals	435
Ordovician		First primitive fishes	480
Cambrian		Large faunas of marine invertebrates	550-570

According to the Oklahoma scheme, if the beginning of the Precambrian era, that is the formation of our solar system, took place at precisely the very minute the new year began — at one second past midnight, January the first — then the first appearance of life of which there are datable remains, that is in the Cambrian era, would not have been until November the 13th at four o'clock in the afternoon. The first reptiles and the great coal forests would follow on December the 6th, appearing at 1:04. The dinosaurs would appear at 3:44 on December the 14th, disappearing seven days later, on December the 21st at 1:12. Whales and apes would make their appearance at thirteen minutes and thirty-six seconds past three on the morning of December the 30th, while early humans would not put in their appearance until three minutes and twelve seconds past ten on New Year's Eve. In this comparison the period called "recent" would then occupy the time which remains in that amazing year — that is, one minute and ten seconds — for 10,000 years. Here is a breath-taking illustration for the familiar phrase, "time flies."[24]

Now, at last, for Teilhard's thoughts on all these things.

NOTES

1. Pierre Teilhard de Chardin, *Christianity and Evolution*, Fr. R. Hague (London: Collins 1971) p. 78.

   Theodosius Dobzhansky, "Teilhard de Chardin as a Scientist" in *Letters to Two Friends*, Teilhard de Chardin, Fr. R.D. 'Ounce (London: Fontana, 1968) p. 226.

3. Sir Arthur Eddington, *The Nature of the Physical Universe* (Cambridge: Cambridge University Press, 1948) Preface.

4. Werner Heisenberg, *Physics and Beyond* (London: Allen and Unwin, 1971).

5. Arthur Koestler, *The Roots of Coincidence*, (London: Hutchison, 1972) p. 53.

6. Koestler, p. 55f.

7. Open University, Science Foundation Course S100, Unit 4. Milton Keynes: The Open University Press, 1970) pg. 20.

8. F.G. Elliott, "The World Vision of Teilhard de Chardin," *The Teilhard Review*, Vol. 1 #2 p. 1.

9. Sir James Jeans, *The Mysterious Universe* (London: Penguin, 1937), p. 148.

10. Rev. John Habgood, "They Changed our Thinking: I Darwin 1809-82) and After," *The Expository Times* Vol. 84, #4, p. 100.

11. Habgood, 105.

12. Theodosius Dobzhansky, *The Biology of Ultimate Concern* (London: Fontana, 1967), p. 36.

13. Elliott, Vol. 1 # p. 11.

14. The British Museum of Natural Science; information given on a 1973 exhibit of the Evolution of the Brain.
15. Theodosius Dobzhansky, "Teilhard and Monot," *The Teilhard Review* (June 1973), p. 37.
16. John Hick, *Biology and the Soul* (Cambridge: Cambridge University Press, 1972), pp. 4-7.
17. Theodosius Dobzhansky, *The Biology of Ultimate Concern* (London: Fontana, 1967), p. 42.
18. Theodosius Dobzhansky, *Mankind Evolving* (New Haven: Yale University Press, 1962) p. 348.
19. W. Russel Hindemarsh, "They Changed Our Thinking: Albert Einstein," *The Expository Times* (April, 1973) Vol. 84, p. 199.
20. Hick, pp. 7-8.
21. Bernard Towers, *Teilhard and Other Writings on Science and Religion* (London: Lutterworth Press, 1966) p. 199.
22. Towers, p. 130.
23. "Geology," Encyclopaedia Britannica, 14th edition (1972), 10:176.
24. Arthur J. Myers from J.L. Kulp, *Oklahoma Geology Notes* Oklahoma Geological Survey (Norman, Oklahoma) p. 134 (1963).

Chapter 2
THE TRUTH FOR TEILHARD: A SUMMARY OF HIS THOUGHT

"*Truth* is simply the complete coherence of the universe in relation to every point contained within it. Why should we be suspicious of or underestimate this coherence just because we ourselvers are the observers? We hear continually of some sort of anthropocentric illusion contrasted with some sort of objective reality. In fact, there is no such distinction. Man's truth is the truth of the universe for man; in other words, it is simply truth."[1]

"Evolution, which offers a passage to something that escapes total death, is the hand of God drawing us to himself."[2]

Teilhard Finds Life Meaningful

In the previous chapter we have seen the vast complex process that is going on and has gone on in our universe for a much more enormous number of years than we had previously been able to realize. Surely this fact gives us a greater sense of wonder before the phenomenon of life, especially our own human life to which all this struggle has moved over these vast aeons of space and time. Now more than ever, we must feel the pressure of the age-old questions: Has life any meaning? Is there any purpose in this incredibly complex system? Has my own life significance at all in the seemingly impersonal, inexorable process going on? To these big questions to which not just religious people but all humankind at some time in their lives seek answers Teilhard gives an answer. Out of a life devoted to revealing just how complex the system is and where we are placed in it, he answers a confident, "Yes." Yes, human life has meaning and truly great significance on the whole.

There are, of course, those who would dismiss his answers as dictated by his assumptions as a priest. Knowing that this is so, he wrote a friend "I've been asking myself whether these views are not mere accommodation I have made so as to save my artifice a datum imposed on me by the Christian faith. But, in all truth, I don't think so. To be sure, perhaps I would never have arrived at this view of things but for my religious education . . . none-the-less . . . if, . . . now, all these solid props were to crumble, I could not see things otherwise than I do."[3]

The Old Demand For "Objectivity" Is A View No Longer Valid

There was a day when scientists, and the people persuaded by them, believed that unless a statement or views could be assumed to be made "objectively," with no prior convictions or assumptions about their subject matter being present in the one who put them forward, those views could be dismissed. Lately, however, more and more people are coming to realize that no one can come to any "fact" with a blank mind. Every thought, every observation, every assumption, is "born." All knowledge, as Michael Polanyi, scientist and philosopher, points out in his book, *Personal Knowledge*, is indeed personal. Anselm's statement, "I believe in order that I may know," is being more and more accepted and echoed. Belief is antecedent to knowledge and not knowledge to belief.

This, of course, as Teilhard knew well, does not mean that one can sweep away all need to make accurate and honest assessment of meticulously made observation. I have been at some pains to call witnesses to Teilhard's exquisite concern for accuracy in observation and insistence on material facts rather than opinions. Nevertheless, a "fact" is never a "bare fact", nor even just "material". A fact is a fact plus the person who sees it. When one goes to report, what one sees, how one sees it and what one says depends on the many things that have helped to form the way one thinks, what one thinks, and how one expresses oneself.

A rather amusing and interesting evidence of this appeared in letters to the editor in "The Times" of London during the spring of 1973. It concerned a controversy going on in England over the use of a common cup for the wine at communion. Two people signing their letters "biologist" entered into the fray. Dealing with the data of germs, wine and silver, one attested from his scientific knowledge that the reaction between silver and wine effectively killed any germs there might be on the cup, and the other was equally emphatic that it did no such thing. When doctors disagree . . . . . ?

DeTerra's judgement on Teilhard in *Memories of Teilhard de Chardin* that "he was a unique blend of personal revelation and scientific experience"[4] does not disqualify him from being believed. Indeed, Michael Polanyi, pursuing his thesis that we know more than we can say, tells of how he wrote to Albert Einstein regarding his discovery of the theory of relativity. Scientists have always pictured this as the result of carefully worked-out experiments bringing him to a logical conclusion. However, Einstein himself confirmed Polanyi's guess that he concieved the theory as an intuition, and only afterwards confirmed his hunch by experiment.[5] De Terra states his conviction that Teilhard worked this way. His ". . . scientific work gave the impression that he had already formulated his ideas and was only waiting for external observations to prove them well-founded."

What then was the intuition that Teilhard had?

The Basis For Teilhard's Assertion About Life's Meaningfulness — It Is Moving To A Goal

He believed that the direction of evolution is towards spirit — supremely towards the highest revelation of spirit in the risen Christ. Because of his "mission to the Gentiles" he generally called this Omega, a term they would find meaningful from their scientific background, and bearing no religious bias which might prejudice them against it.

He saw two recurrent movements in the great flux of

things — union and dispersion — the two great forces at the heart of the atom. And, even as the greater strength in the nucleus is the power of attraction which keeps the nucleus stable, so the greater power of attraction — the power of Christ — is causing all things to converge. What they converge on finally is God in Christ. From the risen Christ comes the power which draws the whole of the cosmos towards its destined end.

Up to humans this force worked with no conscious involvement of that which was to be united. With the arrival of Consciousness freedom of choice entered in. From then on it becomes conceivable that refusal to yield to the drawing power of Christ could prevent the final consummation. Like the Bible, however, Teilhard never entirely accepts the possibility of God's failure.

It was for this great end, the union of all things with himself in a voluntary union of love, that God created all things; or perhaps to put it even better, "He caused all things to create themselves." Because of the complete independence of everything in the cosmos, so that everything that is depends on everything that has been, the consummation — when it comes — gathers in all things. This movement is not an escape of the spiritual from the material, but a carrying forward of the material. Even that which is rejected as it seems in the forward movement, for example, all the mutations which seem simply to perish because they appear not to help forward the species, all the sperms which perish in the race to the ovum, have their part. They go, as Blair so well puts it "on the compost heap... what is left behind in that process is not rubbish to be burned. A compost heap makes useful material out of refuse; it remains dynamic."[7] Thus, in the words of Colossians 1:20, "Through him (Christ) God was pleased to reconcile to himself all things," and the "all things" is all-inclusive.

But let us go back and try to trace the general movement of Teilhard's ideas.

To Understand Something, Look Not At Where It Started But At Where It Has Arrived

It had been the custom up to his own time, Teilhard

asserts, to try to understand things by going back to their roots, reducing them to their smallest and most distant points. The result of this, under the scrutiny of modern science, has been to make people see themselves dwarfed by the magnitude of space on the one hand, the infinitude of size on the other, and by the over-reaching vastness of time. Moreover, to go back to beginnings is really not possible. In these enormous reaches, beginnings disappear.

Since with every major development something unexpectedly new appears, is it not (he asks) more reasonable to start, not with the first but with the latest, to see what are its distinctive characteristics? Then one can trace back to see if any path can be found leading up to this end.

Thus Teilhard begins with the latest. On the tree of life humankind is this latest comer. Their newness is thought — not just the power to think which other creatures have to some extent, but the power to know that they know. They are able to think in conceptual terms, which includes the unique and complex ability to make and use words. Humans are also, in other ways, the most complex of all living, and indeed, all things ever known. Physically they are not as specialized as many other creatures. Rather, they are more adaptable. Because of their power of thought, and ability to communicate and to manipulate, they are able to influence and shape their environment, one of the chief formative elements, you will recall, in the process of evolution.

Moreover they stand alone, and have stood alone at the tip of the leading shoot of evolution for at least 2,500,000 years. Since their emergence, there has been no branching out on the bush of life into further species from ours, as had always happened before. Having developed, humans, as we know them, spread all over the world. In the recurrent pattern of union and dispersal there was only this kind of dispersal, not divergence into sub-species, as had occurred at other levels. This makes it seem as if with these some kind of end had been reached.

Looking at the physical make-up of this species, therefore, again one looks at that which occurred last. This, as we have seen, was the enlarged and very complex brain. The enlargement had resulted in a coiling in on itself of the surface of the brain so as to make possible all the complex neural connections which lead to the expression of personhood. Now this is the element which is left over whenever scientists try to place us in some already existing category. What is new is, therefore, qualitative and spiritual rather than material. There is no previous category which will include us whole, which will not reduce us to less than we know we are. The emergence of the human therefore, Teilhard insists, is the appearance of a new phenomenon. What has made possible the newness has been an increase in the complexity of organization of what was already in the system. Is there here a clue to something that is going on all along? Is there here a law to be discovered?

A Study Of Some Late Arrivals Points To The Importance Of Organization

In the process going on in the universe there is a pattern of constant uniting, after there is a flying apart of the whole new unity. Immediately, through chance encounter of some of the particles with each other, there is a further union, this time producing a whole both richer and more complex than before. These movements are repeated over and over until, when a certain degree of complexity is reached, there emerges an entirely new quality. Indeed there is a transformation from one level of being to another. As an illustration of this process Teilhard uses the analogy of water and steam. When, under the influence of heat (energy), a certain complexity of the molecules of water is reached, water becomes steam — a gas rather than a liquid, an entirely new and different phenomenon. Nothing new has been added but what was already there has been organized into more complex arrangement so as to produce a new dimension.

This happened in the evolutionary process with the emergence of life. Fairly recently scientists have discovered that there is no clear dividing line between what is alive and what is not. The same elements are there; what seems to determine whether something is alive or not is not the component parts but their relationship. The virus, for instance, probably the most primitive form of life, seems to belong to the order of the inanimate when it is isolated. However, when it comes into relationship with living matter it is definitely alive. This is a fact Teilhard could not have known since it has been discovered since his time, but he realized that there was such a breakthrough from one state to another, with regard to humankind.

There is nothing in our physical composition different, as we have seen, from the most of the universe. However, under the influence of the basic stuff of that universe — energy, bringing about the complex organization of the brain — something new emerged. It is the ineffable quality of thought, the emergence of personality.

A Certain Degree Of Complexity Produces A New, More Independent Category

As he looked at the other great occasions in the evolution of the universe when something entirely new had emerged, life, Teilhard saw the same thing. In all pre-life, though uniting goes on of atoms to form molecules and these to form crystals, the degree of organization in inanimate things is quite simple compared with that exhibited by the first expression of life, the proteins. Here again, when a certain degree of complexity in organization was reached, a new emergence occurred. It was an emergence so new that a new category was created, a new form of expression had emerged — life.

Again the newness was in terms of qualities which had this in common with those which marked the distinctiveness in humans the quality of "consciousness." It is in this category — life — that we meet the phenomenon of adaptation to environment so important in the process of biological evolution. Moreover, as one goes up the tree of life where, working on the products of dispersion — mutation — natural selection brings about adaptation to environment in producing new species, one finds an ever-increasing degree of "consciousness," of freedom — as it were — from the dominion of that environment. We see it, for instance, in the ability of animals to move, whereas plants do not have this ability.

Thus Teilhard arrives at his theory of complexity-consciousness — i.e., that when a certain degree of complexity has been reached through the double movement of union and dispersion going on in the universe, the resultant product will exhibit a higher degree of self-determination or "consciousness." Living things are more independent than inanimate ones; thinking humans than non-reflective animals. Before Teilhard the appearance of life and thought had always been seen as "improbables." Teilhard's theory, according to the British anatomist, Bernard Towers, made things begin to make sense again.

Teilhard Believes The Process Is Going On — A Greater End

But Teilhard does not stop here. It is when he goes beyond this that more scientists fall out with him. Since he thinks evolution has produced personhood at its leading edge, and this is seen in rudimentary form in life, then the direction of evolution must be towards perfection of consciousness — that is, spirit.

But obviously this end has not been fully attained. We live not in a completed but a "becoming" universe. The same movement is still going on, the movement towards greater complexity of organization to make possible greater emergence of spirit. It is from this point of view that Teilhard looks at what is going on in the world of the twentieth century.

Evidence Of Complexity Arising In The Human Sphere

Physically, he points out, we are becoming more highly organized all the time. There is the increasing growth of our cities as people come together in closer and closer contact in order to make possible those things we demand for our standard of living. This includes not only the production of goods and services but the possibility of education and the growth of the arts. There simply cannot be a fine symphony orchestra, a viable live theatre, a ballet company, or a choral society without a certain density of population.

In order to make possible those things by which we hope to improve the quality of life for everyone, nations have to work more closely together in trade, economics, and politics. We have, in our time, a great growth of international groups of all sorts.

Modern means of transportation have obviously brought people closer together physically. More and more people, especially the young, are learning what the rest of humankind are like — not by books, but by actually living among them. This has had its results spiritually. The recent revulsion against war coming out of the Veitnam conflict was certainly in part the product of such world travel. Added to that, of course, was the influence of instant means of communication by which we are actually able to be in the midst of the horrors of conflicts. War can no longer be conceived of as glamorous. In this respect I found the exhibit at the Guards Museum in London very interesting. There, in the dress of soldiers during the life history of the Guards, one sees a sort of evolution of this attitude. Almost suddenly, it seems, at the beginning of the twentieth century, with the South African War, uniforms become drab and unflattering. The play-aspect of war is being stripped away gradually. It has taken the marvel of mass communication, however, to speed the process up.

The ability we have to express ourselves has produced a new medium of development — information. By feeding information into our "thinking machines" — computers — we are able to extend enormously our range of capabilities. An interesting new thing about this fuel — information — is that, unlike physical energy, it does not gradually disperse as does, for instance, heat or radiation, and disappear. Information increases with use. The more it is passed on the greater it becomes. Moreover, the more it is shared the more it draws together those sharing it, and the more it requires closer cooperation in order to produce more. It is itself a uniting thing.

Few people nowadays are unaware of the steady

increase in population. Teilhard observed that the very shape of the earth is compelling this increasing population to come together in more and more complex organizations to live. Obviously therefore, there is still a movement within the universe bringing individuals together.

Not All Uniting Is Creative: It Must Be Centered

But will this coming together result in a creative unity, the kind that brings into being a new whole?

That depends on the kind of uniting that is going on. As Teilhard looked at the crystal, the most complex form of pre-life, he saw that the formation was that of a chain. When he came to the cell where the boundary to life had been crossed, he found a circular form. The components of the cell have been drawn together, as it were, center to center. In humans we see this same infolding or centration in the structure of their brain, as the cortex, in order to fit into the skull, is curled around, making possible the complex connections of reflective thought. And it is in our thoughts that we individually become for ourselves the center of the universe. Herein lies the power of our "dominion" over all the rest.

But herein, too, lies our danger. Centering on ourselves, whether it be in egoism, in devotion to family, or to city or to nation or to race, or any of the various groupings which are essential to us is the source of great danger. Our very proximity to each other, or ingenuity, and exchange of information have here been made extremely dangerous to the continuation of the process. We need to be not just drawn together, but to some common center outside ourselves. This is the kind of uniting we see at work in the process before us. It is the strange quality of gravity. The very fact that there is the kind of movement that has brought individuals not only together but towards greater consciousness led Teilhard to conclude that there must be a single point which acts like a great "magnet," drawing all things towards greater consciousness. There must be a center acting on all other centers for the shape of things to be as it is.

This Center Must Be Personal Because This Is Man's Attainment

He called this center Omega. Since consciousness is what emerged when the complexity of organization became great enough, Teilhard concludes that there must be in everything what he calls a "within" — that is, a potential for consciousness. This must mean that Omega possesses consciousness in still higher form in order to pull to it all other centers. This then means that Omega must be personal, even super-personal.

There is also another important reason why Omega must be seen in personal terms. When humans became able to shape their own environment then one of the important factors in evolution passed into their hands, as we said before. If those who believe behaviour is another factor in evolution are right, humans would be even more in control of the movement. Whether or not it goes on then, becomes our responsibility — to consent, to desire earnestly, any union which will take place.

Certainly we will not give our wills to any kind of union which threatens what is unique in us, our personalities. The constant cry today, as we find ourselves in crowded cities, more and more organized in colleges, societies and nations, is that we are being de-personalized. More and more people are losing their sense of identity and seeking some way to stop becoming less than persons. Any kind of unity which will rob us of this precious quality we will resist. Indeed, any unity which would make people less than persons would be a backward step, since personhood is that which marked the emergence of humanity. However, in the stream of evolution, once a new break-through has been made there is no reversing the step.

The unity which people will work to further must be one which will make them more personal and draw them center to center with all others. Such a union would have to be a personal one, for only in the union of persons with persons under the power of love is each member of the union more completely a person; only with love are all those things which defeat union overcome.

Omega Must Be Able To Guarantee Change, And The Defeat Of Death

Thus from another direction Teilhard shows that Omega must be personal. It must have the power to change people's attitudes, to overcome their self-centeredness, to transform their animosities, and to be victorious over all that keeps them from being not only their highest selves but ready to form a new whole. They in their freedom must be willing to have this happen. Indeed they must work for it, putting forth all their energy to bring it to pass.

Because this is so, they must be convinced that they're not wasting themselves on something that will not endure. Omega must be able to guarantee that the struggle and sacrifice involved will not be in vain. Death must not have the last word. Teilhard was ever afraid of their losing the will to push on. Some of his most passionate passages are written regarding those he saw as the greatest danger to mankind, to the whole cosmos. The first of these were those who resist change, the pessimistic about the future, the fearful of the present. He was concerned that they would hang back and try to reverse the forward movement. The second were the apathetic. Of the two he feared the second more. The first would not be able to reverse the movement, although they would be lost to it, except in their contribution to the "compost heap." But the help and energy they could contribute would be lost to themselves. Apathy, however, was another matter. Since humans are now responsible for the forward movement, they must cooperate to set free the power that makes for motion. They must cooperate by faith, zeal and love. Should their contribution of energy fail, all would grind to a halt; indeed, all would fly apart under the power of dispersion into the nothingness of multiplicity from which all came.

The graffitti I once saw on a college wall in Cambridge would, I am sure, have made Teilhard's blood run cold, even as it expressed his conviction, "Due to a complete lack of interest, tomorrow has been cancelled." If humanity suspected that death would be the final end of all striving, Teilhard was sure they would not pay the price of effort involved in completing the great design. It was at this point, Teilhard believed, that humanism — great and admirable as he had known it to be in many of his greatest friends — was not enough.

Omega then must not only be personal, indeed suprapersonal — able to inspire love, to draw by love, to transform the human spirit, to unite — but it must be able to guarantee immortality.

Omega Must Be Identified With Christ

It is at this point that Teilhard had to draw on his religious education to find the one who would fulfill all these needs. Omega, he could only conclude, must be the risen Christ.

Because humanists with their passion for humankind have as their goal, "man as he was meant to be," Teilhard had high hopes for his beloved "gentiles." Where else would they find their perfect man except in Christ? Teilhard was confident that when their faithfulness to the highest and best has reached its goal they will find their path has led to the Christ whom Christians believe to be both the perfect human and the perfect revelation of God. Thus Teilhard's conviction that "all that rises must converge" was a fitting text to be printed on the medallion struck in his memory by the French mint.

The Future — The Formation Of A "Mankind"

It is clear, of course, that when Teilhard speaks of the future states into which the great movement forward is going, he must leave the role of scientist and adopt that which a writer in *Teilhard Re-Assessed* sees as his most characteristic one — that of prophet. Like the prophets of the Old Testament, it is through his observation of the flux of things in his own time, and his own experience, that there comes to him the word that he must speak.

Teilhard had had the privilege of being part of many international bodies of scientists and others, who were bound together by their enthusiasm, knowledge, skill, and interest in common projects. He had experienced, not only the need that each member of such a team comes to feel for the other — the oneness of mind and heart that develops in their relationship — but also the enhancement of knowledge and personality which takes place. In Peking, in New York, and in other places where he took his knowledge and skill to contribute to the advance of science, he had experienced a foretaste, as it were, of the next stage in the cosmic development he envisions — the formation of Mankind.

The Place Of The Church In This "Mankind"

For this union, of course, the influence of Omega is essential. It is, he insists, to be seen not just as some moral or legal force, but as biologically essential in providing the energy that has brought about creative union all along the way. In this union, however, as was not the case before, humans in their freedom have to cooperate. We must add our contribution of energy — the energy of faith, hope, and love. This is why apathy, cynicism, and pessimism are so deadly, so dangerous.

For, as energy within the complex had to reach a certain peak in order for life to emerge from pre-life, human from pre-human so within the complex "Mankind" the temperature must rise to make possible the new emergence. This time, however, the energy will not be physical but spiritual — faith, hope, and love. Above all, as Paul insisted, there must be love — love of the finest and highest passing into the very ecstasy of adoration. Then can come the glorious moment when union between Omega and Mankind can occur. The Book of Revelation speaks of this as a marriage, the analogy Teilhard has had all along in mind for personal union. Now the glorified Christ is clothed in his body, Mankind, which in that union is itself transformed into spirit.

In this last emergence the pioneer, of course, was Jesus. By his victory in life and death he not only passed through the barrier into this next stage himself, but he won the victory for all people. By his free choice as a man, by his work and, above all, by his death in perfect faith and love, he has broken through to begin a new species. He is the new Adam, the first-born of a new humankind. He has established a new line. Teilhard uses for this the scientific term "phylum," speaking of it as the "Christian phylum." Into this new phylum we are born, not by physical but by spiritual birth, even as Christ was. It comes about through faith by which the power of God is enabled to work within.

Teilhard, like others who have been members of working groups, had known the experience of oneness as a unit, presaging the coming of the next stage, "Mankind." So, too, he and others had had a foretaste of the final stage, the spiritual. Countless men and women have thrown themselves on Christ in faith and found themselves able to transcend themselves. They have been able to do and be more than they knew themselves capable of in their own power. At that moment they have had what the Bible calls "a pledge" of what is to come. When anyone is so at one with Christ, that person is, St. Paul says, "a new creation." This "new creation" Teilhard accepts literally and in accordance with the pattern he sees in all that is going on in the universe through all time.

The Final Steps — Union With Christ, Union With God

When humankind as a whole is drawn by Christ into unity with himself, the Parousia or Second Coming of Christ will have taken place. Teilhard gives this event the same place of climax it has in Scripture, an importance many small but lively groups of Christians have given to it. However, he has made it make sense, taking its place in the whole scheme of things.

There is yet one more step to be taken before all is complete. Not just humanity, but the whole of the cosmos, our dwelling place, was brought into being for Christ. Therefore, only by its union with him will he have his "fulness." (For this Teilhard uses the term used in the New Testament, the "Pleroma.") Then, as St. Paul says, "comes the end when he delivers up the Kingdom to God the Father."[8] Then the unceasing prayer of the church, "Thy kingdom come," will be answered and "God (will) be all in all."[9]

This is the vision of things that Teilhard puts forward in *The Phenomenon of Man*, and in other writings in which he goes beyond it and expands on it. This is the framework of his thought, woven of scientific observation and experience, of religious study and life.

The Pattern In Evolution Must Be Repeated In Personal Life

What he saw in the universe he sees in the personal interior life. His exposition of this is "The Divine Milieu." Just as the universe is within the influence of the risen and glorified Christ, moved by him through the energy of God, so the individual lives within God, "in (whom) we live and move and have our being."[10] All that keeps us from being aware of this, Teilhard insists, is our inability to see.

The sustained change we call evolution in the universe has its parallel in the interior, personal life. We must be continually on the move from where we are to where we are meant to be. Our goal is unity with God in that final creative union in which will be at once most perfectly ourselves, and in complete and perfect unity with God and with all others even as Christ has drawn us to himself in love.

Christ is drawing everyone as he is drawing the world, but we, being human must cooperate. We must ourselves strive for the finest and best in all our activities. This includes so-called "secular" activities as much as so-called "religious" ones. Teilhard is at great pains to insist that, because the perfection of the world is as much in God's plans as the completion of people, to do one's utmost in the world is to give God glory. This glory is finally complete only with the perfection of the whole universe. What distinguishes Christians who work for God in their daily life from those who work solely for the perfection of their task or out of devotion to that perfection is, Teilhard insists, only a matter of sight. Christians see all work as done for God; the non-believer is not aware of the divine partner nor of the final end of his work.

None must ever rest satisfied on the level which has been reached. For individuals, too, there is an "evolution." They must keep moving from one level to another. All are provided, as it were, with a personal spiral staircase with its landings. They must move from one to another without lingering on any one. Having reached one level, what would have been right and fitting for them to do or be at a previous level may not belong here. Each one has his/her own level so that no one has the right to stand in judgment on the conduct and life of another who may be at a different level. So, too, it is no good to regret "what might have been" or carry the guilt of what one has done earlier. Everything must be left behind, realizing that the present is "born" out of the past.

Movement Comes Through Activity And Through Acceptance

To move from one level to another demands a constant renunciation of what has been attained, a dying that one may live, a losing to find. This does not mean that what we had before found good is not good, simply that it is not now suitable. Teilhard is at great pains to take from Christian renunciation and asceticism any suggestion of a negative. He will have none of the teaching of renunciation for its own sake. One does not give up things because they are evil but because there is something better, more suitable, ahead. And it is ahead to which one belongs. This means a constant struggle. The desire in us for stability, for comfort, for pleasure is very strong. It has only been at great cost that we have arrived where we are. However, for us something much greater than pleasure is in store — the delight and joy of the perfection we can know only as we and God together bring God's work to its fulfilment.

God is to be discovered not just in the work which he and we do together — that is, in human activities. He is to be found in the work God does alone, of which we are simply the receivers. Teilhard calls these "passivities." These are the things which happen to us. They range from our heritage — biological, social, and so on — our place in the whole scheme of things, and the things which happen to us over which we have no control. As we see God also in these and accept them in loving cooperation, we come to know another source of joy and make, as it were, another spiral of our ascent. Just as we make our ascent both by what we do and what we relinquish as we move from one level to another, so we also do in the things we accept in faith and loving cooperation.

Thus we move when what happens to us seems to diminish rather than to increase our life. Such things are suffering, sickness, loss, death. Our part in these must be, first, to do our utmost to overcome them and not let them take our life from us. We must use every weapon we have to do this because these things threaten our integrity. But when we have done all we can and still are not successful in defeating the enemy, we must accept that God is doing for us what we must constantly be doing for ourselves — tearing us away from what is behind; for what lies ahead is more perfect. In this act of acquiescence we will also work for God.

Teilhard sees the process happening in the "diminishments of age" and, supremely, in death. In death — still the greatest enemy since it threatens all that has been attained — the great breakthrough can come. Emptied for the final union, "mankind" may be wholly united with Christ. And when that union has reached its final complexity, there can come the union with God.

This union is not to be confused with anything like the absorption into the "All" found in many Eastern religions. In these all individuality is lost in the whole. What Teilhard envisions is the same creative union he has seen in evolution, in which each part becomes more itself as it becomes one with the whole. Into each union, also, all that went before is brought by each individual. The analogy Teilhard uses for this union is human marriage.

The consummation which Teilhard sees for the individual, as for the cosmos, is not, as MacQuarrie charged in a lecture at Oxford, 1973, the old business of the final escape of spirit *from* matter. This is rather the transformation of matter in all its fulness into spirit. Spirit, according to the Teilhard view, could never have emerged without matter. Matter is vital to it, not to be escaped from and left behind but transformed and included, and this, as Blair's analogy of the compost heap reminds us, includes even that which was discarded as not helpful to further ascent.

Thus, as Scripture has always affirmed, *the purpose and end of everything is "the glory of God."* But Teilhard's theories transform that phrase from something suggestive of a selfish desire on the part of God to be adored by all to a desire for a joy and perfection of all that he has made. It is the fulfilment of the desire of all human beings, of all things. For this moment surely there are no more fitting words than the paean of praise heard by the seer, "Blessing and glory and wisdom and thanksgiving and honour and might be to our God forever and ever! Amen."[11]

NOTES

1. ed. Jeanne Mortier and Marie-Louise Aboux, *Album, Teilhard de Chardin*, (London: Collins, 1966) p. 138.

2. Album, 185.

3. Pierre Teilhard de Chardin, *Letters to Leontine Zanta*, Tr. B. Wall (London: Collins 1969) p. 87-8, LLZ.

4. Helmut de Terra, *Memories of Teilhard de Chardin* (Tr. Brown John) (London: Collins, 1964), p. 121.

5. Michael Polanyi, *Personal Knowledge* (London: Routledge and Kegan Paul, 1958), pp. 9-15.

6. Helmut de Terra, 121.

7. H.A. Blair, "Progress," *Teilhard Reassessed*, ed. Anthony Henson (London: Darton, Longman, Todd, 1970), pp. 97-8.

8. I Corinthians 15:24 (RSV).

9. I Corinthians 15:28 (as quoted by Teilhard).

10. Acts 17:28.

11. Revelation 7:2 (RSV).

N.B. Because of the large number of quotations from Teilhard's works and especially that readers may have immediate information as to the source of each quotation, once a quotation has been fully identified in the notes, the initials of that book and the page where the quotation is found will appear in the text. The identifying initials will be given for each book on its first full appearance in the notes... See above.

A full list of the Teilhard books used in this text also with these identifying initials is to be found on the first page of the Bibliography.

BIBLICAL REFERENCES
Except where otherwise noted all quotations from the Bible are from the Revised Standard Version (New York: Thos. Nelson and Sons, 1952).

Chapter 3
THE ONE AND ONLY FOUNDATION: THE COSMIC CHRIST

"I am deeply attached to Christianity: but I simply think that, in the present conditions, Christ *is kept too small.*"[1] "Christ is not something added to the world as an extra, he is not an embellishment, a king as we now crown kings, the owner of a great estate . . . He is the Alpha and the Omega, the principle and the end, the foundation stone and the keystone, the plenitude and the plenifier. He is the one who consummates all things and gives them their consistence. It is towards Him and through Him, the inner life and light of the world, that the universal convergence of all created spirit is effected in sweat and tears. He is the single centre, precious and consistent, who glitters at the summit that is to crown the world, at the opposite pole from those dim and eternally shrinking regions into which our science ventures when it descends the road of matter and the past."[2]

Teilhard's Thought Is Grounded In His Personal Faith In Jesus Christ

What are we to say of these things? Have they any basis in the Christianity of the Bible, any contribution to make to late twentieth century Christian faith and teaching? Much, I would say, not least because they come out of a very deep and rich Christian faith achieved and held at great cost. The "truth for Teilhard" was rooted and grounded in his Christian faith. He certainly used scientific methods, modes of thought, language and facts, and based much that he said on his scientific findings and his experience as a scientist. This was largely because his greatest concern was to reach those to whom he felt especially called to minister, his colleagues, many of whom were unbelievers, skeptics, or waverers — all with scientific backgrounds, not a few of whom had sought him out in their need. Teilhard, then, knew from experience the truth of the statement by another scientist, Jung, "When you want to talk to a scientist you cannot begin with a religious creed, you have to show the facts and let them draw their own conclusions."[3] However, undergirding all Teilhard's thought was the faith in which he had been nurtured, supremely his deep personal devotion to Jesus Christ.

His own experience of the drawing power of Christ, the fulfillment which came to him in hours of communion, and his own increasing longing for further unity with his Lord, enabled him to see the pattern he saw in the data he collected, analyzed and studied in the field and laboratory. He also knew the enabling and staying power coming from communion with Christ to be effective even in purely physically trying circumstances. And during the long-drawn out mental and emotional agony accompanied by the frustration of his dearest work, by the Church he loved enough to want to reform, only this same power from Christ had kept him going. The fulfillment and coherence he had known imparted to his own life through relationship with Christ, he had also seen come into the lives of those to whom he was a spiritual counsellor. He was aware in his own work that the power to do it came from Christ. His own experience also convinced him that the convergence he saw in the universe exists because of the same Christ. This convergence of . . . the growth of a "humanity" . . . which he had experienced in his scientific group he had also known in the fellowship of those who are one in Christ, despite all the disagreements he had had with the Church.
Surrounding and guiding all these other considerations must have been the experiences of mystical union he himself had had though he never tells of these in the first person. Such self-effacement, Dr. Martin Israel, in his Cambridge lecture on Mysticism (Jan. 23/74), insisted is the mark distinguishing the true from the false mystical experience.

It is possible that Teilhard arrived at the hypothesis of an Omega point by the logical, scientific reasoning he outlines in *The Phenomenon of Man*. From the data he has put forward, there must be, he reasons, some magnetic center by which the whole of the evolutionary scheme hangs together and towards which it moves. Nevertheless, I have little doubt but that he was able to "see" this, because he had had the experience in his own life of being enabled, drawn forward, and drawn towards others by his own deep relationship with Christ.

The Role Of The Mass In Teilhard's Idea Of The "Within"

Equally important was the role of the Mass, The Lord's Supper, in helping him to come to his view of the "within." By this, Teilhard means that there is in everything a core, a potentiality of spirit, an ability to respond to the pull of spirit towards the development of the greater spirit to the end that the "within" takes over the "without" when the process is complete. Material becomes spirit as water becomes steam. This is something more easily followed by those who accept the Roman Catholic view of what happens to the bread of communion at consecration. Christ enters that bread thus transfiguring it so that though to the outward senses it is the same, to the spirit it is a new substance, Christ's flesh.

Although this teaching concerning "transsubstantiation" has, of course, always been a point of division in Christendon, there is no doctrine of communion, however simple it may be, that does not assert that through the faith of the believer who comes to the Lord's Table to open himself to the presence of the Christ, the bread is more than just the symbolic presence of the Lord. The possibility of union is not just metaphorical. It offers an assurance that Christ fulfills all desire for union with himself. It is not just that believers and the bread become one in their partaking; it is in very truth a uniting of believers and the Lord. And believers who are thus united with the Lord can go from the table more themselves, as they were meant to be, because of that union. Moreover, every celebration of the Lord's Supper is seen to be but a "down-payment" as it were, of a supreme communion, a complete oneness at a final feast.

Thus, no matter what one's theology of the sacrament of Holy Communion may be, there is in it some degree of "spiritualizing" of the material bread. In order that Christ should be able in any form or degree to enter the bread of communion, there must be a place for him in that bread. There must have been in the bread some potentiality of its being thus transfigured. In Teilhard's thought, anything which appears in the course of the world's history, must have been there, at least potentially from the very beginning. Thus, he reasons, there must be in every "material thing" down to its lowest form, a "within." Indeed Teilhard, as we will find, sees in what is going on in the mass as, a clue to what is going on in the whole universe.

The Idea Of The "Within" In Scripture

Although Teilhard never makes any reference to the incident of Jesus' transfiguration on the mountain, when the disciples for a brief period saw their master as more and other and greater than they had realized he was, his use of the word "transfigured" at different times, for the change of state whereby, through increased material complexity a higher state of consciousness can be expressed suggest that it was this incident too, which helped him "see." In this moment on the mountain, the "within" of Jesus momentarily shone through and irradiated the "without." And perhaps it is suggestive that something like this is to be seen in the resurrection, since following the first experience Jesus is reported to have warned his disciples not to speak of the incident until after he had risen from the dead.[4]

The Idea Of The "Within" From Our Own Experience

Perhaps we would not find this matter of "the within" and the "without" so mysterious and unreal if we were to think of it in personal terms, in incidents in our own experience. We have all known times when we have seen the face of another "transfigured" before us . . . the face of a mother looking at her child, of a lover at his beloved, or someone who has just become aware of the overwhelming love of God. Such faces are irradiated with an unearthly beauty that startles us into wonder and reverence. At such times we feel we are seeing something holy, "out of this world." We even use the expression that we have seen the "soul in the face."

Teilhard Offers An Alternative To The Orthodox View Of Christ: The Cosmic Christ

Certainly Teilhard makes very clear that one of the prime concerns in all his work is helping others see Christ as he has seen Him. Writing to one of his two "gentile" friends on one of the many occasions when he was being urged to leave the shackles of his church and order, he says, "I am deeply attached to Christianity: But I simply think that in the present conditions, Christ is kept too small (as compared with the world). This they (i.e. Rome) cannot resent (The only trouble is . . . they do *not see the real size of the world . . .*) (LTF 185). Over and over he returns to the "smallness" of the Christ as customarily presented by orthodox christianity. "My whole spiritual construction," he writes to this same friend (LFT 197) "is genuinely built on (or rather culminating into) an enlarged and 'rejuvenated' figure of Christ . . . "

Although Teilhard does not make a great deal of reference to the Bible, there is a group of texts over which he had pondered long and carefully, which were certainly formative of his thought. They are the ones which speak of Christ's relationship to creation, and to all that exists. These texts make such tremendous claims for Jesus that, as Teilhard well points out, it is hard to reconcile them with the Jesus of Nazareth as he is usually presented by the church. It is the "glorified" Christ on whom Teilhard concentrates, the Christ presented in such passages as John 1:3, "Through Him God made all things; not one thing in all creation was made without him."[5]; Colossians 1:16, "by him God made everything in heaven and on earth, visible and invisible, whether thrones or dominions or principalities or authorities . . . all things were created through him and for him." Colossians 1:15,[5] "the first born of all creation;"[5] Colossians 1:18, "he is the beginning;"[5] Colossians 1:17, "he is before all things and in him all things hold together,"[5] and all the passages in the book of Revelation assigning immense significance to Christ as the key to the meaning of the whole process which God initiated at creation and has at last brought to its conclusion. 1 Corinthians 8:6. "one Lord Jesus Christ, through whom are all things and through whom we exist."[5] Hebrews 1:, "a Son . . . through whom (God) created the world."[5] Certainly as a theological student I had heard these passages interpreted as referring to Christ as the personified Word of God, earlier spoken of in the Old Testament as the creative purpose of God, the principle of the divine self-disclosure. Yet, as a figure of speech, this interpretation really did not come alive; the relationship between Jesus and the creation was not at all gripping. It was, for me, otherwise with the vision of Teilhard. He sets these texts in the context of the development of the universe as he, the palaentologist, has seen it.

Christ's Role In A Dynamic Universe Where The Process Is For Personal Union

Because to him the universe is dynamic, a constant becoming, in which the dominant motion is that of uniting in creative union, Teilhard sees the essence of the creative process as unity. From the very beginning therefore he sees God willing the unity of all creation with himself in *a creative*, that is, a "personal" union, a union of love. This requires another "persona" for, for Teilhard, God is supremely personal. In other words, therefore, from the very beginning, as the prologue to the gospel of John asserts, God willed Christ. In order to have Christ he had to have a man, that is *Homo Sapiens*; in order to have *Homo Sapiens* he had to have all those ages of development, that complex and astounding process that moved from primordial hydrogen, the dust of space, the appearance of humanity, the process we call "evolution." I say "had to," in the sense that this was necessary in that it was the will of God; the way the divine creator chose to work.

In speaking earlier of evolution, I have at times used such words as "flow" or "march." A better word for the movement, however, would be the one Teilhard used, "grope," for on the bush of life more branches and twigs come to nothing than go on to bear the fruit of new or later families or species. Nature has to try everything, Teilhard often asserts. The process has been described as perhaps most like the way in which human beings arrive at new concepts when solving problems. They try this and that and the other, either in actual deed or most often in thought. Much more is discarded than can be used. The picture St. Paul gives in the eighth chapter of Romans of the whole of creation, "groaning in travail," is movingly accurate of the process. And yet, as I pointed out previously, Blair's[6] analogy of the "compost heap" is a vivid way of expressing Teilhard's conviction that none of the suffering or loss involved is final. Since the whole process was necessary, in the "necessity" of God's choice, it can truly be said that it was "for Him and through Him" that all exists.

However, the union of Christ with the Father culminating in the cross and expressed in the ascension, is not the end of the story. God's goal was not merely His own union with the risen Jesus, but with the whole of his creation united by and with the Son in all His fulness. Thus is fulfilled the glory of God.

Christ Acts As A Magnet
His Sisters And Brothers Into This Union

At the peak of creation is humankind whose consent, and indeed, commitment to this union must be wooed and won. Because we are, by the love and will of God, an independent creation with our own will and power, can be drawn into union only through our will to do so. We must so trust that we are willing to give ourselves in love to this oneness. In a world in which there is so much threatening our integrity, and finally and worst, the threat of final disintegration in death, we must have a very convincing and powerful proof of the power and love of God to complete what he has set out to do. We must see to believe. Only one who like the risen Christ has met the vicissitudes, the threats, the agonizing conditions of life in the universe as it is, where groping is the rule, and groaning the constant sound, and remained unshattered in his trust in God and oneness with his spirit of love, and over all evil triumphant, could win the trust and love of creatures like us.

Thus Teilhard sees in the risen Christ the "Magnet', the motive power for drawing humanity forward into a new stage of life, the stage into which he himself has passed where spirit is more determinative than "flesh". Since in the development of any new species the environment is a major factor, with the drawing of humanity to the perfection of unity with himself, Christ also draws all creation into himself to its fulfillment and perfection. Christ, therefore is seen, not only as the apex of evolutionary development leading up to his appearance on earth, but as the goal and motive power for all movement from then to the culmination of God's purpose in the mighty unity of all things with Himself.

Christ Is Saviour Of The Whole Cosmos

For Teilhard, Christ has the role not just of being Saviour of mankind as he is usually taught to be, but of the whole cosmos. Until this has been done, salvation is not complete. He is at the same time its crown and the source of power by which it reaches its goal. Again this conception of the role of Christ has its Biblical warrant in passages that strike the cosmic note. Not least of these is that often puzzling phrase in both the Bible and the creeds about Christ's being "seated at the right hand of God". By this figure of speech Teilhard means not only the orthodox idea of honour and authority but more strongly of power. It is the power to get things done, which resides for most people in the right hand. For Teilhard that which draws all creation to its culmination in unity with God, is the power of Christ to draw all into unity with himself, the personal unity of love. And, as I said earlier, of the bliss and reality of this unity, Teilhard himself had had a foretaste, as others have had, in his experiences of mystical union.

In the Christ who fulfils the highest aspirations of humankind and of the things of earth, Teilhard saw humanists reaching their goal. In the one who fulfils all the hopes of the Messiah, perhaps one day, the Jews also would be drawn to humanity at the highest. In the one who united both God and man, as Zaehner points out[7] we have a concept which by every consideration of logic should not be found in the faith of Islam or Buddhism, but yet has crept into the popular practice and thought of both. All, it seems, know in their hearts the Longing of the small child who, being assured of God's presence with her in the dark, preferred her mother's, because she wanted "someone with a face."

Teilhard sees, finally all religions coming together, not in a weak, watered-down syncretism, but in "A general convergence of religions upon a universal Christ who fundamentally satisfies them all: that seems to be the only possible conversion of the world, and the only form in which a religion of the future can be conceived."[8]

The Larger View Of Christ Glorifies All Effort

The idea of Christ as completed only by the bringing of all things to their perfection both helped to explain to Teilhard the real desire of people for perfection in their work, and contributed a necessary corrective to the type of religion which despises the world he found all too prevalent in his own church, as well as in others. When, quite properly such a church holds up the ideal of life dedicated to God, it risks involving its members in an agonizing moral dilemma if it insists on the necessity of choosing between working to perfect the world, or serving God. Teilhard insisted that doing one's very best at whatever is one's task in life, for the betterment of the world, is truly doing it to the glory of God, since it is only through the perfection of the world that God's great purpose can finally be accomplished.

There are many passages and expressions concerning the role of Christ in bringing things to their fulfillment as he fills their "within" and draws them together by drawing them to himself — Ephesians 4:10. "He who descended is also he who ascended far above all the heavens, *that he might fill all things.*" Ephes. 1:10, "to unite all things *in him, things in heaven and things on earth.*" 1 Corinthians 15:28 and Philippians 3:21 speak of all things coming into subjection to Christ; and in Hebrews 1:3 Christ is spoken of as the one who "upholds the world by his word of power". In Colossians 1:17 where it is stated of Christ, "in him all things hold together" Teilhard finds the Biblical expression of his picture of evolution holding together from above.

When all things are united with Christ then the final act can take place. The completed Christ, now in personal and mystical union with all creation, as 1 Corinthians 15:28 puts it, submits himself to God, and God will then, as he first willed it, "be everything to every one". The great and glorious union will be complete.

Christ Unites Even Religions

Without this larger vision of Christ which he felt was fully justified by the vision of Paul and John and other New Testament writers, Teilhard felt that those, who had caught the vision of the vastly enlarged universe revealed by science, would find the Christ of the classical church teaching much too small to claim their allegiance. Indeed, the common emphasis on individual, personal salvation, had already in his time alienated many from the Gospel. Before the "cosmic Christ" however, Teilhard had great hopes that, as the letter to the Philippians (2:10) puts it, "every knee would bow," not just those of Christians but of all faiths, religious or not. Thus Teilhard gives all the hope of being whole whatever their work may be. This, of course, is not an original idea with Teilhard. Church fathers and others, have said it in various ways, not least of all George Herbert, in his familiar lines,

> "who sweeps a room as for thy laws
> makes that and the action fine."

However, again, Teilhard puts flesh and bones into the idea; he integrated it, as all else, with the whole present day view of the universe as we now know it.

Teilhard A Pioneer In His View Of Christ

It was during the noise and confusion, the bestiality and suffering, and also the glory and companionship of sacrifice and a great task shared that Teilhard, as a stretcher-bearer in the First World War, first conceived his vision of the cosmic Christ. It is very interesting to note that this term "cosmic" is continually cropping up in the most recent Biblical commentaries on the "cosmic passages" e.g., *New Century Bible* on the Gospel of John by Barnabas Lindars, 1972; Epistle to the Hebrews by Jean Hering, 1970; Colossians and Philemon by Lohse, 1968; Ephesians, Philippians, Colossians and Philemon by George Johnston, 1967. Even if these people have not consciously been influenced by Teilhard, here is evidence that Teilhard's vision of Christ as the head of a large universe has not been his alone. However, he may have been breaking new ground when he first conceived or, as he may well have felt, "received" it.

Teilhard challenges the orthodox role of Jesus as a winsome and glorious man, some two thousand years behind us, whom we must imitate today. He knows that such a call, too often sounded in Christianity, is impossible. At very least the conditions under which Jesus lived were so much less complex and developed than they are now. Teilhard certainly leaves us the wonderful Jesus of Nazareth, and with this I shall deal in a later chapter, but he gives us someone for life here and now and for all the ages of ages. His is a Christ who is continually developing even as is the universe, growing more and more complex. His is a dynamic Christ who calls us, not to go back to first century Galilee, which is a complete impossibility, even if we would desire to do so, but to go forward with all the best and the finest and highest we have in us and with us. "Christ" he explains . . . "can be attained only through a universe that has been carried to the limits of its capability."[9]

The note of community so sadly neglected in the

Christian doctrine of personal salvation and yet so much a part of Biblical teaching (in the Teilhard interpretation) has been, recovered and enlarged. His community is not just all humankind but the whole cosmos. Yet, in this enormous enterprise, Teilhard insists that the smallest and most seemingly imperfect contribution of the weakest soul aspiring to the best he knows and is capable of, plays its part. Teilhard's Christ is also he who does not "break the bruised reed or snuff out the smoking flax." Thus Teilhard places the Christ whom he so adored at the very center and apex of his system, truly the Alpha and the Omega. He insists, as a fellow-scientist, Coulson, puts it "all nature is needed that Christ should be understood. Christ is needed that all nature should be holy."[10] Is this not a vision of Christ which we need in these days when we have come, belatedly, to be concerned about the environment which we have despoiled?

Perhaps had Teilhard not been silenced by his religious superiors he could have opened our eyes earlier. Or perhaps, as he himself continued to believe even under the most trying circumstances, nothing comes into being before all things are ready for it and its time has come. His time is now.

With Teilhard Things Make Sense Again

One of Teilhard's critics has discounted his thought on the ground that it had been worked out because of a psychological necessity. That analysis may well be true. However I believe that critic wrong in his judgement that this is something which reduces the value of his conclusions.

People's religion is, according to Jung, in the nature of a pattern. Its truth for them resides in the extent to which the knowledge and experience they have and gain, makes a coherent whole, or "makes sense."

The necessity for this "sense" I have found, in my pastoral work, is a very urgent one. When tragedy strikes, the greatest need the bereaved express is the need to know "why?" It is only if and when they can fit this very large and important event into their pattern of thought or adjust or entirely alter their pattern, that they find wholeness again. That new pattern may be a new and deeper faith in God; again it may be a throwing out of all faith, for even those who find the whole business of living absurd and meaningless and are satisfied with this answer, have their pattern. A relief worker, telling of his experience in bringing such basic things as water and food and shelter to the victims of a natural disaster wrote recently that what people left without these basic necessities of life seemed to want most was not something to eat or a place to shelter in, or even someone to love them but an answer to the haunting question, "why?" Sir Alister Hardy, now retired from the Department of Zoology of Oxford University, insists that religion is a biological need; other biologists agree.

If Teilhard, scientist and priest, worked at making a coherent pattern out of his two disciplines of religion and science and the experiences of life they brought him, he was working at a common human problem. The experience of wholeness and integration which this pattern gave him, he saw, not as a work of his own but rather as a revelation, for in discussing the question of revelation, (C & E 160) he says, "the sound of (God's) voice (is) recognizable primarily by the fullness and coherence it contributes to our individual and collective being."

It may be that those scientists who discount Teilhard's work are being described by a member of their own discipline, R.A. Fisher in his Eddington Memorial Lectures of 1950 "Biologists working in their characteristic comparative manner . . . with a limited amount of reflection on [their observations] . . . are on the whole distrustful of speculative generalizations and easily confused by abstractions."[11] Those who seem to feel that Teilhard's findings can be discounted because they supported his deepest aspirations and faith, might well listen to this further word of Fisher, "We should guard ourselves against the assumption which seems to me a perverse one, that the facts when ascertained will necessarily be antagonistic to our aims, hopes or aspirations."[12]

It was during the years of agony and grief, and struggle and the deep comradeship that only the sharing of such things in the closest intimacy can bring, that Teilhard discovered the foundation stone and crown of all his thought, the cosmic Christ. Every finding he made thereafter came as a building stone but to be fitted on, and to prepare, a place for that apex. Some people achieve such a structure by never exposing the finished product to the light of further scrutiny or the test of any more facts, but Teilhard was still adding to his until the day of his death, some thirty-seven full years later. And the master plan was quite able to contain all that he found and experienced.

Some may well object to the Teilhard vision of the "cosmic Christ," that all this could not possibly be what the writers had in mind when they wrote the words, since this vision draws on knowledge very new today. This is certainly true, just as true as that the conception we have of Jesus today is undoubtedly other and probably bigger than that held by the disciples who accompanied him in his lifetime. What the biblical writers were doing was ascribing to Jesus the greatest and highest categories they knew. No title, no description could be big enough to contain his meaning. This is still true today. The difference between then and now is that we realize how immense are the categories even of earth. Too many Christians still see Christ as a single historical individual, Jesus of Nazareth, who did not even receive a mention in secular history. "Christ" places him, as the Biblical writers did, in a cosmic setting. We now have a new knowledge and appreciation of that setting that the Biblical writers could not have had. For each of us, Biblical writers, modern scientists, churchmen, Christians, the Christ will always be greater than we can express.

Christianity is a living faith which means it must ever be growing if it will not die. We believe the Bible to be a living word, as relevent to today's life as it was to life when its words were first written or spoken. Moreover, as Michael Polanyi so well and fully demonstrates in his book *Personal Knowledge*, one characteristic of people is that they know more than they can say. Humans, as more and more biologists and even social scientists are admitting, are more than just mind and body. There is a dimension to them of which they themselves are not always, or fully aware. Sometimes we even say things that are much wiser than we are; we surprise ourselves into saying, as we hear what we have said or written, "I didn't know that I thought or knew that." Sometimes it is only much later that we begin to realize, if we ever do, the size of the truth we have put into words. So I believe it is of much of the Scripture.

Of Teilhard's reflections on the passages about the "cosmic Christ," W.H. Thorpe wrote, "Teilhard and Polanyi understand that Paul in the last three epistles had a vision which neither he himself nor perhaps anyone prior to our own day, has been in a position to comprehend as fully as can now be done."[13]

It *is* an exciting time to be alive, to be in the Church, to be a Christian. Surely not least of the excitements is in beginning to discover that the dimensions of this enormously enlarged world of which we are now aware, do not dwarf but enlarge him whom we love as Lord of life. Whether we know this excitement depends upon our willingness, Teilhard puts it, to adopt a new way of seeing and acting. Teilhard never felt that his way was the only way, or even the best way. In a lecture given in Peking in 1942, shortly after he had finished writing *The Phenomenon of Man*, he said, "The views that I present are still only at their birth. Do not therefore take them as universally accepted or definitive. What I am putting before you are suggestions, rather than affirmations. My principal objective is not to convert you to ideas which are still fluid, but to open horizons for you, to make you think."[14] He knew there were still great and marvelous vistas ahead to be discovered by those who had faith, because he himself had found it so.

NOTES

1. Pierre Teilhard de Chardin, *Letters to Two Friends*, Tr. R. D'Ouince (London: Fontana 1968) p. 185, LTF.

2. Teilhard, *Science and Christ*, Tr. R. Hague (London: Collins, 1965), pp. 34-5 SC.

3. Karl Jung, from a letter written to a Theologian quoted in *God and the Unconscious*, Victor White, (London: Collins, 1960), p. 72.

4. Matthew 17:9, Mark 9:9.

5. Biblical quotations here are as found in *Teilhard*.

6. Blair, *Teilhard Reassessed*, pp. 87-8.
7. R.C. Zaehner, *Concordant Discord* (Oxford, Clarendon, 1970), p. 442.
8. *Teilhard, Christianity and Evolution* Tr. R. Hague (London: Collins, 1971), p. 130 C & E.
9. Teilhard, *Let Me Explain*, Tr. R. Hague and others (London: Collins, 1970), p. 151 LME.
10. C.A. Coulson, *Science and Christian Belief*, (London: Oxford Press, 1955), p. 118.
11. R.A. Fisher, *Creative Aspects of Natural Law* (Eddington Memorial Lecture) (Cambridge: Cambridge University Press, 1950), p. 1.
12. Fisher, p. 6.
13. W. H. Thorpe, *Science, Men and Morals*, (London: Methuen & Co. Ltd., 1965), p. 152.
14. Bernard Towers, *Concerning Teilhard de Chardin, Essays in Science and Religion*, (London: Lutterworth Press, 1966), p. 134.

Chapter 4
THE SEAMLESS ROBE: CREATION, INCARNATION AND REDEMPTION

"Creation, Incarnation, Redemption. Until today these three fundamental mysteries of the Christian faith, while indissolubly linked *in fact* in the history of the world, have remained *logically* independent of one another... seen in this light, the three mysteries become in reality no more... than the three aspects of one and the same fundamental process; they are aspects of a *fourth* mystery, which... is the mystery of the creative union of the world in God." (C & E p. 182-3).

The Christian Story Is A Unity

In his perception of the cosmic Christ Teilhard is possibly breaking new ground for many, or rather, as others realize, pointing us to an emphasis which has been made before but overlooked until now when our new knowledge has made us better able to appreciate it.

This may also be true of his other major emphasis — the wholeness of the Christian story. Although it is possible to divide most books on Christian theology into such topics as "Creation," "Incarnation," "Redemption," and so on, Teilhard's genius for synthesis has never been more clearly shown than in the fact that one simply cannot treat his theology this way. To him the matter of God's dealings with his universe, his cosmos, is as indivisible as the robe Jesus is said to have worn to the cross. For it the soldiers cast lots because to divide it would have been to destroy it.

It is Teilhard's contention that by seeing, for instance, the incarnation or the church, or the last things apart from creation or from each other, we have contributed to the same sort of destructive fragmentation as has happened when we have engaged in the agonizing choice between entirely serving God and doing to the utmost his work in the world. These are, he insists, one and the same thing.

Teilhard, therefore, gave his life to working out for theology in his writing, and for science in his work, a way in which people could "see" that there need be — in fact, there must be — no such separations. From him the words of the marriage service would have had much wider significance than usually given them, "What God has joined together let not man put asunder."

To See This We Must Begin Again With The Human Race

In order to understand Teilhard's theological thought we must begin where he got his clues about evolution with *The Phenomenon of Man*. There are critics who are loud in their condemnation of Teilhard for beginning any study of theology here. This is particularly true of some who make this the bedrock of their rejection of Teilhard. They insist that of course true theology must begin with God. Teilhard is perfectly aware of the impossibility of understanding people without God. It is this very dimension in them that makes it impossible for them to be fitted into any scheme based purely on physics and chemistry that made Teilhard insist that they may be the starting point for understanding the whole process which had produced the human race.

However, in order to help his beloved "gentiles" who thought in scientific terms, Teilhard insisted on arriving at his theology in the way he arrived at scientific truth — dealing with the known and the observable. This is his contribution to theology.

However, in beginning with humans he is not unique;

he is not even un-Biblical. Is not one truth of the incarnation, that for human beings God communicated all they needed to know of themselves and of their creator — indeed, of all things — in a human being? In spite of the Jewish horror of making images, is not the Old Testament so full of figures of speech personifying God that the prophets have constantly to be reminding people that God is not human? Is not one of the foundation stones of revelation that God reveals himself and his will through human history and through his servants the prophets? Moreover, when the old Testament thinkers wished to express their conviction that some great principle of wisdom and creative power lay behind the world, did they not personify this "wisdom?" (Perverbs 8, 9, etc.) Jesus, in his teaching, contributes to and underlines the idea of the personhood of God, and continually tries to help us in our understanding of him by comparing him with human beings. Certainly Jesus makes clear that, in understanding God by looking at human personality, one is beginning, as it were, at the lowest common denominator. "How much more, your Heavenly Father," is how he puts it when he compares the human father's dealings and God's. Perhaps now we would say that God is "transpersonal" — certainly more than "super" personal. Nevertheless, we cannot start from anything greater than the only form of personality we know, the human. Karl Barth, in his book, *The Humanity of God,*[1] witnesses, that we cannot get outside ourselves to understand God.

Teilhard's contribution is his insight that, by studying the "phenomenon of man," we can find the clue to all that has been going on from the beginning and all that lies ahead to the end. Thus we begin to look at his theology from his understanding of *Homo Sapiens.*

Human Uniqueness — Self-Consciousness — Enables Us To Organize The World About Ourselves

The human species stands alone at the top of the bush of life, unqiue in the complexity of physical and chemical organization, also unique in that, with it, thought has come into the cosmos. Increasingly we are having evidence that other forms of life have awareness, and even react to this awareness. For instance a worker with a lie-detector in the United States is reported to have recorded emotional reactions in plants similar to human distress, horror, loneliness, and pain.[2] In animals we have evidence of some degree of thought; but from none of them do we have those inventions by which humans have been able to modify the environment in which they live. That comes from their ability to organize their awareness, from their "consciousness."

In no other creature do we have the full-blown phenomenon of personality which again is the organization of many kinds of awareness. All these have a physical and chemical basis. The seat of the uniqueness of human beings, physically and chemically, is that complex organ, the brain, with its cortex folded in such a way that there can be the incredible number of neural connections which are the stuff of thought. The infolding of the cortex has crowned a process that has been going on from the beginning, from the first moment when primordial hydrogen was drawn into a knot to become the stellar furnace that first produced the elements, to the closing-in of the molecular complexes that marks the appearance of life. Always there have been two pulls on the stuff of the universe — the attraction from the center of one particle to the center of another, and the attraction that has drawn them into ever greater complexity of organization as to a common center. Both these pulls are against the tendency to fly apart, to return to the multiple. Indeed, they make use of it as, when the separations occuring from the encounters of the portions and particles, become richer and more varied combinations in subsequent unions. The results of the two pulls to unity are seen in their peak in the human brain.

This development has produced creatures who in thought center everything around themselves. Is it not true that you and I are the centers of our universe? It is impossible for us to see anything except from within our own selves. Even scientists, who once insisted that nothing was valid which did not strictly exclude the observer, are having more and more to admit that he cannot be excluded. Every observation, however scientific or technical it may be, is affected by the observer. It is by organizing observation, sense data, ideas and thoughts that we are able to live. It is also how we modify and adapt our environment. And it is environment, you will remember, which is one of the prime features affecting all development. Up to humankind, changes have come about in physical arrangement, as the more and more complex body and brain came into being. With the appearance of *Homo Sapiens*, lonely on its stem, no further physical modifications have taken place, and the time charts show how long a period that has been.

The world is a very different one from what it was when our forebears appeared. The life we live, at least on this continent, is as different now from what it was when they first appeared as day is from night. All of this has come from human ability to think, to draw by thought all that is about to the center of the brain, and from that center to make outward changes. It is still a process of organization, of uniting.

This, however, is not the only kind of organization we see as we study our phenomenon. All of us are aware, and perhaps even resentful, of organization as we know it over and over in our own lives in terms of "organizations." I'm sure that most of us feel like a woman I once visited on a Saskatchewan farm who, making the usual diagnosis of the world's sickness, remarked, "There are just too many organizations. What we need is an organization to get rid of them." A more illogical bit of reasoning than that would be hard to find, but it carries its truth. We cannot get along without organization; without it there is chaos.

The Bible Pictures God Organizing

And is not that where the Bible begins the great poem of creation in the first chapter of Genesis, with God and chaos — "the earth, formless and chaotic." Teilhard calls it the "multiple". And what do we see God doing with the chaos? By his word of power he organizes that "multiple" step by step up to the appearance of those made in His image.

Although Teilhard never deals with God directly, since

God, as God, is not a phenomenon which can be studied; he knows God by what he does. Whether or not we are seeing things from the point of view of the scientist watching, as Teilhard does, over the centuries, atom come together with atom, molecule with molecule, organism with organism in ever more complex arrangements, every union bringing into being something new and other than just the sum of that which entered the union, Teilhard sees one over-all creative action taking place in the cosmos — union. It is the union of the single parts coming together which brings things into being. It is their power to attract one another which keeps the whole in existence. It is the greater pull towards more complex union that results in the great break-throughs of life and thought. Moreover, energy, the great and mysterious foundation of all, is also motion in response to attraction.

The key to the universe is not "being", as the philosophers have said, but "uniting." "To be," says Teilhard out of his scientific observation, "is to be united; 'to be' is also 'to unite'."

Pannenburg wonders, in his review of *The Phenomenon of Man*, why Teilhard does not use the model of an electro-magnetic field when he speaks of God as the milieu in which we live. No doubt that idea would be helpful, but Teilhard's point of reference is not physical phenomenon, but human. He knows there is a much more powerful center of unity than even the center of a magnetic field — it is personality. The task of psychiatrists with patients who have "gone all to pieces" is to try to help them pull themselves together, to find with them some center for their life. The more unified persons are the greater their personalities but this unity must be provided by a center beyond themselves. The higher and greater that center, the more they are united with it, the greater their own unity and therefore their personalities. Teilhard, therefore, would never think of God as less than what the Bible always assumes he is — personal.

The Energy-Producing Union Is Love

Moreover, observing people, Teilhard is aware that there is one kind of energy which brings about the sort of union he sees going on in every part of the process of evolution, the union that both preserves the integrity of the uniting parts and enhances their individuality, and brings out of the union something new and greater than a fusion of the two. This energy is love. Love draws together. The aim and delight of love is oneness. Love breaks down barriers. Mutual love draws the most unlikely and different together, as nothing else can. Love draws out and makes blossom the finest and best. We experience this in people. I can remember having a girl whom I had always considered extremely plain and unattractive turn up in my study with her fiance almost unrecognizably beautiful as she spoke with wonder of his love for her. Those who work with and know animals recognize that when they are treated with love they become better than they were. Some time ago a news report in a North American paper told of how a woman attacked by a bear in a National Park kept the animal from tearing her to pieces by talking to it for many hours before help arrived. She had treated it as if it were more than it was, and it responded. There are those who are quite convinced from their own experience or that of others that even plant life responds to those who tend their gardens or house plants with real devotion.

    Most people are aware of the importance of the role of love in human affairs. The humanist acknowledges its vital role in raising women and men to their most human state. Taught by Jesus, Christians have been aware of the love of God as a vital, transforming power in life. They have been aware that to respond to that love is their duty, and to be wholly united with God in love is life's crown. They have also known love of neighbour as the accompanying demand of Christ and a necessity for the coming of the Kingdom of God. But Teilhard sees this much-honoured and abused quality as more vital and formative than even this. "God's love for the world and for each of the elements of the world and the love, too, that the elements of the world have for one another and for God," he writes (LME 94-5), "are more than a secondary effect attached to the process of creation; they represent also both its operative factor and its basic dynamism." And again, in a letter to a friend, "It gives me great strength . . . to recognize that all evolutionary effort can be explained as the justification and the development of a love (of God). It is what my mother told me long ago, but it will have taken me a lifetime to integrate this truth into an organic vision of things."[3]

For Teilhard the love of God is the beginning of all. It is that which has kept and keeps the whole evolutionary process going. It is God's love which will bring all to a conclusion and crown his work.

Creation

With this background, let us now look at some theological concepts.

"In the beginning God created," so runs the familiar account of creation in the authorized version of the Bible. But later translators have acknowledged that the words could as well be translated somewhat as does *The Anchor Bible*, "When God set out to create heaven and earth." Here we have the important implication that this was only the beginning of a process and not a completed one.

Karl Schmitz-Moorman of the University of the Rhur has written, " . . . the very idea of a perfect creation in the beginning does not make sense any more in the contex of our world . . . Gradually, during the last century, man has become ever more conscious that this world is not a world of Being, but of Becoming."[4]

It has been suggested that it was the "telling" (i.e., revealing of the truth) and not the creating which was completed in six days. Thus the argument for instantaneous creation can be discounted and the way opened for a concept of creation as a dynamic process.

For Teilhard creation begins when the "Word" is spoken; it goes on until the great moment when God becomes "all in all."

And it begins with a uniting. It is God's love uniting with himself the multiple in all its various forms that is back of that awe-inspiring process which brought into being our solar system, the earth and all that is on it. Although the first chapter of Genesis is not concerned with scientific details, being a poem of praise to God, nevertheless there is at least a representation of the "dust" of space in the word translated "without form and void," a Hebrew word which corresponds well with Teilhard's "multiple" as he had known it in science. Interestingly, the next word used for the beginnings, "waters," is always in Hebrew a plural form. Thus Genesis pictures God organizing or creating relationship between the individuals and drawing together these pluralities to bring into being all the unities that make the variety of the world. The story in the second chapter of Genesis contains the same thought, as the Creator, using the mist, unites another substance continually used in the Bible both for countless numbers and nothingness, "dust," into the clay from which humankind will be formed.

Whence the "multiple?" Teilhard does not speculate. He merely sees the multiple as that against which God sets the unifying power of his love. It is that into which he pours himself as artists pour themselves into their work. Because it is love, supreme and unbounded love that broods over the multitude, so love gives no less than himself to every particle of his universe to bring it at length to that fullness of life which is to be found only in the perfection which can experience full union with him.

Incarnation And Redemption Within Creation

Here, then, in the creation, we have beginning also both redemption and incarnation. As love can give nothing less than itself, pouring itself out into the beloved, so God pours himself into his creation. Thus there comes into being the center or "within" of every particle which, being love, reaches out to others to draw them one to the other, and to be drawn in turn towards the supreme center of love, bringing ever-increasing complexity of organization.

Although it is supremely seen in the sacrificial love of Christ on the cross that draws all to him and into a new life, that love was drawing the particles of stellar dust to form the basic elements right at the beginning. This, too, is the love of God. And the emptying of himself which we know in the Christ who "emptied himself," (Philippians 2:7) "taking the form of a servant" is a specific revelation to our eyes of that which has always been present in the servant God who lowers himself so as to join himself with the primal particles of matter that they may unite and the great process begin. Thus Teilhard sees the principle of the sacrifice of God to save going right back to the very beginning when supreme unity, as it were, to use Juliet's words, "cuts himself up in little tiny stars" to pour himself into the multiple. Only thus can begin the process which will come to its flower in persons, and in the supreme person, Christ. Only through Christ does he will to draw all things to himself fulfilled and completed.

It is not that God ceases to be himself or to be perfect unity as he unites himself thus with his creation, enabling it, as Huxley says, "to make itself." He does not cease to be himself any more than do creative artists or artisans who literally pour themselves into their work so that they become, for the time, one with their creation. Indeed, as Polanyi points out, only by becoming part of the brush or the tool can anyone do really creative work.

Moreover, those who have given themselves wholly to their creative work know that at no time do they feel more themselves, more whole and complete, more unified and fulfilled, than when they thus pour themselves into their creation. At such times they are also completely without self-concern; but because humans are creatures and not God, it is only for a time that they can sustain the process of self-giving, a process they know only afterwards to be a very costly thing. We can know such moments, then, only fitfully and limitedly. This is what it is to be human. However, should God for one moment withdraw himself, all would return to dust. How thankful we should be that we can praise the "steadfast love" of God that "as it was in the beginning, is now, and ever shall be, world without end."

And so it goes up the scale of complexity until the unit is a person. Always that which pulls the unit together out of the many is the personal, reconciling love of God. That this love will be suffering and sacrificial is well-known to anyone who has ever done personal counselling or engaged in any kind of reconciling. You cannot comfort the grief-stricken, strengthen the dying, plead with the guilt-ridden to accept forgiveness, or try to heal any kind of breach in personal relationships without heavy cost in energy — physical, mental, and spiritual. Every step in the great creative process which is to move through the unity of humankind and Christ — of all with God — is incarnation and redemption. As Teilhard puts it, the humble details of the Bethlehem birth were long foreshadowed, as were also the sufferings of the cross. Truly suffering love was "in the beginning."

The Love Of God Appears As Suitable To Each Unit

Of course, at the level of atom and molecule, of organism and organ, and even of most living creatures, what informs them is not "love" as people would recognize love. It is love such as each unit can contain. In all but humans we see it only as the mysterious force which brings about union, the union with each other, and an ever-striving upward for a larger union bringing into being new forms — the process of evolution.

As we think of this process we may well feel that the idea of "love" should be questioned, remembering that of these new forms brought into being in the process, the majority came to nothing. However, it is only through the process of "trying everything" that the new species are produced which ascend up the scale to reach the climax in that creature which alone can know about the love of God. This process which Teilhard so vividly describes as "groping" is surely the pre-personal form of that about which St. Paul is speaking in his speech in Athens when he describes all people seeking God in the hope that they might "feel after him and find him." The word translated here "feel" could be translated "grope." (Acts 17:17). Paul, of course, is speaking about human endeavours in their religion, but, as I pointed out earlier, our present knowledge reveals to us that such groping goes on at every level. And Teilhard insists that all this groping is indeed, even at its most primitive, a seeking after God.

God's Love Must Be A Suffering Love

To realize that God in his love should also have united himself in love with all those who seek and fail, that he yearns after *all* that he has made, merely enlarges our conception of the divine anguish which we see in visible form on the cross.

I can remember having the poignancy of this brought home just a little when I heard a minister who had been sent in the early days into the coal mining area of the Rockies in Alberta tell about his life. He learned early that, when a siren sounded, it meant there had been a disaster underground. One day when he was out visiting he heard the ominous warning. At first he thought, "Somebody is in terrible danger." And then the truth came home to him, "Those are my people."

For God all are "his." The cost of creation to God can only be measured in the natural disasters that take place all along the arduous climb of evolution in which for every part that fails, as well as for all that succeed, there sounds in the divine heart the cry, "These are my people," for God himself is involved in each one, in love.

The End Of The Process Is Complete: Redemption

Because of the end of the process — the glory and fulfilment towards which the process moves — is the gathering in of all into which God has poured himself in love, brought to its highest and finest and fullest and therefore ready for complete communion with God, the whole process of creation is one vast incarnation, one great clothing of the divine in the stuff of its universe.

It is also one vast redemption, one mighty act of salvation, of making whole, of rescuing from evil. Since the essential work of God is uniting, and that against which God turns his energy and power is the multiple, the work of evil is dissociation or disunity.

The Problem Of Evil

The Bible itself never speculates on the origin of evil.

Evil is just that which God is against; it is that which God's conscious creation for God's sake, is to struggle with. It is all that would take us away from relationship with others and with God. Do we not see God at the very beginning opposing the multiple, the divided, in the chaotic formlessness both of primeval stuff and of the dust? Do we not see the same work being done by the Son? He lets himself be killed as a friend of sinners rather than save himself by supporting the contention of those whose religious system was built on the teaching that God disowned any relationship with those who had broken the law. He died in response to his own need for oneness with the Father. How complete was Jesus' union with God is surely most powerfully attested to in the effect it had on the faith of his disciples. Although they belonged to a race whose distinction from all others was expressed in the ancient creed, "Hear, O Isreal, the Lord our God is one Lord," they found themselves, after association with him, professing "Jesus is Lord." At the same time they found that when they gave their love to him he drew them into such closeness to one another and to others that they were a different kind of people and "men realized they had been with Jesus." (Acts 4:13). Is not the characteristic work of the Holy Spirit, shown over and over in the New Testament, the bringing together into the oneness of community the most disparate and varied elements? Finally, does not the Apocalypse portray at least this — a vast multitude of every variety who are yet completely one in their ecstasy and adoration of God, all members of one community, the new Jerusalem?

From beginning to end the Bible pictures God at work redeeming, rescuing, saving from threat of disintegration, the whole of his creation. Where there is disunity, Teilhard continually asserts, there is nothing. This is not the airy-fairy theorizing of one with a thesis to support. Scientists from every field speak of the importance of integration, including the important integration of personality into an "I". It is an interesting psychological insight, which Teilhard would support and deepen, that the wild, unhuman man whom Jesus met and cured along the tombs at Gadara, told Jesus his name was "legion," meaning a multitude. (Luke 8:26 ff). Surely all of us knows, in some degree, the devastating experience of having things — even at times, ourselves — "fly to pieces." At such times we know complete helplessness, even despair.

At the time when, in 1974, astronomers had been expecting the comet Kahoutek to provide a spectacle in the sky, only to be disappointed, a commentator on BBC4, speaking about comets in general, pointed up this whole relationship between lack of unity and nothingness. "Even," said the commentator, "were we to collide with a comet, we would never know it. A comet is nothing more than a completely formless mass of gas and dust. A comet is the closest thing to nothing that we know."

Without the creative power of God continually upholding and sustaining all by his love — his love for everything — planted deep within all that they may be drawn to and upheld by him so that all may be held together, everything would fly apart into the nothingness of the multiple. Because the multiple is the stuff of which all are made, only a constant battle against it keeps things whole. Salvation, which is not just making, but keeping, things whole is a constant and costly process. Especially is it costly to God, who must ever give of himself to provide the power by which things are created and sustained. Thus creation and salvation go on continually, and both are incarnation as God more and more brings into being that which can express him more fully.

Where Jesus Fits Into The Scheme

Does not this dissolve the work of Jesus Christ as the incarnate Son of God and saviour of man into a nebulous generalization?

Not at all. In Teilhard's thought the Lord Jesus becomes more essential and indispensable for the purpose and plan of God than he is in orthodox thinking and teaching. He has the key place in the whole divine plan. Certainly he is the saviour of the human race as the church has always taught, but because of the relationship Teilhard sees between humanity and the rest of creation, Jesus is seen as the saviour, not just of human kind, but of all that is.

Teilhard Again Begins With Humanity Made For Relationship With God

To see that we must start where the Bible does, "in the beginning," but this time we will be concerned, as Teilhard was, with humans. To do so is to do what the Bible itself does. In both accounts of creation in Genesis they are given a place not dissimilar to that which Teilhard assigns to them. In the first account this creation occupies a much larger part of the text than that of any other creature; this species is the one who crowns material creation, which brings it to its close, and to which the place of lordship is given. In the second, their importance is underlined, not only by the fact that everything which is created is brought into being for them, but that before anything exists at all the prospect of their creation is held before us. (Gen. 2:5).

It is generally conceded that the purpose of the first account of creation is to give glory to God by revealing that all things owe to him their being. I believe that the purpose of the second chapter is to reveal where meaning and continuing life is to be found — in relationship. From the very beginning when out of that dust God makes the clay, uniting its multiplicity, to mould humanity in both its sexes, everything is made for its relationship to the last comers. The trees, the water that sustains life, the garden, providing not only food for their bodies and their need for beauty but their need for work, and the animals — all find meaning for life in their relationship with human beings. And for them, the supreme relationship is with God, united with him center to center.

Humans Also Make To Create

Humans were created both for relationship and to create relationship. They are to find life in relationship and in creating a relationship which is nothing less than the very work of God.

Nevertheless, we are still created not creation. As such, we have limitations which the trees of "knowledge" and of "life" symbolize. By these limitations we will be continually challenged. Therefore, with the love which characterizes all provisions made for us as in this chapter, God reveals that in this challenge lies the risk of death. If we want to know more and be more, we will have to accept death.

If we are to create, we must do as God has done, sacrifice our own unity to enter into a larger one. For all but God himself, this is risking death. Yet in our struggle to know more, the one thing we must long to know — what is good and what is evil — will never be subject to our knowing at all. It can only be realized by faith, by entering with the whole self into the supreme personal relationship with God. By our own volition, individually and together we must die to self in a larger love.

This is what we were made for. The vast process before us has struggled at exorbitant expense to produce this bearer of consciousness, this creature capable of thought, of this degree of freedom. Yet because we are the product of all that has gone before, we, like them, are a fabric woven on the warp of the multiple. The pull of the multiple will be our constant foe which, as Cain is told (Gen. 4:7), he "must master." We are like God in that each of us is also a center, in that we must unify, but also must be unified. For this work we have the equipment of "consciousness."

Interestingly, two physical scientists, Sir Cyril Burt and R.A. Fisher, both see consciousness as having to do with relationship.[5] To us has been given the power to do what God has been doing all along, creating, that is unifying or creating relationship. Our special equipment is not our "without" but our "within", as Genesis 2:7 suggests. This is something as new, in the cosmos, as was life when it appeared.

Man's Power To Create Potential Only

It is T.H. White, the novelist, who puts this all most tellingly in *The Sword In The Stone*. The badger, a scholar, has set out to write a thesis which will once for all settle the question "Which comes first — the chicken or the egg?" His thesis is that it was the egg. Since all embryos are almost identical, he imagines a time when they were all summoned before the Creator to choose what special equipment each would have. For six days they chose — wings, special feet, special eyes, skins, muscles, and so on, until it was man's turn to choose. He said that he trusted the Creator to have made him as he wanted and therefore he asked no other gift. If he wanted to go by air, or sea, or under the ground, as the others did, he would just invent a way to do it. To this the Creator replies, that "Man," [has guessed] "Our riddle." "You will look like an embryo till they bury you, but all others will be embryos before your might; eternally undeveloped, you will always remain *potential* in Our image, able to see some of Our sorrows, and to feel some of Our joys."[6]

Human power is the power of God to unify but, as White puts it, it is his *potentially*; it can become actual only as it is exercised in personal relationship with the Creator. Before people appeared the relationship between God and his creation was that of things and a person. Now that persons have entered the world, the relationship must become personal. There must be personal response from the latest material creation.

"Original Sin" Not Broken Relationship But Imperfect State

But this, too, can come about only through process. Teilhard broke with the teaching of his church, and indeed that of most churches, in denying that there had been any state of perfection in the relationship between God and humanity at its first appearance. He could not accept the idea of a "fall." He did not see "original sin" as a broken relationship that needed mending through the work of Jesus Christ, but as an imperfect state that needed perfecting and transcending.

Moreover, he could not accept that, with the initial transgression, death entered the world. There had been death from the beginning. Indeed, from the number of shoots that amounted to nothing in the upward groping on the bush of life, it would seem that all along death had been the rule, rather than the exception. What did enter the world with humans was consciousness of death, and with this the temptation to pattern life and conduct around the fear of death. With consciousness of death came the temptation to prize stability and seek it rather than to venture forward. Dobzhansky speculates that, as early as consciousness of death appeared, came also consciousness of God, which in its primitive form might be, as Werner Heisenburg puts it, a sort of "compass... (for) man's relation to a central order."[7] Sir Alistair Hardy feels that the religious sense is as fundamental and goes as deep as the instinct of sex. Since consciousness of death and consciousness of God may have appeared close together, it is not surprising that they are often intertwined.

This View And That Of The Bible

Does not all this fly in the face of the Bible's analysis of the situation set forth in the third chapter of Genesis? I do not think so if we are prepared to come to that chapter with an open mind.

As I said earlier, I am convinced that the most important point of the second story of creation which leads into the third, is that the meaning of life is to be found in relationships. In this chapter it is clear that the supreme relationship for humans is relationship with God. Without this they are nothing — dust. Nevertheless, as we find this relationship at the end of the second chapter, it is neither mature, nor even particularly personal, on the human side. They are in every way childish, and they continue to be until the end of the third chapter, though by that time they may be seen to be adolescents. Certainly at no point has there been any kind of *personal* relationship broken.

Because the Jews, who wrote this profound story, saw their relationship with God in terms of the Law, the story gives the impression that the vital, or rather, the deadly thing that has happened is the breaking of a commandment. However, an incident in a confirmation class one time made me see that what is really being shown up here is an immaturity of personal relationship.

As we finished the "Fall" story, one of the class, quickly supported by the others, objected, "Why didn't God forgive them and let them have another chance?" It was some time before they were able to see that nowhere in the account are there any of the necessities for forgiveness. The man and woman take no responsibility at all for their act or its consequences. Apart from their fear of what God can do to them, there is no sign of their concern about their personal relationship with God or what it means to him. They show no desire for close relationship with him. This still has to be developed. They have the equipment for making relationship — consciousness — but they are only potential persons. Much more creation — uniting of the multiple, much more salvation, much more incarnation — must go on in this part of God's creation before it is what he means it to be.

Now that God has willed to have a partner, one on whose cooperation he depends, he must win this cooperation. There is now the chance that this creature, this centered molecule, will refuse him, deny him, defy him. Moreover, since we have power over our environment, any contrary attitude of ours will make it harder for the rest of the creation to respond to God. Thus, with the creation of this creature in God's image there enters into the divine life the cross as a terrible personal tragedy.

I can remember having the meaning of this brought home to me through my relation with one of my well-beloved cats. Although I had never given him anything but good food, he always approached his dish with a caution that looked terribly like suspicion. If he had been my child and not just an animal, I thought, how hurt I would have been to have him distrust me so. How much more must God suffer!

The Necessity Of Revelation

With us then, the work of God enters a new phase. It is still that of creation, redemption, incarnation, but now there must be revelation. If we are to be in partnership with God, indeed if we are to live in God's world at all, we must be able to know; we must become conscious of what is going on. Again, this can happen only as a process.

NOTES

1. Karl Barth, *The Humanity of God*, (London: Fontana, Collins 1967).
2. Vivian Buchan, "ESP's Everywhere," *Healthways*, March 1973.
3. Teilhard, *Human Energy*, Tr. J.M. Cohen (London: Collins, 1969) 72 (footnote) HE.
4. Karl Schmitz-Moorman, "Theological Methods in an Evolutionary World," *The Teilhard Review*. 9:68-9, October 1974.
5. Sir Cyril Burt, "Mind and Consciousness," *The Scientist Speculates*. ed. Irving Good (New York: James H. Heineman Inc., 1962) p. 82. R.A. Fisher, *Creative Aspects of Natural Law* (Eddington Memorial Lectures) (Cambridge: Cambridge University Press, 1950), p. 18.
6. T.H. White, *The Sword in the Stone* (New York: G.H. Putnam's Sons, 1939), p. 291.
7. Werner Heinsenburg, *Physics and Beyond* (London: Allen & Unwin 1971) p. 214.

Chapter 5
WE SEE JESUS

"Now in putting everything in subjection to man, God left nothing outside his control. As it is, we do not yet see everything in subjection to him, but we see Jesus . . ." (Heb. 2:8(b)-9).

"Christ is he who structurally in himself and for all of us, overcomes resistance to unification offered by the multiple, resistant to the rise of spirit inherent in matter. Christ is he who bears the burden, constructionally inevitable, of every sort of creation. He is the symbol and the sign-in-action of progress. The complete and definitive meaning of redemption is *no longer only* to expiate; it is to surmount and conquer. The full mystery of baptism is no longer to cleanse but... to plunge into the fire of the purifying battle 'for being' . . . no longer the shadow, but the sweat and toil, of the Cross. (C & E p 85)

Jesus, The Clue To The Mystery Of Life

For Teilhard, the Christian, the supreme revelation about what is going on in the universe is made in Jesus Christ. However, as he says in *The Future of Man*, "The first Christmas . . . could only have happened between heaven and an earth which was *prepared* socially, politically, and psychologically, to receive Jesus."[1]

The Preparation For Jesus —
The Chosen People

Anyone who has thought about this matter of

preparation, either alone or in Bible study groups, studying the words in Galatians (4:4) regarding the coming of Jesus "in the fullness of time", will no doubt have considered the political and perhaps even the psychological preparation for him. Teilhard's particular contribution is his insistence that one must consider the biological preparation as well.

He is thinking, certainly, of the long preparation of the Jews, of which we are made conscious through the presence of the Old Testament at the beginning of our Bibles. Recent studies of man and his development recognize ". . . the evolution of a non-genetical system of heredity, founded upon the fact that the most complicated brains . . . can . . . make it possible for instructive stimuli from the outside world . . . to be handed on." Thus there can be " . . . the transfer of information through non-genetic channels from one generation to the next."[2] Now we can see even more clearly how Jesus was prepared for by his own race. The fierce insistence of the Jews on reverence for, and obedience to, the one true God, instilled into their children from their earliest years, defended at such cost over centuries of persecution, ridicule, and struggle, was absolutely necessary to prepare his way.

Medawar's statement suggests that those dry geneologies of the Old Testament and the beginnings of Matthew and Luke are not nearly so irrelevant as many Bible readers have thought them to be. It was from these people and no other that Jesus could come, because it was through them that the very particular kind of preparation had been made. Of course, Teilhard insists that this preparation was being made from the very beginning of creation and before. "If God wished to have Christ, to launch a complete universe and scatter life with a lavish hand was no more than he was obliged to do," he writes, [C & E p 32]. In this preparation the appearance of man was a stage, an absolutely vital stage of course, but only a stage. . . . "nothing is more wrong," he writes, "than to treat the human as though it has been biologically stationary since the ending of the Ice Age. It may be that to macroscopic observation nothing has changed during the period in the general arrangement of the cerebral neurons. But, on the other hand, what extraordinary and irreversible increase of collective consciousness is manifest in the appearance of association and opposition of techniques, visions, passions and ideas! What an intensification of reflective life! [FM 287].

If we can read the Old Testament, guided by those who are able to help us see the way the religion of the Jews developed, we become aware that, for them, this "intensification of reflective life" came in the realm of religion which Teilhard defines as "not a strictly individual crisis or choice or institution but represents the long disclosure of God's being through the collective experience of the whole of humanity." (H.E. 47) For the Jews, the pressure of God on man (the generalized sense of moral values common to all men) came to have content which became focused in the Law, interpreted and refined by the prophets but, above all, validated by experience. That it was they and not others who saw God's hand in the events of life, is the proof of God's "choice" of them for, Teilhard writes, "we cannot recognize God's hand and voice in the world without a special sort of super-sense whose existence we should note (if union with God does indeed correspond to a higher degree of life) is perfectly in harmony with all the laws of biology." (C & E 161-2)

Teilhard was a person who believed in such instances of "choice." In a paper prepared for UNESCO he had insisted that there are "better endowed races." Undoubtedly the special endowment of the Jewish people has been this ability to see the hand of God in the experiences through which they passed. Their geniuses were religious geniuses. Their role in God's plan, according to the prophet Isaiah, was to be "witnesses" for God to the whole of humanity. To them had been given a special ability to relate the "within" and the "without" in terms of a rational and personal God rather than, as in the East, in terms impersonal and arbitrary.

Dr. de Lange, of the Department of Oriental Studies, Cambridge, a learned Jewish rabbi, speaking on Judaism in a seminar on comparative religions in the spring of 1974, stated that he felt the strength of Judaism was its ability to make a sensible and wise relationship between the practical and the theoretical, the sacred and the secular, the world and the world to come. If consciousness is, as I have accepted earlier it may well be, the faculty of relationship, this suggests a refinement in the Jews in that area which makes people human. This, in turn, implies that these people are, at the very core, "a better endowed race."

Preparation — Long Before And Outside Of The Hebrews

However, Teilhard sees the preparation for Christ taking place not just in the small corner of the world and the tiny race from which he sprang, or even in the brief centuries spanned by Old Testament history. In a typically lyrical passage quoted in *The Hymn of the Universe*, he puts it this way: "The prodigious expanses of time which preceded the first Christmas were not empty of Christ; they were imbued with the influx of his power. It was the ferment of his conception that stirred up the cosmic masses and directed the initial developments of the biosphere. It was the travail preceding his birth that accelerated the development of instinct and the birth of thought upon the earth. Let us have done with the stupidity which makes a stumbling block of the endless eras of expectancy imposed on us by the Messiah; the fearful, anonymous labours of primitive man, the beauty fashioned through its age-long history by ancient Egypt, the anxious expectancies of Israel, the patient distilling of the attar of oriental mysticism, the endless refining of wisdom by the Greeks: all these were needed before the Flower could blossom on the rod of Jesse and of all humanity. All these preparatory processes were cosmically and biologically necessary that Christ might set foot upon our human stage. And all this labour was set in motion by the active, creative awakening of his soul inasmuch as that human soul had been chosen to breathe life into the universe. When Christ first appeared before men in the arms of Mary he had already stirred up the world."[3]

For Teilhard, Christ is heir, not just to the priceless process of revelation and experience, fortified and purified by suffering and struggle, from his Jewish ancestry, but to all that had been revealed to, achieved and developed and learned by, the whole human race, even as he was the force which set it all in motion. He is indeed the crown of the whole cosmic process up to his appearance in Bethlehem at the beginning of the Christian era.

This view is in accord with modern scientific thought about the appearance of any outstanding figure. When a genius emerged in any age, Thorpe says, his appearance is due not just to a "rare and precious constellation of genes." It needed also the right social environment for their manifestation. As is true for the appearance of anything or anyone else in the universe, Teilhard insists, Jesus could have appeared at no other time or place than he did.

Jesus — Son Of Mary, Son Of God

Does this then mean that Teilhard dismisses the virgin birth as a physical fact? He does not actually discuss the question, but his very high view of the value of chastity in the evolution of spirit would at least suggest that he does not. However, in *Christianity and Evolution* (p. 162) he writes, "In a certain number of cases (the virginity of Mary, Christ's material resurrection, the Ascension, and so on) we get the impression that the Gospel miracles express in concrete form (like Genesis) the "unrepresentable" elements in events as profound as the absorption of the Word into the human phylum . . . this is not simply a matter of symbols; rather it is the expression in image of something which is inexpressible."

To say this is not for one moment to suggest that Jesus is not the Son of God, for God is not flesh but spirit. It is not to say that his birth was not a miracle. Teilhard, like the scientist, Bernard Towers, who speaks of "This incredible adventure on which we all started some nine months before we were born"[5] would have us see all birth as miracle and remember that every one of us is a potential son of God, whose ability to realize that potential has been made possible by the life and death of one whose chosen name for himself was "son of man."

There is no doubt of Teilhard's veneration for Mary, about whom he writes, "The world's energies and substances — so harmoniously adapted and controlled that the supreme Transcendent would seem to germinate entirely from their immanence — concentrated and were purified in the stock of Jesse; from their accumulated and distilled treasures they produced the glittering gem of matter, the Pearl of the Cosmos, and the link with the incarnate personal Absolute — the Blessed Virgin Mary."[6] Certainly he sees in her relation to God, as expressed in her response to the annunciation, the perfection of spirit which enabled God to use her to bear the one who would voluntarily and through the most extreme human effort reveal the divine presence in the world.

It has always seemed to me, however, that while Mary's submission to God is a distillation of the finest and best in the Hebrew devotion to God up to her time, and her openness to this new and threatening future, the crown of all the prophets had pled for, Joseph's relations with God as we see them in the early part of the Gospel of Matthew, are not much less impressive than Mary's. He, too, against all his most cherished and revered convictions, does what he feels God asks of him, and at God's command moves both physically and spiritually in perfect faith.

Teilhard And The Historical Jesus

Teilhard does not deal in much detail with the historical Jesus. This is not surprising. While Teilhard, the scientist, only in his later years became uninterested in the past, Teilhard, the theologian, writes of the Jesus of history, (LTF 48) "in a sense the past does not interest me." He, like Paul, is not concerned with Jesus "after the flesh" (2Cor. 5:16); he feels that this emphasis in the church's theology, which concentrates so much on the synoptic Gospels, has made Jesus too small in our eyes. "If Jesus were not more than 'a father, or brother, a mother, or a sister' to us, I would not have need of him," he writes to a friend (LTF 48). "What I 'ask' of Christ is that He be a Force that is immense, present, universal, as real (more real) than Matter, which I can *adore*; in short, I ask Him to be for me the Universe: complete, concentrated and capable of being adored. This is why, while acknowledging the irreplaceable value of the first three Gospels in presenting the real historical *beginnings* of Christ (with a practical code of moral comparison with Him), I prefer St. John and St. Paul, who really present in the *resurrected* Christ a being as vast as the World of all time. Have you read, for example, the beginning of the Epistle to the Colossians (Chapter 1, verses 12-23), and tried to give it the full organic meaning it requires? Here Christ appears as a true soul of the World. It is only thus that I love Him."

The Historical Jesus Was Necessary For The Emergence Of The Cosmic Church

This does not mean that he sees the life of the man of Nazareth as unimportant. "The more . . . we think of the profound laws of evolution, the more convinced we must be that the universal Christ could not appear at the end of time, at the peak of the world," he writes (C & E 181), "if he had not previously entered it during its development, *through the medium of birth*, in the form of an element. If it is indeed true that it is through Christ-Omega that the universe in movement holds together, then correspondingly, it is from his concrete germ, Man of Nazareth, that Christ-Omega (both theoretically and historically) derives his whole consistence as a hard experiential fact."

He Is Necessary For Winning Human Cooperation

This is a statement that needs a fair bit of unpacking and to do so we need to do some review. It reminds us again of Teilhard's principal thesis that the whole process which he sees going on in evolution reaches its goal in personal union with God through Jesus Christ. Up to the emergence of persons, the movement has gone on without any kind of conscious cooperation from those units being acted on, as God's love drew them each to the other and towards the goal. The work was all being done by God himself alone, for in him still was the attractive force as well as the source of energy. However, once the human emerged equipped with consciousness, the one species with whom God wills to share the task of creation has arrived; but it has yet to be enlisted. It must become conscious of what is going on. It has to be won to work for its furtherance. Humans must not only know the goal, they must so love that goal that they are willing to engage in the very costly process by which progress can be made. Because this is so, they must know that the struggle is worthwhile, how the work is to be accomplished, and be assured that they can attain it.

Since the life they must lead is to be human life, the skills they must use are to be human skills — and, as Polanyi points out,[7] skills can be learned only by example — the revelation given to humanity must be in the form of a fully human life. Moreover, this enterprise will call for commitment. Persons can commit themselves wholly only to persons, for in any other kind of union precious personhood is diminished. With the emergence of persons, the energy of God reveals itself as love and, as Teilhard says (LME 81), "Love cannot be born and take permanent root unless it finds a heart, a face." Thus the process going on in the universe is now revealed as "spirit becoming Presence."

The New Humanity Capable Of Relationship With God Must Come Out Of The Old

Moreover, since the plan of God requires the creation of a new humanity which will be capable of entering into personal relationship with Divine Spirit, the work of re-creating it will have to go on from the first within the old humanity. In harmony with all the rest of the process the new can emerge only out of the old, experienced and perfected. With all the rest, there will have to be a union, an increase in complexity, a fresh infusion of energy in order that the gap between states — this time, matter and spirit . . . may be bridged. Jesus, says Teilhard "is the spark leaping between God and the universe."[8] If humanity, the peak of material creation, is to become capable of entering into union with God, then one man must bridge the gap. He must so live the human life as both to perfect it and transmute it by that same formula which St. Paul was to recommend to the Philippians (Ch. 2:12, 13), "work out your own salvation with fear and trembling, for it is God at work within you both to will and to work for his good pleasure."

Jesus, A Son Of Man

Unless we see Jesus beginning as a man, a human being like ourselves, we cannot follow Teilhard's thought here. This is entirely consistent with the Gospels in which Jesus is at great pains to stress his identity with humanity — all of it — above all creaturely, limited people infinitely, and therefore terribly, liable to error. It was, I believe, his consciousness of just this that led Jesus to go to John at the Jordan for baptism. He accepted wholeheartedly, as an adult human being, what he had become conscious of in adolescent fashion in the Temple at the age of twelve, his overwhelming need of God in order to live a wholly human life. The act of accepting baptism marked the complete dedication of his life in response to the pressure of God's love. Nevertheless, it was also Jesus' declaration to himself, and to God, that in his own consciousness he knew his need and in his heart earnestly desired to be wholly and completely empowered by God. Unlike the self-congratulating Pharisee, in the parable about the Pharisee and the penitent publican, Jesus never thought of himself as "not like other men." (Luke 18:11)

Jesus: Conscious of Being a Son of God

And yet, of course, it is exactly here, in the intensity of his own consciousness of himself and his turning of his life over to God, that we have the difference between Jesus and all other persons. In this man, coming at the end of that long line of men and women in whom self-consciousness and God-consciousness had been their most cherished and bloodily purchased heritage, are these two qualities distilled in all their purity. Here they are united into the most perfect union possible in humanity.

Jesus Lets His Consciousness Of The God-Relationship Win A Victory For All Humankind

The consciousness of himself and of God, exhibited by the twelve-year old Jesus in the Temple, is something most adolescents experience if they have had, as Jesus had, the privilege of being raised in an atmosphere where God's presence is acknowledged. What is different is that in the mature Jesus it is the God-consciousness which takes precedence increasingly, over the self-consciousness. In his consciousness, that seat of relationship between the "within" and the "without," Jesus, by his own free choice, gives ever more importance to the evidence from the "within" until in his final acts of response to the love of God and the love of others, he completely empties himself in faith and love on the cross. At the moment when every evidence from without denies even the reality of the "within," the moment of dereliction, he still wills to cry, "Father, into Thy hands I commit my spirit." It is then, and only then, that the pull of the multiple is broken, once for all. The triumphant Jesus breaks the barrier that separates flesh and spirit and pioneers the way to its goal for all mankind. (Hebrews 12:2).

Teilhard felt that the almost exclusive emphasis of the church and her theologians on the suffering and death of Christ as an expiation for sin had hidden the much more vital truth which was not unknown to the early church fathers — that Jesus' work on the cross was the accomplishment of a tremendous victory. He insists that we have too long seen Jesus as the suffering victim rather than the triumphant victor, and would have us make anew the emphasis of some of the drawings of the crucifixion on the catacomb walls of the crucified Lord "reigning" on the cross.

All Of Jesus' Life Is Expiation — Opening Up Closed Relationships

Of course he would not deny that expiation was necessary. There was a heavy burden of the consequences of evil to be taken on and overcome. All through his life we see Jesus doing just that — taking it. Other human beings like me, and maybe you, when others trespass on what we see as our territory, rights, or privacy, pass on the hostility, taking out on others the hurt we feel or fancy we suffer.

I once saw a wonderful cartoon illustrating this perfectly. Mother is busy sewing when she is interrupted by little Nipper. Annoyed, she barks at him. Little Nipper, all ruffled, goes and gets rid of his annoyance by kicking little brother. Little brother takes out his hurt by pulling the cat's tail, and the cat, fur flying, digs fiercely at the back of mother's chair. Thus the vicious chain goes on until someone just "takes it." This means he must not only absorb the alienation from outside but also that which rises from within, and must return rejection with acceptance, hostility with love, and thus replace dispersion with unity.

Relationships Closed For Jesus To Open

Thus Jesus opened up relations, holding open the offer of closer relationship to everyone with whom he came into contact. There, at the cross-roads of the ancient world, he met every manifestation of the disrupting force of evil. In Israel, in his lifetime, there was every influence to work against the unity of persons with persons of persons with God, not least of all from the very people to whom had been given the special equipment to further the process of unity, for Jesus was born at a time when Jewish faithfulness to the Law had hardened official religion into a legalism and an exclusiveness that denied the finest insights the Jews had been given and thus threatened the spiritual progress of the universe. Rightly realizing the treasure they had, but wrongly thinking to preserve it, as people are always tempted to do by the pull of their "warp" against the risks that bring new life, the religious leaders chose two dangerous courses. They interpreted relationship with God in terms of literal obedience to an external law, and relationship with others in terms of their own race. Thinking to preserve what they had, they adopted the closed system in which energy gradually dies. They exposed to the danger of death the finest flower of religion the world had yet developed. Teilhard, commenting on these things in general in our life, writes, "Man's aversion from all promiscuous contact with his like, and his passion for his own selfish development to the exclusion of all else, are dangerous forces of disintegration; they sap the foundation of the world and attack the seed of unity it contains. (WTW 173)

Thus, in the condition of the Jewish faith into which Jesus was born — a faith that, ironically, had been born of the risk and the openness of the Red Sea — there was another element in the "fulness of the time" prepared for Jesus' coming. The cross hung over his head from the very beginning, a catastrophe had been prepared, for ". . . without catastrophe of some kind evolutionary potential would soon be exhausted."[9]

Against this hardening of the Law, the exclusiveness that shut out not only Gentiles but even their own "sinners," Jesus pitted the energies of his life and death, the energies of God he allowed to flow through his own openness to the Father. Thus he made possible a forward step in the plan of God.

Development Even In Jesus

* I believe I see a step in the development of Jesus' thinking about Jewish exclusiveness in his encounter with the Syrophoenician mother seeking help for her daughter. (Matthew 15:21-29) At first Jesus refuses her, saying that his mission is only "to the lost sheep of the house of Israel." Only after her wit, her faith in him, and her persistent love of her daughter have given him time, opportunity, and the right conditions to make those relationships in his own consciousness we all know at some time as "inspiration," Jesus sees his mission in wider terms. These terms were to lead to both his death and his victory.

If this seems to see Jesus in too exclusively human terms, I can only say that, if Jesus is a true man, as Christians have always seen him to be — if he gathers up in himself the

---

*This was written ten months before I read Robinson's *The Human Face of God*, where the same opinion appears.

whole of humanity as its leading shoot, as Teilhard sees him — he, too, must have experienced development. Because we can know him only through the eyes and memory of those who remembered and adored him as he became, it is now practically impossible to mark the developments which occurred. Nevertheless, I am convinced that the encounter with the Syrophoenician woman does mark such a moment, even as a similar moment was decisive in the life of the early church. (Acts 10:9 and ff)

To Bring Humanity Forward Jesus Himself Had To Move

Moreover, if, as Christians believe, Jesus brings humanity into a new dimension of life, he had himself to go through that process with the same equipment that is every one's. Otherwise, how can he raise the process and infuse any power into it? How can he honestly invite us to follow him? For me — and I dare to think Teilhard would have agreed — the modern "mystery play," JESUS CHRIST, SUPERSTAR, makes this point more poignantly clear than anything I have yet encountered. The very human Jesus of that play is one with whom any one can identify, not least of all when, rising from the prayer in Gethsemane, he cries, "Take me before I change my mind." The dreadfulness and creatureliness of the human choice which must be made, always without any assurance of finality, is here superbly illustrated. The way in which the choices of Jesus were gradually and inevitably moving him beyond the merely human is equally well brought out in the play by the continual complaint of Jesus' companions, "I don't understand him." "What's the buzz?" The ending of that play, to which many Christians have objected, could not have been different from what it was, leaving each viewer to make his own answer to the question, "Jesus Christ, Jesus Christ, who are you? What have you sacrificed?" Life's business, as Emerson once put it, "is just the terrible choice." In making his choice of trusting the "within" or the "without" to make the creative relationship between them, Jesus chose to trust the spirit, the "within," even against all the evidence. He trusted spirit to such an extent that he became transparent to it. People no longer saw a man, but God through man; however, everyone has to arrive at this sight of himself/herself. God has made this truth plain in the incarnation.

This same choice of trust must be made by every one placed between matter and spirit on the evolutionary journey to God. Jesus reveals that every one is destined for union with God. By his choice he made the great leap forward possible for all who follow him. Having made the advance, he introduces into the human stream the power to do what he has done. This power is appropriated not physically — i.e., by flesh and blood (as the prologue to St. John's Gospel, verses 12-13, makes clear), but by faith. This should be expected since it was not in the physical but in the spiritual, the realm of consciousness, that the breakthrough into humanity came. Moreover, it is not the physical, but the spiritual, which determines the course of evolution. By giving priority, as Jesus did, at the cost of agonizing struggle with every material pull, to the unseen pull which drew him both to humanity and to God, Jesus broke the shackling hold of the warp, the "multiple," over humanity. As God has chosen to work through humans only, once they appeared this victory had to be made by a genuine human. Also, it could be entered into only by genuine human choice.

Although it is a very imperfect analogy, as all analogies are, Jesus was, for the runner of the human race, what Roger Bannister was for mile-runners, "the pioneer and perfecter of our faith," as Hebrews 12:2 puts it. Jesus was the first in all the world perfectly to fulfill the divine command given to Cain about the evil, the pull of the "multiple," that is at the foundation of all things, "You must master it." (Genesis 4:7)

Jesus' Work Of Suffering Released Creative Energy

In the struggle to master it, submitting himself entirely to divine love, Jesus drew upon the energy of that love, and by his struggle and his suffering he released it into the whole cosmic process. Thus he made available to all in its fulness, "the power to become sons of God." (John 1:12)

Teilhard, out of the experience of his own sufferings, mental and spiritual, and his ponderings on the suffering of his beloved sister Marguerite, a life-long invalid, the griefs which came to his family in their many bereavements, and probably above all, the massive sufferings of the First World War, evolved a very interesting and helpful theory about suffering. He saw it as a catalyst for releasing energy into the cosmos. No one who has suffered, physically or mentally, will deny that it drains people of energy. To suffer calls upon all the energy one has and more. Indeed, how often has one heard someone say with wonder, after a very harrowing experience, "I never thought I could go through such an experience!" The energy given off may well be dissipated in resentment and bitterness, which alienate and break unity with oneself, others, and God. But suffering which is endured and accepted — especially suffering which draws and unites itself with love either of others or God, or both — does release power, not only enabling the sufferer to endure but to transform others.

I once saw this happen on one of my pastoral charges. There a man, stricken with multiple sclerosis at the tragically early age that disease strikes, by his sheer helplessness, bravely endured, refined the community in which he lived. His very helplessness brought out the best in his neighbours and friends. His suffering was a channel of the power of God to raise men beyond their present state. In his presence they were kinder, more considerate and unselfish, than they ordinarily were.

Supremely on the cross, the climax and culmination of a life of suffering, Jesus made himself the channel of God's energy of love. He also added to it his own work in battling the warp upon which his own humanity, like the humanity of all, was woven. He had to battle also the evil of the environment in which he lived, an evil which had been intensified by the choice of those before him. No wonder then the cross is a source of power — a transformer in every sense of the word. Here is power, human and divine, united for one end, the raising of the world to God, and no hint of disunion taps any of that energy off. Not the least vestige of self was left to come between the man Jesus and God. In his death Jesus perfectly "hollowed himself out," as Teilhard puts it, for the entrance of God in all his fulness. He then became the full expression of God's love in human form; from him henceforth could come the energy for the transformation of human kind, the Holy Spirit.

Jesus — The Center Of Attraction Drawing Forward

But Teilhard assigns to Christ another role as well, to be the nucleus which can attract and hold the world of humankind. That he can do this Teilhard asserts from the twin grounds of science and Christian experience. In science, he points out (S & C 110), complete consistency defines a natural center. The fact that Christ has been examined as no other and yet still exhibits an *"endless capacity of harmonizing the whole physical and psychological order of our universe* can have but one explanation. The Christ who gradually reveals himself to the Christian thought is not a phantasy or a symbol (*if that were so he would be found in some way wanting or would cease to satisfy us*); he is, or at least he introduces, the reality of what, through the whole structure of human activity, we are awaiting."

An African woman first introduced to the revelation of Jesus about the fatherhood of God, once said the same thing in profoundly simple language, "I always knew God was like that; why hasn't someone told us this before?"

From another part of the world, Japan, comes the report, through a representative of a Bible Society, that when the first Christian missionaries landed they found a convert already made. Through reading a New Testament which had been washed ashore he had become committed to Jesus Christ, whom he found to be the answer to all his longing.

The Importance Of Jesus' Life

Although, like the gospel writers, Teilhard places most emphasis in his writing on the passion and death of Jesus, he recognizes the significance of Jesus' life and person. In the life of the historical Jesus he writes, "We see the Master of the world, leading ... an elemental life but ... leading the total life of the universe ... by experiencing it."[10] "You, Jesus," he says again, (WTW 211) "are the epitome and the crown of all perfection, human and cosmic. No flash of beauty, no enchantment of goodness, no element of force, but finds in you its ultimate refinement and consummation."

His Decision-Making

I spoke earlier of the element of decision-making in Jesus' life, as in every life. Rollo May, one of the great modern psychiatrists, sees as an aspect of a new dynamic, the old principle, "*decision precedes insight and knowledge.*"[11] It is interesting to note that the only incident in the gospels from Jesus' youth shows him making what, from his parents' reaction to it, would seem to be his first big independent decision (Luke 2:41-50) — to stay behind in the Temple to ask questions. This is followed by his decision to respond to John's summons to baptism, his decision in the temptations, and so on. That these decisions led to greater insight and knowledge is made plain by the Gospels, which over and over record men's amazement at the depths of Jesus' insight and knowledge. "He knew what was in man," says St. John (2:24). "Where did this man get these things?" ask his neighbours (Mark 7:8ff). Both Matthew and Mark record that people were aware that "he spoke with authority, and not as the scribes." (Matt. 7:29, Mark 1:22). And the faith Jesus inspired in the Roman centurion who came to ask for help for his sick servant (Mark 7:8ff) comes from the fact that he, a soldier under a higher command, recognizes in Jesus one who could do more than an ordinary man because he was in touch with a higher authority.

The Miracles

This brings us to the question of the miracles which occupy so much space in the gospel records. Once they served to awaken faith, as Teilhard notes (C & E 160) but now they largely prove barriers to it. Some years ago, when I was teaching a teenage Sunday School class, the day came when they decided to trust me enough to come out with the doubts they had about miracles. "This business of walking on the water," one objected. "I've tried it and it just doesn't work." I conceded that that was likely, and then we explored the fact that he was not able to be very much like Jesus in his relationships with people and the general conduct of his life either. We looked at various explanations of the stilling of the storm, such as the possibility that Jesus had known it was going to happen from his observation of how weather developed in that part of the lake and simply pretended to make it stop to impress them. They wouldn't accept this because they had experienced Jesus' integrity for themselves. They at last came to the conclusion that the greatest of all the miracles of Jesus was the kind of person he *was*.

This is directly in the line of Teilhard's thinking. We have just seen evidences from psychology and from the gospels that Jesus knew more. Teilhard says over and over, to know more is to be more. Again, if it is the love of God which is the energy moving all things and Jesus himself, by his own free will, placed himself in that love without limit so that in him there was a new degree of integrity and a closer contact with the power of God, then anyone near him is in a powerful field of attraction. As Teilhard puts it (FM 220) in the vicinity of Jesus "we shall be entering a new world of relationship where the hitherto impossible may become simple, being enacted in other dimensions and another environment."

If Jesus is, indeed, as Teilhard sees him, ahead of humanity in the evolutionary process then, as we continue to learn more about the way in which the universe works, Polanyi's views about our doubts may well be valid. "Some of these doubts may turn out one day to have been as wanton, as bigoted and dogmatic as those of which we have now been cured."[12]

A student of the phenomenon of brain-washing in China, claims that thoughts and words have previously unimagined powers to penetrate to the very depths of personality. Such a revelation should warn us about labelling things "impossible" or "unreasonable." Moreover, with Jesus we have to deal with the powers of faith and of love. Speaking about extrasensory perception, Price has said, ". . . the idea 'that such things do not happen' expresses itself by preventing the phenomen from occurring, or at least making it more difficult for them to occur. In an age of faith, when the general opinion is credulous instead of sceptical, it is presumably the other way around. It really is easier for "queer events to happen just because everybody thinks they do happen."[13]

If, as Teilhard believes, Jesus had insight into, knowledge of, and relationship with, a higher dimension of life and its laws and lived in harmony with these, it seems to me not only possible but inevitable that the disorder he found would be brought out of chaos by the power to which Jesus submitted without any reservation — the love of God, the force unifying all creation.

Jesus, Himself The At-One-Ment

In Jesus we have the at-one-ment between the purpose of God for humankind and its fulfilment. Here is a man with "everything in subjection under his feet." (Hebrews 2:8). By his full acceptance of the cost of creation, which his suffering on the cross reveals Jesus broke through the barrier into the realm of spirit. Thus he makes it possible for us to do "greater works" than he had done "because I go to the Father." (John 14:12).

Moreover, being the one whose perfection fulfills all our dreams and hopes and the mighty plan of God, Jesus is himself the justification of the whole costly process God set in motion at creation. As we have noted many times, as all of us are aware in our passage through life, the cost is a very high one. Supremely, of course, this cost is revealed to us on the cross. "The Cross, . . . " writes Teilhard (C & E 163) "is now the symbol not merely of the dark retrogressive side of the universe in genesis but also and even more of its triumphant and luminous side . . . symbol of progress and victory won through mistakes, disappointments and hard work." It reveals to us not only the depths of our own nature, with all their horror and darkness, and our utter need of a divine partner, but also what it is in us to be, what therefore we will never be satisfied without becoming, and the cost that must be paid to reach that satisfaction. Once for all the cross should reveal to us that life is not "a bowl of cherries" but an enormously costly battle exacting a very heavy cost. The perfection of the man Jesus is the "justification" of that price.

Jesus Enables Us To See That The Cost Of The Struggle Is Worth It

Without Jesus, we, the reflective element of the cosmos, might well conclude, as many have, that the whole evolutionary process is too cruel and too costly. But Jesus of Nazareth, perfect man, is indeed God's justification of all that has gone before. Jesus Christ, risen and triumphant, is the justification we must have to maintain our zest for life in face of all the labour, pains, griefs, and strife by which alone we can do our part in bringing God's purpose to its fulfilment for "the doctrine of the Cross is that . . . human life . . . leads somewhere, and that . . . upward . . . towards the highest possible spiritualization by means of the greatest possible effort." (DM 102). It opens our eyes not only to the direction in which things are moving, but to the demands and cost of meeting those demands, of accepting that direction, and to the potentialities at our disposal. Jesus, crucified, risen and ascended, is our justification for undertaking the life to which the Cross challenges us. For the Cross is, also, as Teilhard points out, a principle of selection among humankind, as it was during the lifetime of Jesus. When he began in his ministry to talk about the cost of following him, men went away; but Jesus himself was and is the justification of those who remain because, with Peter, they have come to know he "has the words of eternal life." (John 6:68). His life reveals what the whole process in which the universe is involved is about, what it is striving to produce, and in his attractiveness we can find that process, as Teilhard has said, "loveable." His resurrection reveals the other essential for us to keep our zest for life and effort, the assurance that the good is not wasted, the struggle is not in vain.

The Resurrection's Assurance of Victory
Christianity's Great Contribution

It is here supremely, that Teilhard sees the contribution Christianity has to make to humankind. Without the assurance that death, disintegration, is not the end, people will not continue to strive with the expensive and agonizing striving which is involved in creation. There are those, I know, who feel this is nonsense, but they have not yet met the dreadful drain of real and ultimate hopelessness. Even logic itself has to yield this point, as a debate held at Cambridge Senate House in 1965 between Dr. Patrick Corbett of the Department of Philosophy, University of Bradford, representing the humanist point of view, and Dr. Donald Mackinnon of the Divinity Faculty, Cambridge University, made clear.

It Shows Us We Live In An Open-Ended Universe

Everyone needs to know the truths the resurrection of Jesus displays — that is, that we live in an open-ended universe, one in which the law of decreasing energy and therefore of disintegration, does not have the last word. But, as the Christian religion teaches, this pull against the forward movement can be overcome only by the way Jesus taught and lived, the way of humility, of openness towards that which is "within" and that which is ahead; the dedication of oneself to the finest and best one knows, no matter what the price or what the evidence presented; by obedience to the rule of love of God and others.

When Jesus, in his baptism, identified himself with humanity, acknowledging his sense of creatureliness with all, and his need for God, and dedicated himself to the will of God as a man, he began the work of creative union, of creating a complexity out of which a new state of consciousness could arise   By his own free choice he lived by that new consciousness. Out of his love and concern for God and others he chose, in the temptations, the most powerful way to convey the conditions by which life was to be lived, the ways of teaching and preaching, of communication. He would help all to know more that they might be more. As he said, "These things I have spoken to you, that my joy may be in you, and that your joy may be full," (John 15:11), and again, "I came that they might have life and have it more abundantly." (John 10:10).

We Need To Know More And More

That humans are equipped to learn more than what they need to live as physical beings, with their chief concern what they eat and wear, is revealed by the findings of science. The psychologist, May, illustrates this from his field, pointing out that when the cortex is impaired patients concentrate on the concrete — i.e., the less than human.[14] Jesus warned us not to concentrate on the concrete. God, he said, had looked after this side. In this, then, he was not talking impractical idealism at all, as some people charge, but what the Canadian novelist, Basil Partridge, has called "the common sense of a lively belief in Christ Crucified.[15]

Teilhard sees the life and particularly the suffering and death of Jesus as providing revelation that all may know more. In addition, he sees him making a tremendous contributon to the energy available in the universe, to overcome the pull of the "multiple," the law of decreasing energy. It is simply not true, as some contend, that in denying the Fall and in his emphasis on the victorious rather than the expiatory side of the Cross, Teilhard is underestimating the power and dreadfulness of evil. He is deeply conscious of what it cost Jesus to win the victory. He acknowledges its dominant presence in all as the very warp on which their humanity is woven. Christ's victory over evil in life and death is, in very truth, as John's gospel continually reiterates, the judgment on giving in to evil, since Jesus, whose potentialities all have, overcame it. He reveals what we can do, what we fail to do, and how we can overcome the enemy, by living the same life of abandonment of self in love of God and others as he did.

Jesus Makes What We Need
Possible To Use

If Jesus did only this, however, he would be not good news but bad; but he does more than reveal what we have within us to be, and how we should be able to do it; he makes what we ought to be possible to us. The goal of evolution is spirit. Jesus is God's supreme revelation. As we accept this revelation as relevant to us and for our lives we are brought nearer the goal for, as Teilhard writes (WTW 256), "Revelation creates spirit to the degree that it enlightens them." However, Teilhard sees and emphasizes the other function Jesus performs in bringing us to "new birth." By his own personal triumph in living perfectly a wholly human life, by the extreme effort of his suffering and death in perfect unity with God and his 'neighbours' by which the final conditions for his transformation into the final state of spirit are produced, Jesus takes the place designed for him from the beginning as the Omega point of the evolutionary process. He becomes not only the goal and crown of creation, but the working and energizing point of attraction for the whole of the cosmos. He fulfils that role which John (12:32) says he forecast for himself, "I, if I be lifted up, will draw all men to me." His function as the Omega, the attractive center of the convergent universe, now has a face for all who will believe in him, who in his baptism joined himself to the earth and to all in their creatureliness; who in his own life exerted human potentialities to their limit in the only way they can be released — through cooperation with God, having reached the summit of human perfection, took that perfection with him beyond the barriers between matter and spirit, and there was released from time and space to be present to us. Thus he can fulfil the function of the Omega point, that of the "magnet," the point of convergence — for, as Teilhard says (P of M 296), "To be supremely attractive Omega must be supremely present."

The work which the human Jesus did during his lifetime in Palestine — that of transforming lives, of making them whole, of drawing them into association with each other and into new and more potent relationship with the world, he continues to perform. He becomes a zone of attraction which can draw them through the barriers of mutual repulsion into "a new world of relationship." And since that is finally relationship with God, the result of his "being lifted up" is indeed — for those who believe — "eternal life." (John 3:14-15).

Jesus, Awakening People's Love, Draws Them Into New Relationship

Through his human life and death, his teaching by word and life of the love and acceptance — the Fatherhood of God — Jesus awakens love. This is a tremendously important function of the incarnate Christ, for we must remember, in Teilhard's thought, individuals must become willingly, joyfully, and lovingly part of "Mankind" before that complexity results which will make possible union with Omega to fill out the fulness of Christ — the Pleroma. The individual must be rescued from that state of mutual repulsion, of aversion and hostility to others of his kind which, as a center, he naturally has. Only love, such as Christ has shown, the greatest love 'that lays down his life for his friends' (John 15:13) can awaken the kind of love that makes "man . . . the most magnificently synthesizeable of all the elements ever constructed by nature." (A. of E. 71).

Thus it is that belief in Christ, acceptance of him "as one's personal saviour," is indeed a "new birth," as Jesus tells Nicodemus. (John 3:3). Because with the appearance of humans the factors influencing evolution are less and less material and more and more spiritual; it is by faith that men and women become the "new creatures" about which St. Paul speaks. (2 Cor. 5:17). Those who by faith come into the zone of attraction of the Christ-Omega are formed into what Teilhard calls "the Christian phylum." By this he means that those who, by their deliberate and voluntary acceptance of Jesus Christ as their Saviour and Lord, to become part of his church, constitute a new and clearly differentiated species within the human race, even as St. Paul and St. John suggest. The love-energy of Christ, freely accepted by them and awaking their love, has brought about an alteration, not in their bodies, their "without" — for with the arrival of *Homo Sapiens* that phase of evolution had come to a close — but in the "within." There has begun to come about in each one an integration of the whole person — now especially including the emotions — a coiling in, which has, in the past, brought forth a newness; this time it is a new kind of person.

This In Turn Creates A New Order Of Persons

Teilhard thinks of this transforming work of Jesus as operative, not just morally and intellectually — as is usual — but organically. He believes that the work of Christ in life and death had a transforming effect on the make-up of the human species, and justifies this belief from his scientific knowledge. "Just as in living bodies a cell, at first similar to other cells, can gradually come to be preponderant in the organism, so the particular humanity of Christ was able (at least at Resurrection) to take on, to acquire, a universal morphological [i.e., formative] effect." (C & E 41).

The special gift of Christ is seen throughout the New Testament as the Holy Spirit. It is his to give, however, only after the Resurrection. First he had to live the life of perfect trust in, and love of, God and others. Then he had to die in the same spirit, yielding up his human spirit to God according to what he felt to be God's will. So Jesus cooperated with God in the sanctification of the human spirit. Thus, the gift which previously God had given only to a few privileged individuals became Christ's to make available to all who, placing themselves by faith within the zone of his influence, would be enabled to receive it. So there came about that great moment in Acts (2:15ff) when Peter would see the fulfilment of the prophecy of Joel — the pouring out of the spirit on all flesh. No longer, as Jesus himself was to say (Matthew 11:12) would the Kingdom of God have to be won by violence. Every human spirit could be made holy through faith in him who was himself the very Kingdom of God.

So the strength of humanity reaches its intended pitch, as the relationship for which it was created is at length established. All the disorder in creation (Genesis 3) has its remedy now available for, as Martin Buber puts it, "Man's will to profit and to be powerful have their natural and proper effect so long as they are linked up with and upheld by, his will to enter into relation."[16]

Jesus performs his transforming work on people's wills. He pours out his love energy so to strengthen their consciousness to unify mind, will, and heart, that with the whole self they yearn to enter into that relationship for which he made and so come to be what they were meant to be.

As a character in the T.S. Eliot play THE CONFIDENTIAL CLERK puts it, "if someone else sees me as I really am, I might become myself."[11] Jesus assures us this is what God does. He sees us and treats us as if we already were what he made us to be and thus enables us to fulfill our destiny.

The New Relationship Is Only The Beginning

However, with the birth of faith in Jesus, the "new creature" is only *born*. It is not fully grown. Since those changes and alterations which Christ is making in the members of his species are not external but internal, not physical but spiritual, only Christ himself knows his own. (John 13:18). The one mark which Jesus said would distinguish those who were his was "love for one another." (John 13:35). Thus is provided the condition whereby the next development in evolution can take place — the forming of a united mankind, a new union in which individuals, entering in love into a larger whole, will become more themselves.. This will happen because "creative union," the kind Teilhard sees coming into being through the process of evolution, has had this effect. Out of this larger union will come a body of such complexity that a new state is prepared for. All, therefore, is prepared for the second coming of Christ to make plain the nature of the power behind the universe; to offer the opportunity of fulfilment in a new union with himself. This time, however, his revelation and invitation are made not to individuals, but to the whole integrated humanity.

The Second Coming Provides Occasion For "The Fall"

It is at the moment of Christ's second coming, when the meaning and end of the whole process is revealed that Teilhard sees the possibility of a Fall, of a cosmic tragedy. All along the way people are free to choose love or hate, Christ or themselves, what seems to them to be their own advantage and safety in stability or separation, or the way of life which is abandonment of self to ever higher union. All along the way there is the possibility of separation and therefore the disintegration, but the final and greatest choice, the one requiring the greatest effort of all, is the choice between humankind's adoration of itself, and of Christ. Right up to the end the possibility of final tragedy remains open. Nevertheless, with the Bible, Teilhard insists that the initial victory of Christ ensures the fulfilment of God's plan. Teilhard is an optimist. This is not surprising, for he was also a mystic, and as Martin Israel, in his lecture in the open series on Mysticism (Cambridge University 1974) said, "No mystic can be a pessimist."

You will notice that in the seamlessness of Teilhard's theology we have quickly passed through three important areas of salvation and the last things. In order to put them into relation it was necessary thus to weave them together. However, I will go back a little and deal with what Teilhard has to say about each.

Salvation — Final Union With God

The salvation which Teilhard envisages is certainly salvation from death (disintegration) and hell, though it is with the greatest reluctance, at the end of *The Phenomenon of Man*, Teilhard accepts the idea of anyone's suffering eternal separation and disintegration. When, with the emergence of the human thought appeared in the universe, Teilhard believes that the threshold has been passed whereby death can bring annihilation. Writing to Leontine Zanta he says, "To dissolve the soul seems to me, in all sincerity, infinitely more difficult than to split the atom." (p. 87). He feels this way because he sees the soul as a stage much farther up the scale in its centeredness and therefore in its unity than the atom. This means then, that if people do not choose to go God's way and yield themselves to his power to transform them more and more into that which is fit for union with himself, they will inevitably choose the pangs and path of eternal separation.

Teilhard therefore was not a "universalist," at least in his mind. In his heart he found the result of his logic hard to take. He knew too much about the rigid principle of selection which goes on in the process of evolution to entertain an idea of universal salvation. However, he did insist, what Christians have always believed, that when they are yielded to God in trust and love, failures, mistakes, and even sins, can be used by God in his great plan. Over and over he quotes the words of St. Paul to the Romans, "In everything God works for good with those who love God, who are called according to his purpose." (Romans 8:28). In the scheme of things before people the element of chance in the play of large numbers necessary for new combinations to produce new forms may seem to entail a terrible, tragic waste, until one is aware of the essential part played even by those which are not "chosen" to continue; for instance, the important role of the sperm, which literally pave the way, making it possible for one of their number to reach the ovum, in the process of conception. In the non-human realm the individual had no choice as to what happened to it, whether it would be chosen or not. With the advent of humanity even this was put into their control; they had to make the choices. Moreover, equipped with consciousness, an awareness of the central order, as Paul insists (Romans 1:19, 20), we are aware that there is a principle of choice — a right and a wrong, often confusedly, but nevertheless certainly. We can choose to go God's way or our own — "the way of progress through extreme effort" — or the way of seeming ease and pleasure to death. Because the latter is the obverse side of the love of God, that love which is intent on rescuing us from the disintegration of the "multiple," it is no surprise that the Bible, in its teaching as to the personhood of God, speaks of this as God's wrath. It is indeed that against which God turns his wrath, that against which he puts the power of his love, the power that made and governs the universe, the power behind all the "laws of nature."

The wonderful thing which the teaching and cross of Jesus make plain is that, when by free choice we turn from our own to God's way, putting his life into God's zone of attraction which he has entrusted to the risen Christ, even those things which before have been, as it were, "minus signs" become "plus signs."

How wise was that child who, for the first time after she had started to learn mathematical signs at school, noticed the cross at the front of her church! "Why," she asked her father, "do we have a plus in our church?" The cross is the world's supreme sign of enrichment.

However, right up to the end, when the final opportunity of choice comes between yielding oneself to loving union with Christ Omega or seeking to exercise dominion over all, the human will has the power to say "no." But that to which the human will says "no" in the final judgment we make will not be simply the acceptance or rejection of Jesus of Nazareth as he is presented by all or even any Christian group; it will be to the love of God urging his creation ever on and forward to the goal of complete and final union with himself in an ecstasy of adoration, love, and praise.

This union is, however, not the union of individuals *as individuals* with God. The pattern Teilhard has seen in the universe all along — of union creating complexity, making possible higher consciousness — he projects into the future. Union with God presupposes a breakthrough into a new realm, that can only be accomplished through the kind of union Jesus Christ, demanding of his followers, makes possible to them — a union of love one with another. Teilhard thus sees the next step in the process of creative union, the creation of a "Mankind." As before, when molecule was joined to molecule to bring into being a new physical whole, so the complex molecules which humans scientifically are, are united not in a physical union (since that state is now past), but a spiritual union of all that is uniquely human — of mind and heart, into a new whole. Like all the wholes previously brought into being by the uniting power of God's love, this whole will be something greater than the sum of the parts; and in it also, as before, each part will be completely and more perfectly itself while completely and perfectly part of the whole. The result of this union will be the final preparation for the culmination of the process God revealed in Jesus Christ — Incarnation. The formation and transformation of "Mankind" will bring into being a body to be indwelt by the glorified Christ. For the Christ whose resurrection was "the center throwing off its original shell of complication" (A of E 45), "Mankind" will be a glorified Body, "the fulness of him who fills all in all." (Ephesians 1:23).

Just as earlier in the process, molecule had united with molecule in a centered whole which was complex enough to be the vehicle of life, and then, in the realm of life, a creature complex and centered enough had produced a whole, complex enough to be an expression of thought, so once again, in the realm of thinking beings, a whole will come into being, complex and centered enough to be the dwelling place of the highest of all, the glorified Christ.

Teilhard, you see, agrees with those groups who insist, on the basis of the words in Revelation 7:4, that the completion of all things requires a multitude, though I doubt that he would be as certain as they are about knowing the number. The important emphasis here is that "salvation" is not a strictly individual thing. He would also agree, again with passages in the Book of Revelation, about a great and final conflict, a mighty act of decision on the part of "Mankind," a crisis of judgment.

He envisions "Mankind" coming in two streams, as it were, to the crisis when the purpose of the whole process is revealed in Christ's coming to claim this body prepared for him. This is Teilhard's version of the second coming of Christ, the Parousia. In one stream are those who, having seen and yielded to the love of God in Jesus Christ, have been enabled by his spirit to unite themselves closer and closer in love with other men and the world for which Christ died. This part of "Mankind" is Christianity, "a 'phylum' of love in nature," Teilhard calls it. (H. E. 15). For this part of "Mankind" the glorified Christ has been their Omega; they have been conscious of him as their goal ad magnet. They have, as John says (5:24), "passed through the judgment." The second stream consists of those who have not said to Jesus, "Lord, Lord," possibly because of the failure of the church in its presentation of the Gospel, but who "*dare to set* the center of their being outside themselves . . . to love another more than themselves, . . . dare to pass through death to life." (WTW 112). These "have done the will of the Father," (Matthew 7:21-22). At the time of the second coming of Christ both these streams will find they have converged on the same goal. The Omega of the non-Christian will be revealed at the Parousia to be the Christ of the Christian. The process in which all humanity, indeed all the universe, has been involved will now be known to all as the preparation for a final Incarnation, the union of mankind with Christ.

But, while the formation of all earlier "complexities" was of non-conscious beings who had no part in their selection, those involved this time are free. Whether they yield themselves to this final union is a matter of their judgment, a final judgment, "the choice between arrogant autonomy and loving excentration," as Teilhard puts it (FM 19), to fulfill themselves collectively upon themselves or personally on another greater than themselves. Surely this is the invitation offered to "those on the right hand" in Jesus' parable of the Last Judgment (Matthew 25:34), "Come, you blessed of my Father — inherit the kingdom prepared for you from the foundation of the world." It is at this point that the mighty conflict, pictured by the Book of Revelation, can occur. Because "Thought has never completely united upon itself here below, . . . " the 'noosphere' [Teilhard's name for the thinking part of creation] . . . may "split into two zones, each attracted to an opposite pole of adoration . . . universal love would only vivify and detach finally a fraction of the noosphere so as to consummate it — the part which decided to 'cross the threshold,' to get outside itself into the other." (PM 317). Then comes the final and decisive division in the great twin movements of unification and division which have gone on since God initiated creation. Here, at length, creation-redemption-incarnation have reached their fulfilment and end.

No Christian will quarrel with Teilhard about the movement of creation towards such an end. This is part and parcel of orthodox Christian doctrine. However, it is not just to Christian doctrine or the Bible that Teilhard points, but to what is going on in the world and society as he cries, "Come and see!"

Teilhard Sees Mankind Now Coming Into Being

Because I have found that many people — even those who confess that after reading Teilhard, they did not understand him — were set on fire by the signs of hope he sees in the world, I want to spend a little time now looking at the late twentieth century through his eyes.

"Mankind," he insists, is coming into being before our eyes. Though Teilhard naturally thinks of developments taking place in the kind of time we saw illustrated in the charts at the end of chapter three, he knew a rapid speeding up had taken place in the last fifty years. Such things as the crowding together of people through sheer increase of population on this round, limited earth, the growth of cities, the rapid means of transportation and communication which have caused the earth to "shrink," have made it absolutely necessary for us to devise some means of living together as one.

The rise of thought in research has led to scientific discoveries that have both enabled us to do this and made it more necessary. Not least among those is the splitting of the atom. Teilhard's delighted reaction to the first time this was done led some people to reject him without fully appreciating what he had said. Certainly he rejoiced in the tremendous achievement brought about through this extension of human knowledge, the ability we had developed, at the cost of great effort and cooperation. Believing, as he did, that the historic incarnation had revealed to us that into our hands had been placed responsibility for the direction and forwarding of evolution, he rejoiced in this evidence that people had at last discovered the way to control and use the energies with which they had to work. Moreover, he rejoiced that, with such a decisively destructive weapon in our hands, we would be forced to learn to live in unity, to give up war as a means of settling disputes and differences. It was his conviction that any development that brings about unity has its contribution to make to God's great final purpose. This view caused him to direct some praise to another quarter, again alienating some, to the totalitarian regimes in Italy and Germany before and during the Second World War, and Russia after it. His praise was for the unity of organization achieved by Hitler and Mussolini, and later by Stalin; certainly it did not extend to their methods. Indeed, he used them in his argument that love, and only love, is the basis for the true union of mankind. Nevertheless, he saw in these and all other such experiments, part of the "groping" process inherent in evolution.

This is the way, Teilhard insists, that we must also see the many blots and blemishes in modern life over which we often despair; the dehumanizing and depersonalizing effects of many of the movements which are forcing or bringing us to work and live together ever more closely and dependently — all the way from consolidated schools, unions, multinational corporations, and economic communities, to scientific endeavours which can now be carried out only by huge teams formed on a multinational basis. Anyone who has ever been part of a large group united in any enterprise — an orchestra, a choir, a sports team, a research team, or a group in industry — can attest to the feeling of exhilaration, the sense of greater personal fulfilment and expanded ability such an experience gives. Research done into motivation for work has shown that one of the strongest incentives to good work is acceptance by one's group, a desire to be part of the production team. The experience of anyone who has done Bible study or any other kind of study in a group has surely been that passages which had been lifeless or obscure in private reading came alive. Perhaps there is more wisdom in the adage, "Two heads are better than one" — the wisdom of Teilhard who foretells the advance of evolution towards a higher sphere in the formation of individuals into "Mankind."

But no one needs to have emphasized surely, that Teilhard is right in seeing love as the only force which will bring this unity into being. Although sometimes it seems we are far away yet from this, the recent repudiation of war, the first really widespread repudiation in history on the part of young people and others influenced by the new means of communication — television, radio, the printed page, and world travel — is surely a hopeful sign. A young man, just finished his education and early apprenticeship in industry on a world tour, significantly wrote to his mother that his was the first generation for whom such freedom as his had been possible. Previously young men of his age had been drafted off to war. With this thought in mind, and a background of Teilhard's thought, I found it extremely interesting to go through the Guards' Museum in London looking at the uniforms worn by fighting men over several centuries. As one went from period to period it became obvious that, slowly but surely, men were becoming disillusioned about the glamour of war. The uniforms became drabber and less like costumes for a fancy dress ball until, at the beginning of the twentieth century, seemingly very suddenly there came the earth-coloured khaki with little, if any, relieving decoration.

Christians Have A Duty To Look For And Encourage All Signs Of Mankind

Rather than constantly bemoaning those things which are forcing people into closer and closer association — as Christians, alas, far too often do — we can, if we will, see signs of hope and take seriously our mission to encourage and further every move towards unity in love in our world. This should mean especially making the church a living proof that a community of love is a possibility; that it is indeed a reality, and thereby infuse into society the one element which can make a community of humankind.

Certainly there are many setbacks and much to discourage one; setbacks are a characteristic of evolution. The higher we go in its path, the steeper and more hazardous the road. As Boulding writes, "The process of moral learning is a long uphill climb, and the hill seems to get steeper and slipperier as we climb it."[18] The fact that collective mankind — whether in nation, parliament, trade union, or even church — is often less developed morally, less effective, less spiritual than individuals should not discourage us if we will remember that these are examples of a very new, very undeveloped kind of creature. Moreover, if we also remember Teilhard's idea that everything has as its warp "the multiple" against which God — and therefore, we — must continually struggle, we will not be quite so shocked or disillusioned when creation seems slow and even non-existent. Christians, of all people, should know how great is the cost of progress.

Nevertheless, progress there is if we know what to look for, and the signs of its coming — the rise of spirit. It is here that some feel they find the greatest reason for criticism of Teilhard's ideas. "If progress is towards spirit," they complain, "how is it we do not find things getting better and better?" Such people are equating "spirit" with "Holy Spirit." Let us remember there is also evil spirit, and if spirit be evil — as it may well be when it chooses to direct itself towards separation and hostility — then, as Jesus says of the eye that is evil, "How great is that darkness!" The part which those of good will, particularly Christians, must be sure to play in a world such as ours is to make sure that in every way, by the greatest possible effort, they work for all those things which will ensure that the evil, dehumanizing, depersonalizing features in society are eliminated, and the good, the fine, and the lovely — that which is most Christ-like — has a chance to rise and grow.

Because Teilhard was under no illusion as to the evil people can do — and evil, he knew, would become more fearsome, with more terrible consequences, as their capabilities increased and the pressures forcing them into closer and more complex forms of organization raised the spiritual temperature — he devoted his life to making people see where they were going. Especially was he concerned that the church, the guardian and trusted transmitter of God's revelation, should become, not the stumbling block to progress she has so often been, but its guide into constructive and illuminated channels. Here, one notes with sorrow, he was a "prophet without honour in his own country."

The Future Teilhard Envisions

However, as I pointed out in an earlier chapter, among those engaged in "future's" research today his work is very influential. What sort of future did he foresee? In many of his writings he is at great pains to dispel any idea of a materialistic "paradise." In *Hymn Of The Universe* (99-100 in a passage taken from F. of M.) he writes, "Let us admit this frankly, once and for all: what most discredits faith in progress in the eyes of men today, over and above its reticences and its helplessness in meeting the cry of the 'last days of the human species,' is the unfortunate tendency still shown by its adepts to distort into pitiful millenarianisms all that is most valid and most noble in our now permanently awakened expectation of the future appearance of some form of 'ultra-humanity.' An era of abundance and euphoria — a Golden Age — is, they suggest, all that evolution could hold in reserve for us. And it is but right that our hearts should sink at the thought of so 'bourgeois' an ideal.

In face of this strictly 'pagan' materialism and naturalism it becomes a pressing duty to remind ourselves once again that, if the laws of biogenesis of their nature suppose and effectively bring about an economic improvement in human living conditions, it is not any question of *well-being*, it is solely a thirst for *greater-being* that by psychological necessity can save the thinking world from the *taedium vitae*.

He was sure this "boredom" would arise if people were to direct their skills, knowledge, and increasing consciousness only to the production and enjoyment of more and more things. Such boredom would make them give up the struggle for the higher and finer and turn their energies to the destructive ends of searching for more pleasure instead of more life. Such direction could only culminate in cosmic and personal destruction. Some of the things we deplore in our present society are fulfilments of just this fear.

Out of his own experience Teilhard was sure that what people really want is more life, and that this life more abundant could be found only in union with the source of all life, God himself. It has been most interesting for me to find, in my reading in the field of science in preparing this work, how many — dealing with the question of the future and where things are going — come to this same conclusion. The scientist Thorpe, for example, writes, "The most strenuous attempts to carry logical thought to its utmost limits culminates in mysticism."[19] Because the mystic has often been portrayed in pious literature as someone so eccentric and withdrawn as to be less than human, it is comforting to hear Thorpe quoting Polanyi, speak in very different terms: "... the mystic differs in degree but not in kind from more ordinary men ... The characteristics of the true mystic include perspective and proportion, sanity and stability. The test of a true mystical ecstasy lies not in its outward sign but in its inward grace."[20] The pathologist, Martin Israel — himself a modern mystic (Cambridge Divinity School Open Lectures, 1974) — has said that the test of the validity of a mystical experience is whether the mystic returns to the ordinary ways of life a more effective person. Accounts of Teilhard's life and character by those who knew him well present this kind of mystic.

Because of his mystical experience of the power of God, seen by others as the process of evolution, causing all things to converge and rise towards spirit, Teilhard believed there lay ahead for our planet the appearance of a super-humanity, "Mankind," and finally, as the end of our planet, "a psychic rather than a material turning about — possibly like a death — which will in fact be a liberation from the material phase of history and elevation in God." (H.E. 47). As the Bible puts it (I Thess. 1:10), "in the great day (the Lord) comes to be glorified among his own and adored among all believers."

The Consummation — A Great Act Of Worship

Although it is far from clear whether Teilhard sees the consummation of the plan of God in one or two stages, it does seem possible that the latter is his view. First, there is the converging of all things in Christ, a second Incarnation. As he says, "To understand the Incarnation begin at the end; look at Paul and John ... the vision they see ... the building up of a living church — of a mystical body — of a consummated totality, of a pleroma." (C & E 67). In this state too, possibly, he sees a development still going on until the end comes in which, as St. Paul puts it (I Cor. 15), "He (that is, Christ) must reign until he has put all his enemies under his feet." Then, "when all things are subject to him, the Son himself will also be subjected to him who put all things under him, that God may be everything to every one. (I cor. 15:25, 28). All ends, therefore, in a glorious unity of the whole. The great act of creation-redemption ends, as God in Jesus Christ had revealed to men it was to end, in a glorious incarnation. As Teilhard wrote, "The Incarnation will be complete only when the part of the chosen substance contained in every object . . . shall have rejoined the final center of its completion." (D.M. 62). Thus he makes no suggestion that the material is to be despised or avoided. Rather, it is to be sublimated and transcended when it has been brought to its perfection.

Judgment

As Teilhard remains true to scripture in his vision of the end as a sublime act of worship, he agrees with the scriptural insistence on judgment. And he is definite about the criteria by which judgment is made. "Not all directions are good for our advance . . . Here we part company with the whole-hearted individualists, the egoists who seek to grow by excluding or diminishing their fellows, individually, nationally or racially. Life moves towards unification. Our hope can only be realized if it finds expression in greater cohesion, and greater human solidarity." (F of M 75).

He does not speculate about the final state of either the rejected . . . those who exclude themselves — or the redeemed. However, in *Science and Christ* (85) he writes, "The monads will join in a headlong rush to the place irrevocably appointed for them by the total adulthood of things and the inexorable irreversibility of the whole history of the world — some, spiritualized matter, in the limitless fulfilment of an eternal communion — others, materialized spirit in the conscious torment of endless decomposition." And, elsewhere, ". . . nothing is more in harmony with the outlook of a universe in evolution. Every evolution . . . involves selection and rejection . . . there can be loss . . . to assert the existence of hell is simply a negative way of saying that by physical and organic necessity, we can attain our happiness and fulfilment only by being true to the movement which carries us along, and so reaching the term of our evolution, (that is a full consciousness of all in all), or supreme death (that is, a consciousness infinitely disunited in itself) . . . Hell is and has meaning only insofar as it occupies in our outlook . . . the opposite pole from God." (C & E 164-5).

Heaven

About "heaven" Teilhard appears to have the same difficulty I can remember being experienced by the decorations committee preparing for open house at the theological college I attended. Very rashly they had chosen the "last things" for their theme! They had no trouble at all with the section of the common room they had designated for hell, but no one could come up with anything at all to put into heaven!

Apart from many references to "ecstasy," "adoration," and "worship," only a few passages possibly contain some lead as to his thinking on the subject. The lyrical passage in *Hymn Of The Universe*, about the ecstasy of union with all things in God suggests at least the colour and atmosphere with which he invests heaven, when the constant prayer will be fulfilled, "Thy will be done in earth, as in heaven." "Let us leave the surface and, without leaving the world, plunge into God. There, and from there, in him and through him, we shall hold all things and have command of all things, we shall find again the essence and the splendour of all the flowers, the lights, we have had to surrender here and now in order to be faithful to life. Those beings whom here and now we despair of ever reaching and influencing, they too will be there, united together at that central point in their being which is at once the most vulnerable, the most enriching. There, even the least of our desires and our endeavours will be gathered and preserved, and be able to evoke instantaneous vibration from the very heart of the universe." (127).

Personally I believe that, had Teilhard ever chosen — as did C.S. Lewis — to try to picture in parable form the future state beyond the material, he would have produced something very like *The Great Divorce*.

The Consummation Not Limited To Earth

There is one more thing that could be said about

Teilhard's view of the consummation of the creation-redemption-incarnation process. He did not limit it to our planet. Though he died in 1955 and wrote the following words in 1920, he had a concern about the place of other parts of the cosmos that would match the concern of any who have seen men walk on the moon and invade the reaches of outer space. "All that I can entertain is a possibility of a multi-aspect Redemption which would be realized as one and the same Redemption on all the stars . . . Unless we introduced a relativity into time, we should have to admit, surely, that Christ has still to be incarnate in some as yet unformed star?" (no matter what) . . . Christ is all or nothing." C & E 44.

NOTES

1. Teilhard, *The Future of Man*, Tr. N. Denny (London: Fontana Collins, 1970), p. 280. Footnote FM.

2. Sir Peter Medawar, *The Future of Man* (London: Methuen & Co. 1960), p. 96.

3. Teilhard, *The Hymn of the Universe*, Tr. C. Vann (London: Fontana Collins, 1970) pp. 70-1 HU.

4. Thorpe, *Science, Men and Morals*, p. 150.

5. Towers, *Concerning Teilhard de Chardin*, p. 110.

6. Teilhard, *Writings in Time of War*, Tr. R. Hague (London: Collins 1970), p. 147 WTW.

7. Michael Polanyi, *Personal Knowledge*, p. 53.

8. Teilhard, *Activation of Energy*, Tr. R. Hague (London: Collins, 1970), p. 147 AE.

9. Kenneth Boulding, *The Meaning of the Twentieth Century* (London: Allan & Urwin, 1965), p. 147.

10. Teilhard, *The Divine Milieu*, Tr. B. Wall (London: Fontana, Collins, 1967), p. 103 DM.

11. Rollo May, *Psychology and the Human Dilemma*

(Princeton: Van Nostrand 1967) p. 134.

12. Polanyi, 275.
13. H.H. Price, *Survival and the Idea of Another World* quoted by Rosalind Heywood, *The Sixth Sense* (London: Chatto & Windus, 1966) p. 219.
14. May, 195.
15. Basil Partridge, *Chaplet of Grace* (Philadelphia: The Westminster Press, 1956) p. 43.
16. Martin Buber, *I and Thou*, Tr. R.G. Smith (Edinburg: T & T Clark, 1958) p. 48.
17. T.S. Eliot, *The Confidential Clerk* (London: Faber & Faber, 1954) p. 57.
18. Boulding, 146-7.
19. Thorpe, 147.
20. Thorpe, 146.

Chapter 6
HIS GARMENT OF FLESH: THE CHURCH

"Whatever may be the merits of other religions, it is an undeniable fact — explain it how you will — that the most ardent focus of love that has yet appeared in the world, burns here and now at the heart of God's Church."[1]

Teilhard's Devotion To His Own Church

So far I have said little or nothing about the role of the church in Teilhard's thought. He who, at such cost to himself in mental and spiritual anguish, refused to cut himself off from the church or even from his order within it, could never accord to the church a place of little or no importance in his theology, even though that church thwarted his heart's desire.

Although he deplored and fought until his death against the narrowness and blindness of the hierarchy, he never wavered in his devotion to it, specifically to his own branch, the Roman Catholic Church. Here he felt, despite all the weakness of which he was well aware, "the axis of Christianity" was to be found. "There are, no doubt," he writes (C & E 168), "many individuals outside Catholicism who recognize and love Christ and are therefore united to him as much as (and even more than) some Catholics. But these individuals are not grouped together in the 'cephalized' unity of a *body* which reacts vitally, as an organic whole, to the combined forces of Christ and mankind." This was written in Peking in 1944 when he had lived out of touch for some time with movements going on in the rest of the world.

Against this one needs to remember, as was pointed out in an earlier chapter, that Vatican II, which officially acknowledged as Christian, "separated brethren," and led the Roman Catholic Church into many areas of cooperation in the ecumenical movement, has been acknowledged as greatly influenced by Teilhard's thought. As Bernard Towers rightly points out, "The ecumenical movement is deeply Teilhardian in character."[2] In it we see the convergence of which he makes so much in his whole way of thinking.

The Church As An Organic Whole: "The Living Church"

Nevertheless, there was logic in his assertion of priority for Roman Catholicism, even as there was logic as well as heart in his steadfast refusal to desert his church. The fact that the Roman Church could act as "an organic whole" was vital to his view of the church. He saw this "body of Christ," not just as a metaphorical thing, but as a physical entity, as real and organically inter-related as any physical body. He insists that "the man who is true to Christ's teaching can ... and ... indeed ... must — understand the mystical union of the elect in Christ as combining the warm flexibility of social relationships with the imperative rigour and irreversibility of the physical and biological laws or attractive forces operating in the present universe." (C & E 69). The bonds which hold Christians together and Christians to Christ, he contends, "are more than just common agreement and affection." The body of Christ is not to be thought of as a vast association — a family on a very large scale ... " (C & E 69) rather, he had written back during the years of the First World War (WTW 51-2), "the mystical body of Christ should be conceived as a physical Reality *in the strongest sense the word can bear.* Jesus — Master — you are the dominating influence that penetrates and holds and draws us through the inmost core of our most imperative and most deep-rooted desires."

The Church Forms The Leading Edge Of The Universe, Rising To The Omega Point

Teilhard believed in, and saw evidences of, the creation of a "Mankind" through the attractive power of God's love exercised through the risen Christ, though known by various other names. In the community of the church, brought into being and held together by the acknowledged love of God, he sees an intensification of the general process, an *"ultra-socialization"* at a deeper level, "its influence animating and assembling in their most sublime form all the spiritual elements of the Noosphere." (LME 98). The role of the church he sees to be essential in the whole working out of God's purpose, since in the church is to be found the rise of a specifically new state of consciousness. This is in line with the process he has traced all along; from a greater complexity arising through the "centering in" of the molecules forming the whole at each stage of development, a new state of consciousness has come into being. In this new complexity, the church, the new consciousness is Christian love. "If the love of God were extinguished in the souls of the faithful," he writes (P of M 324), "the enormous edifice of rites, of heirarchy and of doctrines that comprise the Church would instantly revert to the dust from which it rose."[3] Elsewhere (A of E 118) he points out that in the church also we have a new state in the development of reflective thought which first appeared with the coming of *Homo Sapiens* and was the distinguishing mark. "In the living thought of the church we can see the reflection, adapted to our evolutionary state, of the thought of God . . ." Since for Teilhard love is like the blood of spiritual evolution, and thought the product and touchstone of evolutionary advance, the church, being the creation and home of the highest manifestation of each, takes her place . . . " not just the teaching Church . . . but the living Church; (as) the seed of super-vitalization planted at the heart of the noosphere by the appearance in history of Jesus Christ an even more interior cone (than mankind) impregnating and taking possession of, and gradually uplifting the rising mass of the world . . . " (A of E 149). Teilhard pictures the whole of the complex of humanity and the cosmos as a cone rising and converging on its goal, the divine center of attraction. Within this cone is a core made up of the church. Rising ever upwards towards union with God drawn by his love to which it responds through its own love expressed in worship and service, its ever-deepening knowledge of Him, the church becomes for the whole of the edifice which God is creating "the central axis of universal convergence and the exact meeting point between the Universe and Omega point." (LME 98). This high view of the church Teilhard derives from the New Testament teaching about the church as the Body of Christ, who is the redeemer and reconciler of the world.

In this view Teilhard is supported by the opinions of Barth "What Jesus Christ is for God and for us, on earth and in time, He is as Lord of this community, as King of this people, as Head of this body and of all its members . . . He is all these as the Reconciler and Redeemer of the whole world. He is all these, however, in the strange communion of these strange saints."[4]

The Faults And Weaknesses Of The Church: The Teaching Church

Teilhard is quite aware both of the "strangeness" of the church and of its saints and he frequently writes both to his friends and to the hierarchy of his own church about his fears and his suggestions for changes . . . "the church will waste away," he writes to Leontine Zanta, "so long as she does not escape from the factitious world of verbal theology, of quantitative sacramentalism, and over-refined devotions in which she is enveloped, so as to reincarnate herself in the real aspirations of mankind . . . I can't get away from the evidence that the moment has come when the Christian impulse should 'save Christ' from the hands of the clerics so that the world may be saved" (LLZ 34-5) ". . . our little churches hide the earth from us . . . There are some who want to identify Christian orthodoxy with . . . respect for the tiniest wheels of a little microcosm constructed centuries ago . . . I have declared war on it . . . I don't quite know how I'll set about waging this war now that my possibilities of outside action have become more and more restricted . . . Sometimes I think the best way of making an attitude triumph is to live it as faithfully as possible." (LLZ 79) "Men love only those who heal or liberate them," he writes to one of his "two friends." "The church often forgets to imitate Jesus christ in this last point." (LTF 49)

In a lecture (reported by Cuenot) he speaks for those for whose faith he deeply yearned, his companions in the field and laboratory, many of whom he thought of as his "gentiles" to whom, like Paul of old, he was sent to bring the Gospel. "There are increasingly large sections of humanity (the most progressive too) on which Christianity can no longer make any impression because it has become lukewarm."[5]

It was the church's refusal to modify its dogma to take note of developments in learning and science, its insistence on continuing to express the truths of the faith in terms drawn from a view of the universe long since left behind by science, that Teilhard found most objectionable. What he feared most, however, was lukewarmness in Christians, as he feared boredom, a loss of zest for life, in humanists and people in general, and for the same reason. Without zest for life humans would no longer push forward either themselves or the world for whose progress he now sees humankind responsible. Without the warmth of love, of which the Christian church is to be both the teacher and the example and, as it were, the "radiator," that energy which will bring about both the rise and convergence of the cosmos on its goal will be lost.

Such is the key place Teilhard assigns to the church in the evolutionary perfecting of God's great plan and purpose. No wonder he would not desert it. As he confesses to Leontine Zanta, having gone through a "crisis of anti-clericalism, not to say anti-Christianity, . . . Given that my only rule of appreciation and practice is tending more and more to become, 'Believe in the spirit,' it would indeed be unjust to see the Church as the one thing in the world which lacked it." (LLZ 91)

In *Let Me Explain* he distinguishes between "the living church" and the "teaching church." It was of the living church he was writing when he spoke of the church as the organic Body of Christ; it was the teaching church to which he directed his criticisms and suggestions for amendment, for it was in this church's custody and transmission of the truths of

Christianity, supremely in the acted "word" of communion, in its teaching and worship, that Teilhard saw its importance.

Other Faiths: Their Strengths And Weaknesses

Early in his life Teilhard had had little appreciation of the value of faiths other than Christianity. However, no man as sensitive and broad in feeling as he could have moved about the world and lived among so many different cultures and not have his horizons widened. He could write of himself in 1945 (Album 171), "Whatever the country or the creed or the social position of the person I approach, so long as the same fire of expectancy glows in him as it does in me, then a fundamental and total contact is immediately established."

He felt strongly, as he indicates in this quotation, the vital importance of "expectancy." He feared that in its teaching and life the church, too often, showed no signs of expecting anything. It was this he hoped to persuade it to feel, as he married his view of continuing evolution with the note of expectancy so strong in the New Testament, but too often abandoned by the more orthodox churches to splinter groups who both materialize and distort the hopes.

It is this note of hope through which he tries to help his "gentile" friends, feeling that if they reached forward they would eventually find the highest and best he knew. Thus he writes to one of them dismayed by the "parasitic network" "that encumbers present day religious confession," (LTF 30) "for you, as for every one, there is only one road that can lead you to God, and this is the fidelity to remain constantly true to yourself, to what you feel is highest in you. Do not worry about the rest. The road will open before you as you go." (LTF 31).

And it was because of the note of expectancy and hope contained in the faith of the modern humanist, including the doctrinaire communist, that not only drew Teilhard to a fellow-feeling with them in his lifetime, but has made possible, since his death, dialogues between communists and Christians. About the Christian pantheist to whom he felt closest he complained that they did not follow their creed through to its logical conclusion. That, he felt, would have led them to discover at the end of the road, personality and immortality. These alone would justify the gift of themselves to their faith that that faith requires. Without these two beliefs Teilhard can only write (LME 92), "When I turn to the human pantheism of today, I feel that the lowering sky is pressing down on me and stifling me."

As he examines the religions of the East, Teilhard concedes that their "incomparable greatness lies in their having been second to none in vibrating with the passion for unity" (LME 90), but he sees this great weakness in Hinduism, the renunciation of effort, in the teaching that "personalization and earthly progress are so many diseases of the soul." (LME 90) He is at great pains always to distinguish the union of the cosmos with Christ in the Pleroma from the Hindu absorption in the All. Union with Christ, he writes, does not swallow up our individuality. We can think in terms of a cell. Each has its own shape and activity yet cannot be explained or live in the full sense outside the complete body. Each self is itself plus ourselves. Over and over and over, against the danger of confusing his teaching with familiar forms of pantheism, he insists that the union which he envisions at every stage "differentiates" and does not absorb, because it is the union of love. (C & E 69-70)

In Islam Teilhard values the way in which it has retained "the idea of the existence of God and the greatness of God . . . the seed from which everything may one day be born again." (LME 89). However, he charges that today Islam offers itself as a "principle of fixation and stagnation" and thus has made "this God as ineffective and sterile as non-being for all that concerns the knowledge and betterment of the world." (LME 89)

All forms of agnosticism, Confucianism, and cults of personal enjoyment and interior perfection he also finds deficient. In ruling out faith in some future consummation of the world, ". . . they all have the common fault of cutting off the flow of life-sap which they should direct into the proper channels and help to rise." (LME 89)

Christianity Fulfils The Requisites For Continuing The Cosmic Course

Christianity alone fulfills all the requisites for continuing the great struggle which began with the initiation of creation and will come to a close in an ecstacy of union with God. Thus he writes (LTF 179), "Christianity . . . is bound to win someway, no other type of faith that has so far been developed in mankind is equally able to make the world around us (in spite of its immensity, apparent blindness, and ruthlessness) sweet and *warm* inside (because it is personal, lovable, and loving at its upper term and in its essence). The real threat for humanity is not a refrigerating earth, but an 'internally' impersonal, icy World. And, if I am right, this is not a question of 'wishfulness,' but a strict biological question of survival." Without love, which alone can provide for an earth become personal, he was to say over and over that complexity out of which the next stage of evolution can develop — spirit — can never appear. Without spirit there can be no union with Christ-Omega, no final union with God whom the Christian Gospel, in its essence, teaches us to know and love as "Father."

Therefore Other Faiths Will Converge On Christianity Provided It Keeps Its Attractive Power

Because of these qualities in Christianity Teilhard envisions a convergence of other religions on it, each bringing with it its own particular gift. It is interesting to note that recently Thorpe has seen evidences that this vision is beginning to become a reality: "In many eastern countries there is now a tendency to a re-interpretation of human history in a manner more consistent with the Christian vein of thought, though not of course openly acknowledging it. It arises out of the fact that, after centuries of social stagnation, there is the drive towards political and economic freedom which is beginning to touch the awareness of everyone."[6]   R. C. Zaehner Spalding, Professor of Eastern Religion and Ethics, in his Gifford Lecture said, ". . . later developments of . . . these religions (i.e.,

Hindu, Buddhist, Moslem) show that each has evolved . . . a theory of Divine incarnation and of a Divine Mediator between God and Man . . . a genuine parallelism . . . but in all religions except Christianity it develops in logical opposition to the dominant view of each of the sacred books. . . . In each case the need for an incarnate God seems to have been so strongly felt that the doctrine of Incarnation made its appearance in surroundings where it had no rightful place."[7]

However, the Christianity Teilhard sees drawing others to it must also show itself the dynamic faith it is because it is love-centered and love-empowered. It must cease to emphasize the evil of matter, teaching us to despise and condemn the world. True, eventually, the world must be transformed into a higher state, but it will be a world brought to perfection by the dedicated efforts of those Christians and others who love God "through the world." Teilhard, as one would expect, deplores the over-emphasis on individual personal salvation so often made by churches. Certainly he knows salvation has to be personal, and none held it more important than he. But for the Christian to see it as the be-all and end-all of the work of Christ is, for him, not only a denial of much that is basic in the New Testament but to have a very narrow and impoverished view of that work. Indeed, re-birth of any Christian to a selfish enjoyment of his/her relationship with Christ is, for Teilhard, an impossibility. The moment of new birth being like the moment of first birth, is into a community, that family of which Jesus spoke in words which seem very harsh if we hear them only as a repudiation of his physical next-of-kin, "Who is my mother and who are my brothers? Whoever does the will of my Father in Heaven is my mother and sister and my brother." (Matthew 12:48,50). As we have seen in the case of the Biblical descriptions of the church as Christ's body, so with this matter of Christ's family; Teilhard sees it as no metaphorical or external relationship. For him, incorporation into Christ's family by faith means becoming biologically a member of a new species. He has called this, in many places, "the phylum* of love." All our future development depends on our being in this "phylum."

* Any broad basic division of the plant or animal kingdom.

Being Part Of A Whole Is An Essential Characteristic In The Universe

As we understand the function of Christ as the attractive force in the universe; as we see faith placing the believer in the zone of that attraction; as we understand the necessity of being part of the whole in order to be included in the consummation of God's plan — we can understand that Teilhard would have accepted the affirmation, so distasteful when taken in its exclusive sense, "outside the church there is no salvation."

He can help us see this idea in new terms even as he invites us to see the words "salvation" and "damnation" differently. "Salvation and damnation are no longer simply blessings or curses that fall arbitrarily on the being, from outside," he writes (C & E 73). "... more formidable ... they affect the whole relationship of the element to the center of universal cohesion ... either incorporation into it which brings fulfilment, or severance from it which brings the loss of organic structure." If this seems like an extreme statement we must realize that Teilhard is writing against the background of scientific knowledge of a world in which ... "physical reality (is) a complex structured activity rather than ... an aggregate of material points;" " ... the unit of matter is a structure of structures; ... the vehicle of individuality is form or structure, ... not a separate, isolated, material entity."[8]

Teilhard's assumption is that we live in a *universe* and that therefore we should expect to find one principle at work in every part of it — as much in the spiritual as in the physical realm — seemingly different but, in Teilhard's view, really one realm. Certainly, the witness of the Apocalypse is that human perfection and fulfilment are to be found, not in splendid isolation, but through inclusion in a new community of which God himself is both center and light; while the lot of those who have chosen to cut themselves off from society by living by principles which harmed society is to "stay outside." (Rev. 22:14,15).

The Church Is Imperfect Because Still Developing

Certainly the earthly community of the church has its imperfections. Any body made up of human beings still very much in the process of becoming truly human under the influence of him who provides the measure for humanity, cannot help being imperfect. But there is, in Teilhard's way of thinking, another reason why the church on earth exhibits painful flaws and weaknesses. It is, itself, like gradually-forming "Mankind" of which it is the core, a very new entity in this evolving universe. Before it are many centuries of growth and therefore of change and development, through painful "groping" and struggle — the path of evolutionary progress. Like all other bodies, like nations, associations and communities, it is made up of "human molecules." It is even younger, as an entity, than "Mankind," still very incomplete, and shares with that evolving body the warp of the "multiple" as well as the newness of its youth. It, too, has to battle its own version of the problem of evil inherent in her warp. Teilhard never forgets or underestimates the power of evil, as much in the church as in any other body based on "matter." Nevertheless, as I said, he is an optimist, not only because he is a Christian who sees Christ's victory as a "down payment" on the final victory, but as a scientist. Though he is speaking of the earlier development, the appearance of life, Henderson writes that only in the kind of physical and geographical environment found on this planet, an environment which has developed "by the merest chance, "could life have been generated and evolved. There is a sense in which the outcome of evolution was implicit from the beginning."[9] For Teilhard, the appearance of life is the guarantee of "eternal life" in the consummation of the Marriage of the Lamb, the triumph of God's love. From this triumph he would not exclude even those who have, at the last, chosen the way of opposition, of damnation," . . . to be damned is not to be annihilated, who can say what mysterious complement may not be added to the Body of Christ by that immortal loss?" (WTW 214).

As part of the great process still going on, Teilhard then

can accept the church as it is, while still doing all that he can to try to keep it from yielding to the temptation omnipresent in creation, to remain static, to try to avoid the risks involved in moving forward. As one convinced of his responsibility for the direction and continuance of evolution, he never ceased until death his attempts to move the church.

Christianity Must Also Continue To Develop

In Christianity also, Teilhard felt, there must be development. Indeed, he felt such development to be close at hand. Writing to a friend (LTF 30) in 1926, he says that in the parasitic network which encumbers present day religious confession he sees something which, in the biological realm, foretells a sloughing off. Moreover, the fact that Christianity has now enjoyed two thousand years of existence seems to him significant. "... it must," he writes, "obey an organic rhythm to which everything in nature would appear to be subject, and precisely because it is immortal, the time has come when it cannot continue to exist without being rejuvenated and refashioned." He does not envison this happening by a change in its structure but rather "by the assimilation of new elements." "We must consider . . . how it may be possible . . . for the guiding principles of Christianity to be expanded without being distorted, to the dimensions of a universe which has been fantastically enlarged and integrated by modern scientific thought." (C & E 176)

Suggestion For Development: Re-examination Of The Value Of Creation To God

He has his own suggestions for the emphases which should be made in Christian teaching in the late twentieth century. First, he feels, there must be a re-examination of the value of the creation to God. As Christianity has traditionally presented it; creation — including that of the human race — is something which God might or might not have undertaken. For him to have done it or not to have done it would have made no difference to him. It is presented as a sheer act of mercy. This very "mercy" is not a small part of the problem. The sufferings and the hazards people have always known to be present in the world, have always presented them with a problem. Now that we are aware, through our greater knowledge of the universe and of the amount of suffering, and the extent of the hazards involved in the "vast enterprise of the cosmos," the idea that none of this is of any real value to God offends both our intellects and our hearts to the point of undermining "our zest for action." [C & E 154]

All this strain on faith is not called for; indeed, it is flying in the face of the teaching of many largely ignored Scripture passages which speak of the filling out of the fulness of the divine. If, in the way Teilhard has outlined, we see the creation as a vast act of incarnation in which the completed and fulfilled cosmos is drawn into mystical union with the Creator as the final term, we can both justify to our God-given intellects the vast suffering and agony inherent in the process and give ourselves completely to the sacrifice required of us as a gift to God, the sacrifice to which our Lord Jesus Christ both led us and enables us. To see the risen Christ as both the magnet drawing all to him through the perfection of his manhood, and the Omega in union with whom all things will find their fulfilment, Teilhard argues, while preserving the importance and the personal warmth of Jesus, assigns to him the role he is certainly given in the thought of much of the New Testament. This note is missed, he insists, when we confine ourselves to the human Jesus of the synoptic gospels. Yet, when aware of this emphasis we look at the synoptic gospels afresh, we hear the same note that is sounded continually through the gospel musical, JESUS CHRIST, SUPERSTAR, and expressed in the constant refrain, "I don't understand him."

The Emphasis Of The Bible Confirmed In Science

Certainly the way in which Teilhard has presented "love" both human and divine, makes of the supreme command of Christ — love for God and for one's neighbour — no longer a valuable exhortation but a statement of the very core of things, a matter of life and death, eternal life and eternal death. This is equally true about the ethical teachings of both Old and New Testaments. During my reading in preparation for this book I have found my own faith greatly exhilarated as I have seen how the findings of modern science confirm the life-and-death values of Biblical commands, exhortations, and insights. If the present day generation — not least of all, modern youth — could be allowed to see the church acknowledging in the way it expresses its doctrine, these new insights into the nature of things, I am convinced they would be much more ready, because of their greater scientific knowledge, to accept and honour the insights and guidance of the Bible. It is up to those of us who teach them to be ready and eager to make and welcome such changes.

About God

One of the places where Teilhard believes there must be change is in the church's teaching about God. With good reason he observes that many Christians feel that the image of God being offered is not worthy of the universe they know. He was an intimate and indeed, a confidante, of many men and women who were well-versed in the mysteries and miracles of the universe in which concept of time and space have, in the last century and a half, become incredibly extended. He knew himself the truth of the words of Sir John Seely that the God worshipped by the astronomer and the geologist, dwelling as they do in the immensities of space and time, is greater and more wonderful than the God of the average Christian. Teilhard is concerned about the image in the minds of that average Christian. Because he believes that "whatever may be said our century is religious — probably more religious than any other. The one thing it needs is a God it can adore."[10] Teilhard tried, himself, to do what he called the church to do at a time when his attempts were being thwarted by the church, "make a constructive standpoint . . . based on a rejuvenated presentation of God . . ." (LTF 150).

In 1950 he sums up his ideas on this subject in a prayer quoted in *Let Me Explain* (161), "Lord of consistence and union, you whose *distinguishing mark* and *essence* is the power indefinitely to grow greater, without distortion or loss of continuity, to the measure of the mysterious Matter whose Heart you will fill and all whose movements you ultimately control — Lord of my childhood and Lord of my last days — God, complete in relation to yourself and yet, for us, continually being born — God, who because you offer yourself to our worship as 'evolver' and 'evolving,' are henceforth the only being that can satisfy us — we sweep away at last the clouds that still hide you — the clouds of hostile prejudice and those, too, of false creeds."

God — Living And Therefore Changing

Here we see Teilhard challenging the idea of the changeless, static God. This is not surprising. Teilhard is writing about the God who, the Bible continually insists, is the *living* God, in contrast to the deadness of idols. This is the God the Bible insists is *One*, in marked contrast to the multiplicity of heathen deities. Modern sciences, particularly physics and biology, have given us new ideas of these two qualities of life and oneness we should not ignore.

If the teaching of the Bible were to contradict all idea of change, of course one might argue that, just because this is the state we find in the universe, we do not necessarily have to find it at the heart of that universe, in the one who is also infinitely above it. However, the Bible does not at all support that kind of changelessness. The Old Testament is rich in allusions to God's "compassion," which, by its very nature being a response to the changing condition of his people and their "passions," involves change, as a great passage containing such an allusion from the prophet Hosea (11:8) specifically shows: "How can I give you up, O Ephraim! My heart recoils within me; my compassion grows warm and tender. I will not execute my fierce anger. I will not again destroy Ephraim, for I am God and not man." Here the prophet argues that the very ability and readiness of God to change is evidence of his being "God and not man." Moreover, the New Testament teaching culminating in the great statement of John (1 John 4:8), "God is love," makes the idea of unchangeableness impossible. Nothing is more dynamic, less static, than love. Certainly there is changelessness in the fact that God is always love, but that very changelessness implies, rather than denies, development. Even on the human level, the more one loves, the wider one's love extends, the greater the development in the lover. Though God is "not man," nevertheless, Jesus taught us, what God himself revealed to us in his supreme revelation in the Man of Nazareth, that we can and must argue from the human to God. We *are* made in God's image. As Buber puts it "... we know unshakably in our hearts that there is the becoming of the God that is."[11]

Changeless In His Attraction

Certainly there is — and Teilhard would be the first to insist on this — a changelessness in God, the changelessness suggested by the physicist Heisenburg when, in conversation with his friends he speaks of "the central order ... with which we commune" (as) "the magnetic force" drawing mankind to *'the orderly'* we think of as the good."[12] This is the movement toward unity that Teilhard, observing it in his paleontological research, sees as *the* direction found throughout the universe. Here, indeed, there is "no variation or shadow due to change." (James 1:7). God, "the center of centers," as Teilhard constantly calls him, is through the energy of his love drawing each element towards the other and all towards himself "in ever greater order and coherence," to culminate at last in a great unity in which "God will be all in all." (1 Cor. 15:28).

There is never any changing, any wavering in the direction, the power and the goodness of that love. Even "the wrath of God," so often mentioned in Scripture and often a stumbling block to those reading it, Teilhard is able to define in terms of this universal attraction, "the side of Spirit we meet as we fall back." (WTW 195). It is our experience in God's love of that quality for which George MacDonald, (to whom C. S. Lewis gives much credit for his conversion) continually uses the term, "inexorable"[13] — a term which I can well imagine scientists would see in the "natural laws" of the universe. Here is the changelessness. God's love is always directed towards the welfare, the unity of his creation. If we choose the opposite direction to unity, we run head-on into the force of that changelessness; if we will not change we will dash ourselves to pieces against that changelessness. As the evangelist, Charles Templeton, is reported to have said once to a group of young people, "Young people, you do not break God's laws; you are broken on them." Not his choice, but ours, turns love to wrath.

For Teilhard, God is the Prime Mover, the one who sets into motion the whole process of creation-redemption-incarnation which the scientists see as evolution. God is also "the Gatherer and Consolidator ahead of us, of evolution."[14] In his "rejuvenation" of the idea of God he would add to the idea of "the God above," "the God ahead." Not for Teilhard any summons to "go back" to God. The only way we are to reach God, he insists, is by pushing forward with all our powers, the perfection of God's creation. To Teilhard perfection is measured by what contributes most to personality, whose supreme example we see in Jesus Christ. And since personality is the result of complexity brought about by unity in love, all that is loving, all that works for unity in love, deserves our extreme and dedicated effort.

Unity Means Personalization

Naturally, because he saw unity as issuing in personalization, God — who is One, the only perfect unity — *must* be personal. To be the goal and motivating force in a universe which moves by love and in response to love, God can be nothing less than personal. Indeed, as he writes, "God must be conceived in the *direction* of *super-person* . . . as vast as the universe, as warm as a human heart, and incomparably more besides. This is all we can say." And in explanation of the term, "super-person," he says, "that is an extension of the good qualities and not of the individual limitations." (LTF 13). Cuenot quotes Teilhard as having said (244) "God is a person, God is a person . . . A God not a person would not be God."[15]

Orthodox Teaching Stresses Roles — Not Relations

Teilhard was constant in his protest against the way that the teaching of the church too often reduced this personal aspect by tying it to specific and often outmoded roles. "For ninety percent of those who view him from outside, the Christian God looks like a great landowner administering his estate, the world. Now this conventional picture, which is too well justified by appearances, corresponds in no way to the dogmatic basis, or point of view, of the Gospels." (LME 99). Again, he charges that Christian thinking about our relationship with God is at a level that is "neolithic." There has been a change in the background which has robbed the words we use for God "of their spiritual value; 'King,' 'Father,' have lost their magic for us. We can think of the relation they imply as too external to us. In future, our age can only worship something more penetrating, more organic, vaster, something that rises above every human value." For instance, he suggests, instead of thinking — as we use the word "father" for God — "he who rules, fosters, pardons, rewards . . . why not go further and say 'he who vitalizes and engenders'?" (C & E 182)

Thus, in his writings from the First World War, he says "God, who is as immense and all-embracing as matter and at the same time as warm and intimate as a soul, is the Center who spreads through all things . . ." (WTW 48). This recalls to us Teilhard's idea of the creation by the love of God, the servant God who, humbling himself to be joined to the least particle of world stuff, becomes "the within" which joins particle to particle until, at length, in the complex human "molecule" the condition of consciousness makes possible the expression of spirit; and in one as God means all to become — Jesus Christ — the relationship is so perfect that Holy Spirit finds expression. "Spirit becoming presence" is one of Teilhard's expressions encompassing all he sees going on in evolution.

God, The Goal Ahead

Yet the God who, at creation, begins clothing himself in

his world, remains — for Teilhard — the God above and also ahead. Indeed, in his wonderful devotional book, *The Divine Milieu*, described by some as a great spiritual classic, Teilhard translates those words quoted by Paul (Acts 17:28), God, "in whom we live and move and have our being," in a way that enables us to take them literally, as we could never do before. God, he insists, is "the milieu" in which we live. Although he never — as Pannenberg, in his criticism of this book, points out — uses as a model for this idea of God the electro-magnetic field, he could have done so had he wished. We are all of us charged particles within this field, because of the spirit within us. God's magnetism continually seeks to draw us to him, and thus to each other, to the perfection of union destined by his love. This magnetism, this drawing power, God assigns to be exercised by the glorified Jesus Christ, risen and triumphant. From him, then, also issues — as from God — the gift of the Holy Spirit to men and women who recognize the power at work within themselves and offer themselves in joyous and loving cooperation to God as "friends," sons and daughters who know what the Father is doing. All are in this "milieu" of God's love, but not all recognize it, or will to be "God's fellow workmen." (1Cor. 3:9). The choice is open, until the fulness of time, to will to go God's way, cooperating against the pull of the "multiple" within, or, yielding to it and suffering from it, eternal disintegration.

The Roles Of The Trinity

The God of Teilhard — Father, giving energy to all; Son, drawing all things forward and upward to himself; and Holy Spirit within all, potentially and realized by recognition and acceptance by all, transforming them and uniting them in readiness for full union with the risen Christ — is the threefold God of classical Christianity. Yet, as Teilhard points out, this "concept *strengthens* our idea of divine oneness by giving it the structure (or, rather, the structural, built, character) which is the mark of all living unity." . . . (C & E 157-8). Within God himself there is that diversity in unity which is not only characteristic of every phase of evolution as we know it —

especially in living things — but that unity in which every individuality will be perfected and made more individual, towards which all things move in God's divine purpose.

Providence: How God Acts

For Teilhard, God is indeed the transcendent God, the omnipotent God, but it is an omnipotence which, by God's free choice in creation, is conditioned by the way in which he has chosen to create. In other words, Teilhard insists, God obeys his own laws. Indeed," . . . God does not make; He makes things make themselves." "Since the First Cause is not involved in effects, it acts upon individual *natures* and on the movement of the *whole*." (C & E 28). This is the quality in God's action which makes it possible for people to fail to see God's hand in any or all creation or activity.

Although Teilhard did not use the scientific model of the electro-magnetic field to define the relation of God to his creation, he does use a mechanical model to set out his views of God's action on his universe, his providence. (C & E 25-35). We are asked to imagine the universe as a sphere filled with living springs upon which God can at any time exert pressure over the whole sphere which will infallibly produce some modification at any point he wishes. Since the pressure seems to come from all directions at once, we cannot pin down the point at which the hand of God is apparent; it could be seen as destiny or fate. So he sees God's working from the "outside" to bring about his will. But God is not limited to working thus; he controls the universe, not only as a whole at once, but individually at the core of each element, "the within." Yet so interior is his working that it can seem to the "spring" itself and to its neighbours, that it is acting alone.

So extensive and so deep is the action of God that "scientifically we shall never be able to see God." But this does not mean that we *cannot* see him at work. Just as in the miraculous there is an exceptional expansion of nature — much greater than could result from the normal function of created factors and stimuli — so, when human faculties are extended so as to actualize "in our minds the supra-sensible world" (that is, 'the within' of all things), not by the deepening of reason alone, but by "a sharpening of the moral sensibilities and a complete loyalty to ever-rising truth," we will see "the Divine underlying the abnormal," the potentiality in every material thing.

The God whom we will see, Teilhard insists, is not a God who works arbitrarily, but one who, working through certain laws of development, by his deep-reaching and all embracing influence can integrate all good and evil to his divine ends. In a universe that is still coming into being through the unification of the multiple, it is inevitable that there will be evil. As Jesus himself said, "It is necessary that temptations come." (Matthew 18:7). This does not for one moment — as Jesus goes on to make clear — excuse, "but woe to that man by whom they come," but it does help with the vexatious — in the realm of our reason. In trying to help us understand how God can work within his inexorable laws and yet be able to exercise "special providence" for the believer, Teilhard says, "Even if the threads are unbreakable or elastic only to a point, the fabric itself is infinitely supple in the hands of the Creator provided that we, on our side, show ourselves to be faithful creatures. Let a man live at a distance from God, and the universe remains neutral or hostile to him. But let a man believe in God and immediately all around him the elements, even the irksome — of the inevitable organize themselves into a friendly whole, ordered to the ultimate success of life. For the believer everything is still, externally and individually, what it is for all the world; and yet God's power solicitously adapts the whole to serve him. At every moment, in some way, it re-creates the universe for the man who prays to it." [C & E 34-5]. Once again we are reminded of Teilhard's love of that wonderful verse so dear to many Christians, (Romans 8:28), "We know that in everything God works for good with those who love him, who are called according to his purpose." Teilhard knew this truth about God from warm personal experience, so he writes to Leontine Zanta, "As for morale, after a period of eclipse in the turmoil of material things, I feel I'm in pretty good shape; which means that I have a fairly intense perception of 'the taste for being.' Once again, the great animating Power, to which it is so good to entrust ourselves, seems — in a motherly way — to have brought the inner and outer forces of the world into harmony around me." (LLZ 85-86).

God Engaged In A Struggle To Complete His Incarnation In The Cosmos

The God of Teilhard is a God who engages still in an enormous and costly struggle of which the life and death of Jesus Christ were a revelation afforded to humankind to enlist their very necessary cooperation. In this revelation, we see the cost of that struggle; here we see the justification of the cost; here, too, we see the power of God to make even evil serve his mighty ends, his power to keep all good. This God indeed is the one of whom Jesus said, "My Father works," (John 5:17). The work he is engaged in is no sham battle, even though the outcome is assured, for the Father's will is that he shall lose none of his own. So he continues to work through the Son of his love, by the power of His spirit, until at length the great work of Creation-Redemption-Incarnation is ended, until "he has . . . gathered about Him the last folds of the garment of flesh and love woven for him by his faithful." (FM 320).

NOTES

1. Teilhard, *Let Me Explain*, Tr. R. Hague and Others London: Collins, 1970) p 95 LME

2. Towers, *Concerning Teilhard etc.* 37

3. Teilhard, *The Phenomenon of Man*, Tr. B. Wall (London: Fontana Collins, 1970) p 324 PM

4. Karl Barth, *The Humanity of God* (London: Fontana, Collins, 1967) p 64.

5. Claude Cuenot, *Teilhard de Chardin: A Biographical Study*, Tr. V. Colimore (London: Burns and Oates, Helicon Press, 1965) p 374.

6. Thorpe, *Science, Man and Morals*, 141.

7. R. C. Zaehner, *Concordant Discord* (Oxford: Clarendon Press, 1970) p 442.

8. Errol Harris, *The Foundations of Metaphysics in Science (London: Allen & Unwin, 1965) p 138, p 141, p 138.*

9. L. J. Henderson, *The Fitness of the Environment* quoted by Errol Harris, *The Foundations of Metaphysics in Science* p 277.

10. Cuenot, 368

11. Martin Buber, *I and Thou*, p 82.

12. Werner Heisenburg, *Physics and Beyond,* pp 214, 217.

13. C. S. Lewis, editor, *George MacDonald, An Anthology* (London: Geoffrey Bles, 1955) p 23.

14. Teilhard, *Man's Place in Nature*, Tr. R. Hague (London: Fontana, Collins, 1971) p 121 MPN

15. Claude Cuenot, p 244.

Chapter 7

"A NEW FORMULA FOR HOLINESS"

Part I:

THE CHRISTIAN LIFE

"What all of us, more or less, are lacking at present is a new formula to express what is meant by Holiness."[1]

"We are each one of us placed . . . at a specific point defined by the present moment in the history of the world, the place of our birth, and our individual vocation. And *from that starting point* variously situated at different levels, the task assigned to us is to climb towards the light, passing through, so as to attain God . . . Matter falls into two distinct zones, differentiated according to our efforts: the zone, already left behind or arrived at . . . the zone offered to our renewed efforts towards progress, search, conquest, 'divinization' . . . and the frontier between these two zones is essentially relative and shifting. That which is good, sanctifying and spiritual for my brother below or beside me on the mountain side can be . . . bad for me . . . What I rightly allowed myself yesterday I must perhaps deny myself today . . . the soul can only re-join God after having traversed a *specific path* through matter . . . Each one of us has his Jacob's ladder." [DM 108].

As Teilhard's theology was based firmly in the idea of the continuing creation-redemption-incarnation, so also is his teaching about the life all must lead, especially those who are Christians. Under the attractive influence of the glorified

Christ through whom the Creator continues his great work of unifying and drawing all things to himself, each individual soul is being drawn up his/her own "Jacob's ladder," as he puts it, through a universe which is saturated through and through with God. Not for Teilhard is the world "the wilderness," the "vale of tears," the "desert land" of so many Christian hymns. He will not either, have those similar descriptions of the material world as "evil" and "fallen," and as obstacles, lures, and occasions for stumbling. Teilhard takes very seriously the judgment of the Creator on his initial creation, as expressed in the first chapter of Genesis: "God saw everything that he had made and, behold, it was very good." If the "goodness" becomes a trap or a stone of stumbling, it is people's own choice — the choice of turning their faces from "the glory that is to be revealed" at the end of their upward journey, through succumbing to the temptations to seek security or pleasure in immobility, or to use what they find for selfish ends.

The New Formula — Based On
THE DIVINE MILIEU

In the first of two books he prepared for publication which he describes as "an essay on the interior of life," *The Divine Milieu*, Teilhard sets out a conception of the Christian life on which he never turned his back or made any substantial change later. It is a book addressed, as he puts it, "not specifically... to Christians who are firmly established in their faith and have nothing more to learn about its beliefs. It is written for the waverers, both inside and outside; that is to say, for those who, instead of giving themselves wholly to the Church, either hesitate on its threshold or turn away in hope of going beyond it." (DM 43).

For such people he sets out what he conceives to be "a new formula to express what is meant by Holiness."[1]

The Divided Life Superseded

Teilhard was troubled by the clear teaching in his own

tradition that Christians had to make a choice which cut them into two. They could either spend their lives "serving God" in the holiness of turning their backs on the world, cutting themselves off from concern with its material progress and well-being, which they must see as of very doubtful value or even as evil; or they could settle for being second-class citizens of God's kingdom, living their ordinary making-a-living lives in the material world, serving it and themselves, and then adding to this life an additional and separate section of so-called "religious duties."

Although this may seem to Protestants a peculiarly Roman Catholic dilemma since, technically, we do not have a class of people called "religious," it has been my experience that such distinctions exist in people's minds, especially regarding their clergy. Many church people demand standards of conduct and self-denial from their clergy they would never dream of expecting from themselves; and not a few seem to feel that there is something fundamentally different about the needs of their ministers. I can well recall the remark of a woman whom I was visiting, when I recommended the practice of prayer, saying that I personally could not live without it. Looking at me as if I were something let loose from a zoo, she remarked, "Oh, that's all right for you!" In addition, I am aware that there are many sincere and devoted Protestants who feel that, because they have demanding duties in earning their living and looking after their families, they do not have the time or strength to do "work for God," as they put it, such as they feel they ought to be doing.

All Of Life Oriented To The Fulfilment Of God's Purposes

As we should realize by now from a study of Teilhard's theology, he would have none of this division of life into the service of God or of the world."... What is sanctity," he writes, "in a creature if not to adhere to God with the maximum of his strength, — and what does the maximum adherence to God mean if not the fulfilment — in the world organized around Christ — of the exact function, be it lowly or eminent, to which that creature is destined both by natural endowment and supernatural gift?" (DM 66)

In a universe which in its every aspect — from atom to social grouping — holds together from above and ahead through the magnetic attraction of God through the risen Christ, every creature *does* live "in a world organized around Christ." However, only the Christian who, through the gift of the ability to receive God's revelation in Jesus of Nazareth, realizes that this is so. As we saw earlier, Teilhard believes that at the time of the Second Coming this revelation will be made to all. To the Christian then, it is given to know "the secrets of the Kingdom of God" but, Teilhard insists, all things, all people, live in that kingdom, immersed in it as in the atmosphere in which the world is bathed. All of God's creation is a "divine milieu." Within the "magnetic field" of God, as it were, everything "lives and moves and has its being."

If we would, as Christians, respond with love, devotion, and gratitude to the love of God by which we are surrounded, how must we live? First, says Teilhard, we need to accept the fact that we live in a world of "becoming," of which we ourselves are part. It is one universe. We are products of it. We came on the scene exactly at the moment and in the place we could have emerged and at no other. Therefore we set out from that particular spot and time on the same upward climb that is the movement of the whole creation towards such perfection of spirit as will lead at length to the union of all things with God in Christ. In this personal climb, as in that of the universe, everything has its place and contribution. There is no division of "sacred" and "secular." Just as the complexity of physical structure made possible the emergence of thought and personality, so the further complexity of all these in "Mankind" will make possible the emergence of greater personality and spirit. This will only occur, of course, provided each individual is true to the finest and best he/she knows and never ceases in effort or in aspiration to cherish and cultivate all that makes for the growth of spirit and the heightening and deepening of personality. And much of this work will, of necessity, be done in the realm most people, under the old system of classification, would call "the secular world." How does one know the things which will promote "spirit" and "personality?" Both are supremely to be found, of course, in God, and of him, St. Paul insists (Romans 1:21), every one has some knowledge. To his "gentile" friends Teilhard was continually saying that they should be true to the highest and finest they knew — to their very best selves — for he had great faith in the power of God both within and without his creatures. The God who had chosen to perfect his creation only with the help of humanity has equipped his fellow-workers with all that is needful. He is a God of love.

But to Christians there has been given a special gift, and therefore a very great responsibility. In Jesus Christ they have in its most understandable and lovable form, that for which they must strive. Here is the human who fulfils God's dream for all, and here too, is the power to reach that goal. For Christians the goal — being persons — is supremely lovable, lovely, and loving. By accepting and responding to that love they place themselves under the influence of the energy that holds the universe together and moves it forward, the energy of divine love.

Moreover, because they can know, through the revelation in Jesus Christ, that the universe — perfected and unified until it can follow the risen Christ into the realm of spirit — is needed to fill out the "fulness of Christ," providing him with his glorified Body, the Christians have a motive for their efforts which others have not. They can do all they do for love, the love of Jesus Christ, of God, whose work they are doing and to whose fulness they are contributing. In Teilhard's scheme, the idea of doing things "for the glory of God" is not a mere metaphor. By the choice of the Creator himself all efforts, however small or insignificant they may be, are needful for bringing all things to their intended end. "We serve to complete (creation) even by the humblest work of our hands," he writes (DM 62). "That is ultimately the meaning and value of our acts. Owing to the inter-relation between matter, soul, and Christ, we bring part of the being which he desires back to God in *whatever we do*. With each of our works ... we bring to Christ a little fulfilment." And again, "Any increase (in one's self or in things) is translated into some increase in my power to love, and some progress in Christ's blessed hold upon the universe. Our work appears to us, in the main, as a way of earning our daily bread... through it we complete in ourselves the subject of the divine union; and through it again we somehow make to grow in stature the divine term of the one with whom we are united, our Lord Jesus Christ... whatever our role as man may be... we can, if we are Christians, speed toward the object of our work as though towards an opening on to the supreme fulfilment of our beings." (DM 63).

We need to recall again that Teilhard sees the whole of creation as one. It has needed every part and every particle from the very primeval dust onwards to bring forth Homo Sapiens on the earth. It needs everything and everyone to bring to fulfilment the glorious unity of God and his creation towards which the Creator has been working in his universe from the beginning.

For Teilhard, therefore, everything and everyone and every work is sacred. This does not mean that all are working for the kingdom or that everything a person does, or fails to do, will find its place in the final union. We are free to choose. We live in a world haunted by God. God is in all things, working for their fulfilment and perfection. Christians who love God and would serve him offer themselves as instruments to do this work of God. We will love and serve the world for God's sake.

Some Misunderstandings Of What "Living For God" Means

Teilhard had undoubtedly suffered from the opinion non-Christians have of their Christian colleagues in the so-called "secular field," that Christians, serving God first, are only half-hearted in their work. Rather than ever seeming to earn such a charge, Christians should cherish the things of earth and work without ceasing for their perfection with a devotion even greater than others, since we know that it is through a creation brought to perfection that the purposes of God can alone be fulfilled.

Dorothy Sayers, in her play, *The Zeal of Thine House*,[3] has an extreme illustration of the sort of thing against which Teilhard is trying to warn Christians. When the architect of a cathedral has to be lifted by a pulley to the ceiling to examine some detail of the work, the task of paying out the rope and watching over his safety is given to a monk who, unfortunately, disapproves highly of the architect's way of life. Instead of watching carefully the work he has been given, the monk decides to engage in his "religious" duty of prayer and thus he misses seeing the dangerously frayed rope that, passing over the pulley, pulls apart and plunges the architect to a life of suffering.

That "ordinary" Christians are tempted to make this break between their work as "Christians" and their everyday activities, I had brought home to me when I was ministering to a small community in which were living a group of people who often paid calls on their neighbours for the purpose of trying to change their religious persuasions. They called this "visiting as Christians," as distinct from other calls they might make on the same neighbours. One day some of my congregation asked me, "How should *we* 'visit as Christians'?" I could only reply, "I hope you will never visit as anything else!"

All On Their Own Private Pilgrimage

For Teilhard, to do anything as a Christian means to do it at the peak of one's effort, as well as one possibly can, whatever it is. And for him this would mean different outward things for different people, and also for the same people at different times.

You see, Teilhard saw every one engaged not only in the great movement of creation towards its fulfilment in God, but in a personal, private pilgrimage as well. Just as the whole cosmos is being drawn upwards towards its perfection by Christ, so every one is being wooed forward by the same attractive power. Whether there is responsive movement or not is the pilgrim's own free choice. But all on pilgrimage are lured by Christ into an ever more spiritual and personal state, into ever more perfect centering of on life on Christ. And as this movement of "infolding in the lower stages of evolution had produced greater complexity-consciousness, so the centering of the personal life on Christ enables the expression of greater consciousness — spirit and personality. This is what Teilhard means as he writes "every man . . . *makes his own soul* throughout all his earthly days." (DM 60-1). It is interesting to note that psychologists agree that, for fulness of personality, integration on a higher personality outside oneself is essential; and that Hick, in his *Biology and the Soul* — written so much later than Teilhard's work — agrees that the soul is not a separate added entity.[4]

Because we each come into the world at our own particular point, with our own personal, private equipment and gifts, prepared for us literally since the foundation of the world, each starts from a different place and is able to move at a different rate. This means, says Teilhard, that what is "good and sanctifying and spiritual for my brother below or beside me on the mountain side, can be material, misleading or bad for me. What I rightly allowed myself yesterday, I must perhaps deny myself today... actions which would have been a grave betrayal in [a saint]... may well be models for me if I am to follow in the footsteps of these saints. In other words, the soul can only rejoin God after having traversed a *specific path* through matter..." (DM 108).

Against this background it is easy to see the logic in our Lord's warning that, in judging others, we judge ourselves; it also emphasizes the folly of taking our standards from those about us. This also means that, for Teilhard, morality cannot be a static thing. When humanity was seen as "finished" rather than as "becoming," he writes (HE 106), the purpose of morality was to "preserve and protect the individual." Now that we realize it is in process of becoming, its purpose is to "guide him so effectively in the direction of his anticipated fulfilment that the 'quantity of personality' still diffuse in humanity may be released in fulness and security. The moralist was, up to now, a jurist and a tight-rope walker. He becomes the technician and engineer of the spiritual energies of the world. The highest morality is hence-forth that which will best develop the phenomenon of motion to its upper limits. No longer to protect but to develop by awaking and convergence, the individual riches of the earth." (HE 106). He calls his morality a "morality of movement," contrasted with the older "morality of balance." Of it he writes, "Many things seemed allowed by the morality of balance, which we find to be forbidden by the morality of movement... a man could...

(decide) to use or leave dormant that part of life which belonged to him . . . now . . . no promise or custom is lawful which does not tend to *the service* of the power within it. . . . Riches only become good (as) they work for the benefit of the spirit." [Honesty is no longer enough]. Love no longer must be satisfied with the founding of a material family. "It must now consider its fundamental object to give that love just the incalculable spiritual power that it is capable of developing between husband and wife . . . it will forbid . . . [the individual] a neutral and "inoffensive existence and compel him strenuously to free his autonomy and personality to the uttermost . . . many things . . . forbidden by the morality of balance become virtually permitted or even obligatory by the morality of movement precisely because [the morality of balance] was satisfied with order . . . (and) did not trouble to find out whether some spiritual possibilities were not excluded . . . Out of timidity or playing for safety it allowed a world of energy to be lost in every realm. In a morality of movement, everything that contains an ascending force of consciousness is recognized under that head and within those limits as fundamentally good: all that has to be done is to isolate that goodness by analysis and to disengage it by sublimation . . . to limit *force* (unless for the purpose of obtaining even more force), is sin.*"

Dangers On The Path

This may sound very dangerous and, of course, it is. Teilhard is at pains to ensure that everyone who reads him is aware that we live in a world of infinite risk, where without risk there can be no more creation, indeed no more life. Indeed, he sees refusal to take risk as one of the most dangerous of all courses, even as did Jesus who appears to have said over and over, "Whoever would save his life will lose it." However, Teilhard does not envisage his system of morality as being

*Force here signifies energy and love. (H.E. 107-8).

without guidelines. "A morality of balance," he writes, "may logically be agnostic and engrossed in possession of the present moment. A morality of movement necessarily inclines towards the future, in pursuit of a God." (HE 109). As we have seen in previous chapters, he is concerned to help make people's conception of this God as attractive and "big" enough so that the morality of movement will be creative and not destructive.

Moreover, though Teilhard never writes specifically about the need of the Christian to be faithful in the discipline of church attendance, he does speak of the importance of worship in giving the vision of God and of the teaching mission of the church. It is, he writes, important to hear and learn the ethical principles of the gospel, for he writes thus of them, "The ethical principles which hitherto we have regarded as appendages superimposed more or less by our own free will upon the laws of biology, are now showing themselves . . . to be conditions of survival for the human race." (FM 212).

Guidelines For The Danger Of Individualism

Among these, of course, Teilhard makes much of Christ's repeated command to love. Indeed, he believes that such are conditions in the universe that, while these words could, for centuries, be presented as a code of moral perfection or perhaps as a practical method of diminishing the pains or frictions of this early life, now, since the existence of the noosphere* on the one hand and the necessity of preserving it on the other have been revealed to our minds, the voice which speaks takes on a more imperious tone. It no longer says, "Love one another in order to be perfect," but adds, "Love one another or you perish." It is love alone which holds the particles of earth together. It is love which provides the warmth, the energy by which the forward movement of all things cancels out the backward, death-drawing pull of the multiple. In entrusting to people partnership with him in the

---

* The thinking portion or layer of creation as there are the atmosphere, the lithosphere, the biosphere, etc. Noosphere is Teilhard's word.

creation of all things, God has need of their love, the love he both gives and makes possible. But they must will love, else they will destroy all that has been done, and every hope of the fulfilment of God's plan as it depends on them; so Teilhard sees and writes further, "to go on putting our hopes in a social order obtained by external violence would simply mean to abandon all hope of carrying the spirit of earth to its limits." (HE 153). Thus, to "see" what Teilhard "sees" is to understand more fully the urgency of Christ's command.

It is realizing this movement that illumines the Christian concept of duty. "So long as our conception of the universe remains static, the basis of duty remains extremely obscure," he writes. . . . "In a spiritually evolutionary scheme of the universe . . . the answer is quite simple. For the human unit the *initial* basis of obligation is the fact of being born and developing as a function of a cosmic stream. We must act, and in a certain way, because our individual destinies are dependent on a universal destiny. Duty, in its origin, is nothing but the reflection of the universe in the atom." (HE 29).

Here he would have us realize what responsibility is ours by reflecting on the prodigious effort and sacrifice which brought us into being. It took the whole universe since creation to produce each one of us. We are each the end of an enormous cosmic effort. Everything on which our lives depend now — our comfort and our enjoyment — has also been so produced. This thought is beautifully brought out in the poem which begins, "Kneel always when you light a fire," especially in the line, "For here, again, is sacrifice for your delight."[5]

No one has the right to treat anything without reverence and without responsibility, for whether that sacrifice and effort will be for nothing depends on our choices — whether we will choose to continue the struggle for greater unity and higher consciousness, or be a drag on the ascending spiral. We can doom all that went before and all that should come after by our refusal to continue the work of uniting-through-love, which brought into being the atom, and the universe, the great atom. Up to *homo sapiens*, the individual existed for the mass. Now the human race — those precious, self-conscious, centered individuals, tempted always to preserve their individuality and to enjoy their exalted position — may well choose to stop and "pitch their tents on the first summit conquered, enjoy . . . his . . . exaltation, the intoxication of raising himself to the highest point of the universe. The temptation is quite natural. But let him beware! . . . because of the autonomy he has attained, he is always dominated by another, higher unity from which he cannot free himself on pain of death precious though it is, the human monad remains vitally subjected to the law . . . (which brought him into being) . . . man must believe in humanity more than in himself or else he will lose hope." (HE 30-1). And for Teilhard loss of hope is death of the spirit that keeps us in the race.

There is in us, Teilhard insists, an "irresistible instinct in our hearts which leads us towards unity," (PM 292), a sense and thrill of oneness, the keynote of pure poetry and pure religion. In our day we have tended to dismiss this sense of our oneness with all that is about us as romantic nonsense, but such a severance from our roots has brought us face to face with the spectre of ecological disaster. We are now becoming painfully aware that the instinct of poet, artist, and seer that bade us look at "sister earth" with fellow-feeling was right, while the hard-hearted exploiter was wrong. All things have conspired together to produce us, but all are holy because their end is greater than they or we.

This realization should lead us back to being more concerned about the love of neighbour on which Jesus laid so much stress. Yet, as Teilhard confesses for himself, . . . there is . . . a mutual repulsion dominant within the human mass . . . the 'other' usually appears to be the worst danger that our personality meets . . ." "The man in the street gets in my way because I collide with him as a possible rival" . . . "The other must be got out of the way." (HE 78). Here, of course, is the great truth about us all contained in the ancient story of Cain and Abel in the fourth chapter of Genesis. It is interesting to see it placed so sagely almost immediately after the appearance of self-consciousness, that quality which comes from the centeredness that also makes us fear the other whose centeredness is a rival to our own.

But for individuals to let this natural feeling rule them is fatal. Progress below the human has come about only through union. Love of neighbour — though of course it was not "love" as we know it — was the secret of life's coming into being. Because ours is only a stage and not an end in the process, for us to try to remain in selfish isolation is biological suicide. The difficulty, of course, is that now we must will to enter into the saving oneness. We must desire, in direct opposition to our strongest instincts and feelings, to become part of a larger whole. Just how dangerous is selfishness, the cult of individualism, in the biological realm to which we belong, is revealed by the fact that the cells of cancer appear to be cells which, having developed as all living cells do for earlier unions, instead of entering into further union for the well-being of the whole body have "again taken up pursuit of their individual development to the detriment of the whole."[6] Progress in the past — and therefore, we must assume, for the future — has come about only as contacts were made between particles which, by uniting, enriched others and themselves. The particles which failed to enter into unity died as the pull of the multiple dragged them down into the nothingness of disintegration. Human beings are part of this whole process; we must learn its lessons and obey the signals it gives.

Guidelines Through The Dangers Of Sexuality

For instance, the presence of some sexual attraction in the world, with its enormous strength to *move* people, points to human need for passing into a greater than oneself. In this area we become acutely aware of our needs of others in order to complete ourselves. Teilhard has a very high view of the relations between men and women. He sees the role of woman as of extreme importance in stimulating and calling forth man from love of himself. Yet he is also aware that this love, if allowed to concentrate on itself, has its own dangers. Love, being energy, is as dangerous as is all energy. Indeed, he speaks of sexual love as "that terrifying energy in which the power that causes the universe to converge on itself passes through us." (HE 74). We need rules to guide us in our mastery of it. The first of these is that "love, in conformity with the general laws of creative union, contributes to the spiritual differentiation of the two beings it brings together. The one must not absorb the other, still less should the two lose themselves in enjoyment of physical possession. . . ." (HE 74). The reason Teilhard warns against this second danger is, of course, bound up with his view of the relationship in the ascending universe between physical and spiritual; to use love, the spirit, for mere physical possession, would be to reverse the direction of required movement in the universe and thus yield to the pull of death. "The only right love is that between couples whose passion leads them both, one through the other, to a higher possession of their being. The gravity of offences against love is not that they outrage some sort of modesty or virtue. It is that they fritter away, by neglect or lust, the universe's reserves of personalization." (HE 74). Equal danger, he feels, comes when couples yield to their delight in finding each other "among a swarm of other beings" and "enclose themselves in jealous possession of their mutual gain," [and] "try instinctively to shut themselves into one another to the exclusion of the rest . . . even if they succeed in over-coming the voluptous temptations of absorption and repose," they are involved in a dangerous illusion — that they can use the powers of the universe given for making *all* one — for "a two-person universe." (HE 75). The same temptations to individualism and egoism that assault individuals and couples can also assault other groups, such as families.

In each case the dangers are equally great, because it is a matter of flying in the face of the law of the universe which continually moves towards greater union, and thus — and thus alone — overcomes the pull of disintegration and death.

First, through learning the truth about the oneness of the creation and its movement and destiny, there can be awakened and stimulated a sense of humanity. The basis of the instinctive feeling of oneness to which romantic ideas appeal can be broadened to include all humankind as its members realize the role it plays in their own development and in the future of the universe. When individuals come to see themselves not as the final product of the universe but as part of the larger whole still in the process of making, they can begin to be rescued from their destructive egoisms by finding a common purpose with others. "I shall like (my fellow man) as soon as I see him as a partner in the struggle." (HE 78). For individuals to come together in the mutual love of friendship there needs to be the basis of a common interest. Knowledge and acceptance of the common task of humankind can provide this. Moreover, in friendship there is a great potential for the growth of "humanity" because, as Teilhard writes, it "is completely different from . . . passionate love, which is by nature exclusive . . . founded on duality. . . . Friendship remains constitutionly open to a growing multiplicity." (HE 79). Friendship is based on all kinds of mutual interests, concerns, and goals. Thus it offers hope for the future by making the individual open to others, and affords the vital opportunity to give oneself to something greater than mere self.

Supremely, of course, the one who redeems through all these means and redeems each kind of love is "the loving center of all convergence," God as he is experienced in Jesus Christ. To have found the center of one's life and love in him is to be rescued from all the dangers and discords that come from emphasis on individual rights and egoisms. "It is impossible to love Christ," writes Teilhard, "without loving others." (DM 144).

Looking at the strife which has been, and still is, in the world between "Christians," it is obvious that the words in *Hymn of the Universe* (88) are equally important: "It is also impossible to love either God or our neighbour without our being obliged to help in the progress of the earthly synthesis of spirit in its physical totality, for it is precisely the advances made in this moment of synthesis that permit us to draw closer to one another and at the same time raise us up towards God." Our experiences with pollution in both the physical environment and human relations suggest that we need Teilhard's view of the work of God through Christ as drawing all things together in spiritual union. If we realize, as he teaches, that everyone — not just psychologically but organically — is part of a whole, we might take more seriously than we do Christ's insistence on our need to guard not only our deeds but our words, our thoughts, and the attitudes we allow ourselves, in reverence for the world and for others. "Like particles immersed in one and the same spiritual fluid, souls cannot think or pray or act or move without waves being produced, even by the most insignificant among them, which set others in motion; inevitably, behind each soul a wave is formed which draws other souls either towards good or towards evil." (WTW 48). No wonder Jesus re-interpreted the Jewish laws about murder, adultery, and slander to include as equally dangerous to social life and spiritual union with God the thoughts which not only give rise to deeds, but thoughts which are as deadly as deeds themselves.

For Teilhard, the love of neighbour commanded by Christ is much larger than just goodwill towards him. It is the Christian's duty, not just because of Christ's command, but because on it depends our love of God, as the Epistle of James makes so bitingly clear. Our love of God, must certainly show itself in our cooperation with him in his work of drawing us to himself in union with others, his drawing us out of the material into the spiritual state in which alone we can be united with him. And this final unity depends on the completion of our union with others. Love of neighbour is the only way to combat the pull to disintegration and death which is in our very fiber and that of the universe: evil, the enemy of God. "In your excessive self-love," Teilhard writes ". . . you are like a molecule closed in upon itself incapable of entering easily into any new combination. God looks to you to be more open and more pliant. If you are to enter into him you need to be freer, and more eager. Have done then with your egoism and your fear of suffering. Love others as you love yourself, that is to say, admit them into yourself, all of them, even those whom, if you were a pagan, you would exclude." (LME 137)

One of the works of the glorified Christ then is to enable us to love others. The thing he commands he makes possible, always. And this is also true of the relationship of men and women in marriage. Because we were made for a much wider love than just one for one, to try to find satisfaction in sexual love alone, and even in one other, is to run into all the dangers and damage we know in our sex-ridden age. Love, a spiritual energy, meant to draw us towards greater spiritual development, will inevitably be destructive, being turned backwards. Love, meant to bring about the goal of spirit through wide and wider union, channelled towards one, will lead either to growing dissatisfaction or the search for more and more amorous adventures, in both of which courses there lies the threat of disintegration. There is only one safe course for sexual love, and that is to be directed also towards the living center of all union. "Love," says Teilhard, (HE 76) "is a three-term function: man, woman, and God. Its whole perfection and success is bound up with the harmonious balance of these three elements."

Teilhard sees this interplay of love of men and women and God not only serving to raise humanity higher, but playing a part in that problem at the moment facing the earth — the population explosion. The role of sexuality, in leading to the reproduction of the human species, Teilhard sees as a transitory one. It was necessary because there had to be a density of human "molecules" for the purpose of personalization, even as such complexity had played its part all the way along. However, the very size of the earth and the limits of its resources are now telling us that physical complexity has nearly reached its limits. This, to Teilhard, indicates that the maturity of personality is approaching when ". . . men will have to realize that it is for them not simply a question of controlling births, but of increasing to the uttermost the quantity of love liberated from the duty of reproduction . . . Without ceasing to be physical, in order to remain physical love will make itself more spiritual." (HE 77).

Thus Teilhard's scientific treatment of love as "human energy" finds itself in the Christian camp, pointing us to the necessity of prior love of God and to the virtue of chastity. Even the gift of sexuality and of human love must be deliberately turned to the well-being of humanity as a whole, and thus to the greater glory of God.

Because the power of sexual love is so great, and therefore its potential to further God's purpose so enormous, Teilhard feels that, in what we allow it to do to us, is where we meet one of the greatest tests of our loyalty to God. Here, above all, we must resist the pull to the lower levels of materialism — selfishness, pleasure, exclusiveness, and all that destroys or impedes further unity. Here we must resist, control, and direct our own actions, feelings, and spirit to those things which produce and build up unity — not only in ourselves and in the beloved — but also in the universe. That wise third chapter of Genesis illustrates in parable form how potent for good or ill is the relationship between man and woman. For guidance and help people can, therefore, look to the Bible. They can judge and direct the quality of their love by such passages as Paul's definition of it (I Cor. 13), or his essay on the fruits of the spirit in Galatians 5: 13-26. Sexual love, Teilhard feels, must — with all other forms of "human energy" — rise from matter to spirit. Since evolution is now a human responsibility, each must direct this powerful drive so that it contributes to, and results in, that unity which ends in the glory of God.

It is interesting to compare this view of Teilhard with that set forth in a science-fiction novel of the first half of this century, set in the most advanced of the planets. There men and women control and direct their sexual drive for the higher good of their planet. Of course, especially in this matter, would we think of the reply of Jesus to the question of the Pharisees regarding the final marital status of the woman who had seven husbands. (Mark 12: 25ff). Here Jesus suggests that, in the higher state for which people are destined, there will be something much wider for human sexuality than the one-to-one relationship we know on earth. Teilhard is suggesting that we must begin to think in these terms here and now.

For Teilhard then, as for St. Paul (I Cor. 13), love is the supremely important spirit. However, he insists, it must be love with both faith and hope in attendance, and love given power, scope and purpose by devotion to the ends and purposes of God — to that which lies ahead. This orientation he sees as vital for, "to go on putting our hope in a social order obtained by external violence would simply mean to abandon all hope of carrying the spirit of earth to its limits." (HE 153).

The Role Of The Church

Since both union with God and others are absolutely essential to the continuation of the development of humanity this universe whose goal is spirit, it is not difficult to see why Teilhard attaches such importance to the church and its functions. In its teaching role, as we have already seen, it keeps before them the ethical principles of the Gospel, but of course it does much more than that. It enables them to learn more of God and the ways he has revealed to them through the ages about the laws governing life. Many of these, in the light of modern research, as well as the view of Teilhard, are coming to be seen as more than just important to the one who "happens to be interested in religion."

In addition, the church — like the family — affords the opportunity to learn to live in oneness with a small portion of humankind, under the influence of a common bond of unity. It enables them to know the uniting power of the love of friendship, under the even stronger power of the love of Christ. Thus membership in a church community is extremely essential for one who would live to the greater glory of God, in the creation of humanity.

However, of even greater importance than its role as the teacher, enabling us to be greater by knowing more and providing us with an experience of living in unity, is the role of the church in providing opportunities for worship for times when union with God is the special intention and goal of all activity. He believes that union with God both increases and directs energy, making it possible to function more effectively. Moments of efficient and explicit commerce with God — prayers, the sacraments — when our vision of God is renewed — enable us to maintain this union in our daily life. From all that has gone before one would expect that Teilhard would especially value that sacrament of the church whereby one is, by faith and will, physically united with Christ — the sacrament of the Lord's Supper.

Although he is not explicitly speaking of the sacrament of Holy Communion in this place, for to him all of creation can offer him this blessed union, these words can illuminate for us what a powerful act it is to him. But he would have no one believe that it works without the cooperation of the worshipper. Thus, he writes, "If I seal up the entry into my heart I must dwell in darkness — and not only I — my individual soul — but the whole universe in so far as its activity sustains my organism and awakens my consciousness and in so far also as I act upon it in my turn to draw forth from it the materials of sensation, of ideas, of moral goodness, of holiness of life. But if, on the other hand, *my heart is open to you* [Jesus] . . . through the pure intent of my will the divine must flood into the universe in so far as the universe is centered on me. Since, by virtue of my consent, I shall have become a living particle of the Body of Christ, all that affects me must in the end help on the growth of the total Christ. Christ will flood into and over me, me and *my* cosmos." (WTW 216).

By thus seeing participation in the life of the church — through sacrament, prayers and other acts done there — as not important just for individuals in their own passage from what they are to what God wants them to be, but of vital importance in doing the same things for the universe in its similar passage, Teilhard deepens and widens the value of the things Christians have been taught to love and value, and gives new reasons for viewing their church life as important. When he sees all this as contributing to the 'fulness of Christ," the Christian's beloved, Teilhard can surely help disheartened and discouraged Christians lift up their heads, and through this new image of themselves become more faithful to the things they have always done and perhaps loved. With Teilhard's view of the part they can play for the whole of the universe and for Christ, by doing what they have vowed in their commitment to do — pray, read their Scriptures, receive the sacraments, and worship — Christians can, with reverence and awe, pray for themselves in the words of their Lord, "For their sakes I consecrate myself, that they also may be consecrated." (John 17:19). Of the other duty laid on Christians — to be witnesses — Teilhard writes, "One of the first duties of a Christian is to show by the logic of his religious view, and still more by the logic of his action . . . (that) Christianity . . . is a soul of immense power which bestows significance and beauty and a new lightness on what we are already doing." (DM 70).

The Role Of The Individual Christian: Action

And what does Teilhard see Christians ordinarily doing? The job in which their talents, their vocations, their opportunities have placed them — with heart, soul, strength, and mind, for, to add one's contribution to the perfection of the universe and of oneself is truly, in Teilhard's eyes, to love God. In order to be united with God, one must be and do something. Develop oneself through "the love of everything that is true and beautiful in the creation . . .offer God with 'trembling love' our collaboration." [Summary of DM 95-7].

Because God has chosen to make humanity participate in his work, Teilhard sees any idea of "dropping out" as unthinkable for the Christian. In this universe which is one, to be a servant of God and of our neighbours calls for strenuous effort. "If we are to succeed in submitting to the will of God, we first must make a very great effort." (S & C 72). "Our duty to men *is to act as though there were no limit to our power.* Life has made us conscious collaborators in a creation which is still going on in us, in order to lead us, it would appear, to a goal (even on earth) much more lofty and distant than we had imagined. We must help God with all our strength, and handle matter as though our salvation depended solely upon our industry." (S & C 32). We "tempt God, by hoping to obtain from indolent prayer, from revelation, from miracles, what only natural toil can supply." (WTW 89).

Though the motto of real Christians is "nothing left untried" which may well engage them in enterprises that will misfire, risks that will prove not to have been worthwhile — even when they have taken seriously the revelations made in the Bible of the areas of risks which are too great — they will still not despair. "The worker whose trust is in God knows that no attempt, no aspiration, conceived in grace, is lost: they attain their end by passing through the living center of all useful activity." (WTW 90). Surely what Teilhard means by "conceived in grace" is what the writer of Timothy was talking about as he similarly spoke about his confidence, "I know whom I have believed and I am sure that he is able to keep what I have committed to him, against that day." (II Timothy 1:12). It surely means all activities of those who, knowing their utter need of Christ and yet their responsibility to act, do so often in agonizing uncertainty as to what is God's will — trusting in God's knowledge of their "frame" and in the realization that, while they are very liable to error — and indeed, to worse than error — God's forgiveness ensures that the relationship between him and them is still intact. Then God's power over evil will transmute whatever of error is — in love and trust and recognition of need — submitted to him. It is our duty to act. The wonder of the Gospel is that we can dare to do so, imperfect and weak and liable to error as we are.

Teilhard condemns all refusal to do one's best as a sinful waste of the energy God has given — a wicked betrayal of the enormous effort, sacrifice, and expense by which humanity has appeared in creation. Every one has an obligation, of which the initial basis is "the fact, of being born and developing as a function of the cosmic stream." (HE 29). However, he has a word for those who err on the other side. Thus he writes to Leontine Zanta (60), "I understand your anxiety about being up to the level of your task. This is one of the great human problems. You have to face the matter squarely, in God's truth and light. Don't get lost in vain self-examination about your capacities and value. But tell yourself categorically, . . . that you should *do your best*. As soon as you give what you are capable of giving, you are united in *maximum measure* to the creative Act; you couldn't be a more useful servant . . . don't forget that if we lack power over our inspiration and intelligence, we have in addition the resource of intensifying our intention and our faith. The longer I plod on, the more I realize that on (that) side our power is prodigious."

Teilhard includes among those making this contribution and having available to them this power, a very great variety of people. "Anyone whose aim (is) . . . to subject a little more of matter to spirit has . . . begun to take leave of himself . . . This is also true of the man who rejects mere enjoyment, the line of least resistance, easy possession of things and ideas, and sets out courageously on the path of work and of the inward renewal and ceaseless broadening and perfection of his ideal. And is true of anyone who has given his time, his health, or his life to something greater than himself — a family to be supported, a country to be saved, a truth to be discovered, a cause to be defended." (DM 97-8).

The Role Of The Individual: Renunciation

In the above quotation we meet a second part of Teilhard's list of activities which a Christian will undertake — self-denial and turning away, as well as self-fulfillment and turning to. He speaks of these two activities thus, "Christian attachment and detachment are like the impulse of a springboard from which to mount beyond . . . (in this we need to avoid extremes). Each of us is placed on a slope at a specific point defined by God — our birth places, history, vocation. . . . Our task is to climb through towards the light . . . a given set of created things which are footholds and nourishment for us, sap to be purified, of elements to be associated and borne along with us." (DM 108) (A paraphrase).

This brings us back to a more detailed look at Teilhard's teaching about the interior life as an upward climb, a sort of spiral staircase on which we must continually be moving in response to God's attractive action and through our own effort and choice, from one level to another, ever towards the goal of spiritual union with God. In this climb there can be no lingering in endless enjoyment of what we have attained; otherwise the terrible downward pull will drag us to disintegration. Built into the Christian life is the principle of renunciation, but it is a positive renunciation. One detaches oneself from "material" things, delights, not because they are evil in themselves; they are not; all God has made is good. But wherever one starts on this "slope" to God one must renounce what is on that level in order to gain the higher level. What is on the present level is potentially evil because it may tempt one to try to stay immobile, an impossibility in a dynamic cosmos; what is on a lower level is definitely evil for it will drag one back towards death. Those things are seemly which belong to the level on which one is, a level of mingled matter and spirit. And they are seemly only if one is already pulling up one's stakes preparing to move; renouncing them for higher and finer values and behaviour.

What such a view of life can do for persons is illustrated, I believe, in two incidents from life. One tells of a fairly elderly couple who, though living in the most wretched and reduced circumstances, bore themselves with a grace and air which impressed strangers at once. When one of these enquired how this was, he was told that those people had once been told they came from royal blood and they never forgot it in the things in which their choice was free. The other is the famous story of Martin Luther who, it is reported, whenever he was tempted to sin, used to tell himself, "But you are baptized." In the matter of renouncing things, and yet never labelling them as anything but good, one is reminded of George MacDonald, the man to whom C. S. Lewis said he owed so much in his Christian life. MacDonald was so unpopular as a minister his congregation kept reducing his salary in order to try to get rid of him. He in turn was so sure God's choice of a place for him was in this congregation that he developed a wonderful philosophy for living with his reduced circumstances. He said he must never persuade himself what he could not have was evil. He must go on thinking they were lovely and desirable, and learn to live without them. Again, I think of reflections of the naturalist, Konrad Lorenz, about such things as jealousy, snobbishness, spite, and so on in animal behaviour, about which people so often say, "Animals show human characteristics." Lorenz says we should say of such things, when we see them in humans, that these are animal characteristics which this human has still not risen above.

It is not just the things we recognize as evil, or below us, which we must renounce in our upward climb, however; there are also good things and fine which, if not renounced, will keep us from the better and finer. As Jesus said, "If anyone would come after me, let him deny himself daily and follow me." (Mark 8:34). Not to do so will, Jesus tells us, bring on death, as one succumbs to that deadly downward pull. One reason we need the Bible and the services of the church is that we may have constantly before us the knowledge we most need and cannot have for ourselves because we must ever be moving beyond where we have been and the knowledge we have had, "the knowledge of good and evil." It is when we fail to see ourselves as still in the making and therefore imperfect, with our knowledge imperfect, that we lose our relationship with the God ever out ahead of us, whose attraction keeps us from falling back into nothing.

Thus the Christian life involves not only attaining, but renouncing, for the higher and finer, literally for Christ's sake.

NOTES

1. Jeanne Mortier and Marie-Louise Aboux editors, *Album, Teilhard de Chardin* (London: Collins, 1966) p 140.
2. *Album*, p 140.
3. Dorothy Sayers, *The Zeal of Thine House.* London: Victor Galanz Ltd., 1939.
4. John Hick, 13
5. John Oxenham, "The Sacrament of Fire" in *Poems of the English Race* ed. Raymond MacDonald (New York: Charles Scribner's Sons, 1921) p 395.
6. F. G. Elliott, *Teilhard Review* Vol. I p 9.

Chapter 8

"A NEW FORMULA FOR HOLINESS"

Part II

ESPECIALLY FOR SUFFERERS

"The problem of evil... will always remain one of the most disturbing mysteries of the universe for both our hearts and our minds." "...God cannot ordain that the elements of a world in the course of growth ... should avoid shocks and diminishments, even moral ones... But God will make it good ... he will take his revenge, if one may use the expression — by making evil itself serve a higher good of his faithful... Like an artist who is able to make use of a fault or an impurity in the stone he is sculpturing... so as to produce more exquisite lines ... — *providing we lovingly trust in him* ... Not only our unavoidable ills but our faults, even our most deliberate ones, can be embraced in that transformation, provided always we repent of them. Not everything is immediately good to those who seek God; but everything is capable of becoming good..." (DM 85, 86).

I think that Teilhard is most helpful of all in dealing with those subtractions from life which happen to us and seem to us to impoverish our lives. These he calls "diminishments" ... things like loss, pain, suffering, disappointment, failure, doubt, sorrow, bereavement, disability, the weaknesses brought on by age, and supremely, death.

"The Christian experiences suffering just as other men

do. As others, so must he do his best to lessen and alleviate it, not only by humble prayer but also through the efforts of an industrious and self-confident Science; but when the time comes when suffering is inevitable, then he puts it to good use. There is a wonderful compensation by which physical evil, if humbly accepted, conquers moral evil. In accordance with definable psychological laws, it purifies the soul, spurs it on and detaches it. Finally . . . it effects a mysterious union between the faithful soul and the suffering Christ." (WTW 68). He is keenly aware of the presence of all these in life and sees great significance in them. He has no doubt of their evil. They are not, in themselves, good; therefore he is quite definite that no one should ever deliberately seek out "diminishments" for the sake of diminishing oneself. He deplores, too, the fact that the vocabularly used about the Cross suggests that the Kingdom of God is to come through mourning and the thwarting of energies and aspirations. "This is," he says (DM 102), "un-Christian . . . The doctrine of the Cross is that . . . human life . . . leads somewhere . . . upward . . . toward the highest possible spiritualization by means of the greatest possible effort."

Teilhard's Qualifications To Speak On This Subject

Of these things Teilhard writes, not as an "armchair general" completely separated from the battle, but as one who has experienced much of what he speaks. The heart of his thought was hammered out in the cauldron of the First World War when he insisted on sharing to the full the bloody agony of life in the trenches. His family life was shadowed again and again by deaths, and constantly by the life-long suffering of his favourite sister. He himself knew the diminishments of pain, frustration, and disappointment, in his severe heart attacks, and in the last years he knew the limitations and weaknesses which old age brings. In addition, he was never free of the mental anguish of physical exile from his homeland, and of spiritual loneliness in the complete lack of sympathy, and even the hostility, he received from most of his fellow-churchmen.

And there was always the adamant opposition of his church to what he was convinced was his mission in life — bringing the Gospel to those who had to hear it in the terms of modern thought and scientific knowledge.

About those sufferings of his he was quite open and frank with his intimate correspondents, especially during the latter part of his life, when his failing heart and aging body brought physical suffering his way. "I wish the presence of the sense of God," he writes to one of his friends after a bout of 'flu [LFT 200-1] "would be more efficient to counteract the depressing effects of a cold. But, after all, this is precisely perhaps the very core of the human condition (I mean the dependency of the soul on the body) which has to be faced, and accepted, and followed faithfully to the end." Again, he writes to the same friend from hospital, "If only I could feel more quiet (less anxious physically) internally. Apparently the best cure is to 'take it easy' and try to transform anxiety into some overwhelming feeling of hope and active relaxation in God which, after all, is the logical climax and core of my whole *Weltanschuung* and philosophy." (LTF 202). From a little later period he writes to another friend (LTF 110), "The recurrence of that nervous anxiety which is more or less my birthright (and which returns a little with age) has slowed down my activity a little. But everything passes except the fundamental taste for life, which is the main thing, or as the Gospel says, 'the unique necessity'." And again, "...How weak and vulnerable I feel at this moment. But... is not one of the principles dearest to Christianity that God is all the more likely to act through us, the more aware we are of our helplessness? Now that the 'veil' of my person is beginning to wear thin (because I feel so vulnerable), I have confidence that God will take over for me somehow." (LTF 105). And, in the same vein, he writes in answer to some expression of confidence from a troubled friend, "I am afraid you have too high an idea of me... sometimes I feel terribly weak and helpless, especially these days, but what reassures me a little... is that, as the great St. Paul said again and again, what force and ardor I do have are not me but deeper than me, and are the most active, the more personally vulnerable and fragile I feel. I suspect it is precisely from this profound source that, little by little, you will see the light appear." (LTF 104)

His suffering at the disappointment — indeed the heartbreak — of the church's refusal to let him publish was perhaps a harder blow even than the disabling heart attack which kept him from his African trip and gradually curtailed his activities; or, it may be, that, coming first, these mental sufferings were a preparation for enduring the physical ones. After one of the many times he was forbidden to spread his ideas formally, he writes about the blow, "It is forcing me back on 'the one thing that is necessary'... worship."[1] It seems likely that the advice he gives to a friend comes from what he himself has learned from being thwarted in his own endeavours, "Try... to learn to love and to accept serenely (as the influence of a great loving power) those uncontrollable events which thwart your action, — and you will see that you can come close to peace..." (LTF 83). Remembering that it was China which was both the instrument and the location of his superiors' muzzling him, and the place where he wrote the books he was never allowed to publish and also where he was given the title, "the smiling scientist," it is moving to read these words written to a friend (LTF 87), "Nothing can resist the person who smiles at life... the triumphant smile of a person who knows he will survive, or that at least he will be saved by that which seems to be destroying him."

For Teilhard, the man of action, before whose seemingly endless stores of physical strength and endurance his companions in the field had marvelled, the "diminishments" of age were something he had to work hard to bring himself to accept and overcome. Lubac (11) quotes these phrases from prayers Teilhard made during one of the annual retreats demanded by his order, "To accept, to love interior fragility and old age with its long shadows and the ever-shrinking days ahead ... to love diminishments and decline."[2] And Robert Speight quotes another note of Teilhard's in his biography, regarding the same problem (12), "May he keep me young (for the greater glory of God): (1) Because trials and age come from him; (2) because trials and age lead to him; (3) because trials and age will only touch me as measured out by him. Accept death as it comes to me in Christ. 'To be ready' has never seemed to me to signify anything else than to be stretching forward."[3]

The Meaning Of Suffering And Death

From this last note we see once again how Teilhard sees the problems of "diminishments" from the point of view of his two loves, science and religion. These two, he felt, could help take away the mortal sting of both suffering and death — the sting of meaninglessness. "Illness," he writes (HE 48), "tends to give sufferers the feeling that they are useless and even a burden on the earth. Almost inevitably, they feel as if they have been cast up by the great stream of life, lying by sheer ill-luck, incapable of work or activity. Their state seems to have no meaning." What Teilhard tried over and over to do for such people was to "help dissipate these depressing views by showing them from a hypothetical standpoint the place and use of suffering in the construction even of the visible world." (HE 48).

Once again he reminds us that this is a universe — indeed a cosmos — in process of becoming. Everything that has been, that is, and that will be comes only by means of a transformation, and "a mass experience (and unfortunately a mass suffering) seems to be the condition for a mass transformation." (LTF 132). "If the world in fact represents a work of achievement at present taking place, . . . it is inevitable that there shall be pain . . . [the world's] progress can only take place at the expense of many failures, many wounds. Sufferers of whatever species are the expression of this stern but noble condition. They are not useless and dwarfed. They are simply paying for the forward march and triumph of all." (HE 50). "They are casualties fallen on the field of honour . . . destined and chosen for the task of raising the world above immediate enjoyment towards an even higher light." He points out here that, as St. Paul put it, different members of Christ's body have different functions for which they were formed; so the sufferers have their own very special contribution to make for the whole of the universe — indeed, the cosmos — destined, as he believed, to be the body of the glorified Christ. "Universal labour is indispensable to the accomplishment" (C & E 219, footnote) — the perfection of a world in a state of evolution. Teilhard points out that the presence of the sick, the disabled, the weak, in humanity is the proof of the reality of life in it. If all were in perfect health of body, mind, and spirit, we could only conclude that humanity was as artificial, cut off from growth, as a bouquet in which are found only perfect blooms. Suffering and pain are the price human beings have to pay for being made in the image of the *living* God — for being on the road to the glorious consummation of union with him. For these views Teilhard has support from other people in the scientific field. Peacocke (18), the biochemist, points out " . . . pain appears to be the necessary concomitant of an increase in sensitivity and awareness, which are the prerequisites of the development of consciousness."[4] Indeed, the great advances which enabled mankind to be *Homo Sapiens* — the enlarged head, the erect posture, for instance — have brought with them greater pain in childbirth and all the suffering of "back troubles." We obviously cannot be persons without suffering. May, the psychologist, says, "To be free means to face and bear anxiety . . .,"[5] "freedom requires the capacity to accept, bear and live constructively with anxiety."[6] He also points out that the temptation to escape from this stress through the use of tranquilizers and other drugs "takes away [the] opportunity to learn;" and thus "takes away some of [our] resources."[7]

    Teilhard was conscious, too, of the burden that anxiety lays on people. "Personally," he writes, "I am more and more struck by the tragic condition of a Humanity that is sufficiently reflective to raise the problem of the Future and the beyond, but not yet sufficiently enlightened to be able to answer it . . . this situation is linked with the successive and inevitable phases of the appearance of consciousness in the World. This is a place of half-light, in which one must know how to wait and trust." [LFT 109] Here, I think, there is a word, too, for those burdened with guilt; a salutary reminder of our humanness, of which — the Bible assures us — God is quite aware.

    In somewhat the same way he also deals with the nagging problem of the existence of all these problems in a world belonging to a God of love. In a static universe which God had created all at once, which could therefore have been otherwise than it is had God just chosen to create it so, the problem of suffering and the love of God is an enormous and painful one. But, in a universe in process of becoming, especially one in which that process is to end in union with God — supreme personal spirit — the problem at least has the meaninglessness removed. "If God allows us to suffer, to sin, to doubt, it is because he *cannot*, here and now, cure us and show himself to us. And if he cannot do so, it is exclusively because we are still *incapable*, by reason of the present phase of the universe, of the higher degree of organization and illumination." (C & E 132). "Our doubts," he writes again, "like our misfortunes, are the price we have to pay for the fulfilment of the universe and the very conditions of the fulfilment." (C & E 132). Seeing this constructive side of suffering — that it plays a part in God's great plan — as God has shown in the Cross, Teilhard would remove the burden that has so often been added to those who are already suffering, the burden of guilt. "In the classical interpretation, suffering is first and foremost punishment and expiation . . . born of a *sin* and makes reparation for the sin . . ." In the cosmic life-view, "suffering . . . is primarily the consequence of the work of development, and the price that has to be paid for it." (WTW 71).

But, of course, it is not only to the blood-stained trail of evolution that Teilhard points the sufferer, or the one troubled by the number of these in the world. Supremely, of course, he points to the Cross. "The Cross is not only the symbol of expiation, but the token of growth through suffering." (S & C 123). "On the Cross we are perhaps in danger of seeing only individual suffering, a single act of expiation. The creative power of the death escapes us . . . The cross is the symbol and place of an action whose intensity is beyond expression." (HE 51-2).

Suffering Releases Energy

Once again we are recalled to Teilhard's theory that suffering and effort make available to the whole evolutionary stream the energy needed for it to rise to new heights. Only a new infusion of energy makes possible the attainment of that degree of complexity necessary for a new and higher manifestation of consciousness, of personality and spirit. ". . .

the Christian Saint," he writes, "will be the man who seeks to make all his powers — gold, love or freedom — transcend themselves and cooperate in the consummation of Christ..." (C & E 170) "sublimating" or "spiritualizing" who could do this best?" ... *the sick* and suffering. By nature and temperament, sufferers are in a sense driven out of themselves, compelled to depart from prevailing forms of life... destined and chosen for the task of raising the world above immediate enjoyment towards an ever higher life ... it is those who bear in their weakened bodies the weight of the world in motion." (HE 50). Thus, "... the sick man has in his apparent inactivity a very grand human task to fulfill. He must, of course, never cease to aim at his own cure and recovery ... he must ... use all the strength that remains to him for the different kinds of sometimes extremely productive work that are within his powers. Christian resignation, in fact, is just the opposite of giving up. Once he has resolved to combat his sickness in this way, the sick man must realize that in proportion to his sickness he has a special function to perform, in which no one can replace him, the task of cooperating in the transformation (one might say, conversion) of human suffering. What a vast ocean of human suffering spreads over the entire earth at every moment! Of what is this mass formed? Of blackness, gaps, and rejections? No, let me repeat, of potential energy. In suffering the ascending force of the world is concealed in a very intense form. The whole question is how to liberate it and give it a consciousness of its significance and potentialities. The world would leap high towards God if all the sick together were to turn their pain into a common desire that the Kingdom of God should come to rapid fruition through the conquest and organization of the earth. All the sufferers of the earth joining their sufferings so that the world's pain might become a great and unique act of consciousness, elevation and union. Would not this be one of the highest forms that the mysterious work of creation could take in our sight? Could it not be precisely for this that the creation was completed in Christian eyes by the passion of Jesus?" (HE 51).

Perhaps the deep and wonderful sense of community and the spirit of selfless concern for others, which grow quickly in hospital wards, is one of the manifestations of what Teilhard is talking about here. Here is created the kind of unity of spirit which he sees as necessary for evolutionary advance, the furthering of the purposes of God. Having myself experienced being in hospital in the smaller wards of new North American hospitals and in the larger wards of older English hospitals, I believe that the gain in privacy and possibly in quietness in the former is more than cancelled out by the loss of community and its support. The healing power of the fellowship of suffering more quickly blooms where many are gathered in the common bond of weakness and pain.

The Necessity For Effort

It is against the background of the contribution the sufferer has to make, not just to his own salvation but to that of the whole cosmos, that Teilhard gives his suggestions, often very down-to-earth, to specific sufferers among his friends. Always he makes it very plain that the first duty is to strive with all one's strength against the evil — for evil it is, as Jesus made very plain by spending so much of his strength and time healing diseases. His attitude, and that of Teilhard, is far from that of those who supinely resign themselves from the start (usually, notably, for others), with the assertion that it is "God's will." Very different is the spirit in which Teilhard writes, "At the first approach of the diminishment we cannot hope to find God except by loathing what is coming upon us and doing our best to avoid it. The more we repel suffering at that moment, with our whole heart and our whole strength — without bitterness and revolt, of course — the more closely we cleave to the heart and action of God . . . The failure that follows on laziness, the illness contracted as a result of unjustified imprudence, could not be regarded by anyone as being the *immediate* will of God." (DM 84, footnote incorporated). "There is only one thing we can say to people who mourn their lost dream of material happiness — get down to work!" (WTW 245). Teilhard sees the effort used against suffering as of equal importance with the suffering itself in releasing energy for the great work of constructing the cosmos of God. He believes that the effort we make is what counts:

... God expects us to help ourselves.

These reflections bring to mind several illustrations from different areas of life. When Teilhard speaks of "God's immediate will" with regard to the suffering we bring on ourselves, I am reminded of the very sage comment of George MacDonald, found in C. S. Lewis's anthology. Referring to Jesus' comparison of God's love with that of a father who, though not as good as God, yet can be trusted not to give his son a stone when he asks for bread, he speaks of God's patience with us when we insist that the 'stone' we have set our hearts on having is really "bread" we ought to be allowed to have. Eventually, MacDonald comments, if we persist long enough in our entreaties God will say to us, in effect, "All right! Go ahead and have *your* 'bread'."

When Teilhard speaks of our need of making a good deal of effort if Heaven is to help us, I am reminded of the words so often spoken at AA meetings by a friend in a group with which I was once closely connected. As he mentioned following the AA practice of turning his life over to God to defend him against his enemy for that twenty-four hours, he always added, "And then I say to myself, 'And what are *you* going to do, B?' "

And with regard to finding God only after effort, I remember hearing the testimony of two mothers who had nursed their own seriously ill children. Each one said that, when she had done all she could and out of sheer exhaustion had turned the whole situation over to God, the peace and well-being which she experienced was truly past all understanding.

Teilhard writes of such experiences: "When we have fought to the bitter end . . . and find ourselves halted, beaten, by the forces of this world, then *if we believe* the power with which we clash so agonizingly suddenly ceases to be a blind or evil energy. Hostile matter vanishes. And, in its place, we find the divine Master of the world who, 'under the species and appearance' of each and every event, moulds us, empties us of our self-love, and penetrates into us. (He must grow greater, but we must grow less. John 3:30). This is the most magnificent of the prerogatives of the universal Christ: the power to be operative in us, not only through the natural impulses of life, but also through the shocking disorders of defeat and death."

(S & C 72).

It is in the area between effort and faith — a typically Teilhardian combination of God and humans — that Teilhard warns we must look for God, and not in the suffering itself. "God is not to be found indiscriminately in the things that thwart us in life or the trials we have to suffer, but solely *at the point of balance* between our desperate effort to grow greater and the resistance to our domination we meet from outside. In that area of equilibrium, however, he is born, only *insofar as we believe that he is.*" (S & C 73).

This was the point being made by a minister to whom one of his parishioners complained that she was going blind. "God is taking away my sight," was how she put it. "Don't let him," was the astonishing reply that she received. "But the specialist says there is nothing more that can be done," she answered. "In that case," said her minister, "don't let him take it; give it to him."

Teilhard thus writes to some sufferers, "Do not *brace* yourself against suffering. Try to close your eyes and surrender, as if to a great, loving energy. This attitude is neither weak nor absurd... It is still too soon, no doubt, for you to recover; try to 'sleep' with that *active* sleep of confidence which is that of the seed in the field in winter... this is the true great prayer of moments of great sickness." (LTF 15). "Don't be impatient, however; just keep your mind and heart open in the right direction — the direction that is bigger than you." (LTF 178). "It is useless to want or regret things over which we have no control. Once again it is God's will manifesting itself; all we can do is to abandon ourselves to it in all peace and openness of heart." (M of M 251) "... the best I can find to tell you is always the same — trust blindly and wait patiently, for all things take time; indeed, that is the very reason for the existence of Time in the world. Trust and patience... borne on these two wings you have a chance of seeing the face of God appear within you." (LTF 104). "The Christian experiences suffering just as other men do... He must do his best to alleviate it... but when the time has come when suffering is inevitable, then he puts it to good use... There is a wonderful compensation by which physical evil, if humbly accepted, conquers moral evil. In accordance with definite psychological laws, it purifies the soul, spurs it on and detatches it ... acting as a sacrament acts it effects a mysterious union between the faithful soul and the suffering Christ." (WTW 68). "And, above all, I shall remind those who suffer and mourn that the most direct way of making our life useful is to allow God, in his own good time, to grow within us and, through death, to substitute himself for us." (WTW 221).

There are many ways Teilhard can see suffering "put to good use." In his own case he writes about the bar to his publishing, " ... things are often working in a most funny and unexpected way. In addition to the real 'advertisement' which the present difficulties are for my ideas, there is also the fact that the conflict helps me a lot to focus better and better the problem and its present solution." (LTF 197). He recognized that even the blunders he had made in his own research had had a cleansing effect. "It is pain," he writes, "that, by stimulating beings to react against conditions that are inimical to their full development, forces them to leave unprofitable roads; it stimulates them to undertake fruitful work and induces them to attain common harmony and to adapt themselves to one another in such a way as to avoid conflicts that injure and encroachments that reduce them . . . by detaching man from lower delights (it) forces him to seek joy in consideration of objects that 'worm and rust do not consume'. . . . that makes his soul return to the higher reaches of being and keeps total pressure continually at work against present limits of his development. It is pain that automatically punishes transgressions of life's laws and sees to it that they are expiated. Suffering stimulates, spiritualizes and purifies. The converse, and at the same time the complement, of the appetite for happiness; it is the very life-blood of evolution..." (WTW 43).

One might still feel that Teilhard, the celibate, could not possibly have written thus about the pain from the loss of one dearer than oneself. However, C. S. Lewis, in the moving diary of his reflections following the death of his wife, writes in exactly the same vein. " ... Bereavement is a universal and integral part of our experience of love. It follows marriage as normally as marriage follows courtship, or as autumn follows summer . . . We are 'taken out of ourselves' by our loved one while she is here. Then comes the tragic figure of the dance in which we must learn to be still taken out of ourselves though the bodily presence is withdrawn, to love the very Her, and not fall back to loving the past, or our memory, or our sorrow, or our relief from sorrow, or our own love."[8] To larger relationship . . . as Jesus said about the question of the woman with seven husbands . . . bigger than this?

The Christian Must Take A Positive Attitude

Finally, Teilhard teaches the Christian to take a positive attitude towards the problem of suffering by seeing it as the work specifically asked of the Christian. "If it is undertaken first, in a disposition of pliant surrender and continued in the spirit of conquest, the pursuit of Christ in the world culminates logically in impassioned enfolding, heavy with sorrow, in the arms of the Cross. Eagerly and wholeheartedly, the soul has offered and surrendered itself to all the great currents of nature. When it reaches the term of all that it has gone through and when at long last it can see things with a mature eye, it realizes that no work is more effective, or brings greater peace, than to gather together, in order to soothe it and offer it to God, the suffering of the world; no attitude allows the soul to expand more freely, than to open itself, generously and tenderly — with — and in Christ, *to sympathy with all the suffering* — to 'cosmic compassion'." (WTW 68).

This message that suffering is part and parcel of the Christian life was blessedly brought home to me by two incidents which happened to me early in my ministry. I had been undergoing some kind of stress and discomfort which had made me extremely sorry for myself, not least because I felt that to be where I was had entailed not a little sacrifice for God. On the first occasion I was complaining about this to a fellow minister. With an insight for which I will ever be grateful, she pointed me to the words of Jesus about the vine and the branches: "Every branch that does bear fruit he prunes, that it may bear more fruit." (John 15:2). "Pruning," she pointed out, "must be a very painful experience for the branch, but it is only the branches that bear fruit that are pruned, and the purpose of the pruning is 'that they may bear more fruit'."

On the second occasion I was by myself, making my complaint to God and seeking his sympathy for the hard treatment I was receiving. Suddenly, across the room (whether in the body or out of it, I know no more than did St. Paul about his vision), I saw Jesus. What he looked like I do not remember. I only know that he stood with his palms so turned towards me that I could see the marks of the nails in their center and feel his eyes looking straight at me as he asked, "What did you expect?"

Death Is The Gate

As Teilhard sees in the diminishments of suffering, experiences that enrich rather than impoverish life, so he sees the final diminishment — death. Like suffering, death must be seen as "the enemy" — indeed, the last and most dreadful enemy. It is against the disintegration of death that the whole vast project of God is pursued. "Death," he writes in *The Divine Milieu*, "is the sum and consummation of all our diminishments: it is *evil* itself . . . We must overcome death by finding God in it." (82). Death must, therefore, find its place in the great ongoing process of the union of all things with God. With Christ's acceptance in perfect faith and burning love, the power of death to disintegrate and to destroy was once for all overcome; that which formerly had only served to separate he turned into the most magnificent of all powers to integrate and unite. Fear of death under which humanity had lived and acted from the first moment of consciousness was, by Christ's victory, removed. Death was revealed to be, not the enemy but the gateway to new and more life. This it is, however, only as and when it culminates a life which is a procession of deaths. As we die daily to those things which must be left behind — not because they are in themselves evil, but because life is a constant journeying — then death becomes another and crowning part of that journey — the final in an increasing series of deaths. As we move up and up the spiral staircase from flesh to spirit, we come at length to this final trap-door, as it were, the last great transition. Then "Death . . . reveals itself as representing a simple phase of growth," Teilhard writes. "It marks our ascension into the superhuman sphere of self-consciousness, of personality." (H. E. 104).

Perhaps we dread death because we have refused to practise for it by clinging always to what we have attained. If this is our attitude to life, then truly death will be a terror, for it is the supreme and inevitable proof that there is no immobility.

Indeed, as Teilhard says, (WTW 242), "The disorganization of our flesh is too firmly built into the *whole* of our past, the structure of the cosmos . . . for us to be able, to have the right, to think of escaping from it. The further one progresses in life, the more one changes. And the more one changes, the more one dies. This is precisely the law that governs our development."

That this is not a terrible but a good and loving provision was clearly brought out in a BBC 4 program on March 25, 1973, called "Where Are You Taking Us?", in which a geriologist pointed out that death is built into every cell. The only exception is the cancer cell. It alone goes on indefinitely. Death is part of the process of living, and what does not die introduces into the world what is worse than death.

Yet, as Teilhard points out though everyone must die and death is part of all life, "In spite of their sharing the same superficial appearance . . . there are as many sorts of deaths as there are souls; and some of these deaths are no more than a phase of transformation of life. The whole difference that distinguishes them derives from the way in which the process of organic annihilation is influenced by faith — by the way in which it is physically converted by faith into a more or less direct ascent towards God. Only one effort, and it is one made possible by confidence in Christ, is worth making. It may be expressed thus, 'to believe so resolutely in the virtue of death that we can cause life to rise from the blackest depths of its shadows'." (WTW 242)

We are reminded once more of Teilhard's view of the scheme of things — that the vast process going on from creation to consummation is what old-timers used to call a process of "soul-making" — the production of spirit so refined and transformed as to be capable of union with God. With the appearance of the thinking process and freedom of choice, humans had to accept the goal and cooperate if it was to be reached. They must will and desire transformation within themselves, the passing from "flesh" to spirit. They must put forward the effort required in the transformation by battling the constant, strong pull in the very warp of their being to return to the multiple, by trying to stay where they are. The pull of God through Christ is there, but they must accept the attraction in love.

The final invitation is to death. Although death is inevitable, built into our very cells, if it is to be the gateway to further life and not a disintegration, we must, as Teilhard has said, accept our own death. We must pray as Teilhard does (DM 90), "Teach me to treat my death as an act of communion." Without such a death there can be no union with God. Death is the final and most necessary part of life. "God must, in some way or other, make room for himself, hollowing us out, emptying us, if he is finally to penetrate us. And in order to assimilate us in him he must break the molecules of our being so as to re-cast and re-model us. The function of death is to provide the necessary entrance into our inmost selves. It will make us undergo the required disassociation. It will put us into the state organically needed if the divine fire is to descend upon us. And in that way its fatal power to decompose and dissolve will be harnessed to the most sublime operations of life." (DM 89).

This does not for one moment mean that Teilhard would have any sympathy with that type of Christianity which despises life, turning its back for a morbid preoccupation with death and the delights or horrors of life thereafter. On the contrary, he writes to a friend, "Your love of life is a healthy and magnificent power; and you must jealously guard the spirit of resistance to physical diminishment which helps you bear suffering. But there is still something missing in your attitude; you do not yet sufficiently love *all* of the Universe, to agree, once the inevitable moment has come, to diminish (in appearance) and to pass lovingly into it. We must struggle against death with all our force, for it is our fundamental duty as living creatures. But when, by virtue of a state of things (transitory, no doubt, but linked to a state of growth in the world) death takes us, we must experience that inevitable paroxysm of faith in life that causes us to abandon ourselves to death as falling into a greater life. To love life so much and to trust it so completely that we embrace it, throw ourselves into it, even in death — this is the only attitude that can calm and fortify you; to love extravagantly what is greater than oneself. Every union, especially with a greater power, involves a kind of death of self.... Death is acceptable only if it represents the physically necessary passage towards a union — the condition of a metamorphosis." (LTF 78-9).

It is the assurance which the resurrection of Jesus Christ gives, that life does not lead to a dead end, which made Teilhard so sure that in the end only an Omega identical with the risen and glorified Christ would ensure the continuance of evolution. Only the assurance that all effort is not going to end in the disintegration of death will maintain in us the zest for life through which we will continue to pay the enormous cost of progress. To know that "Death surrenders us totally to God, it makes us enter into him..." enables us to play our part in the last great choice we have on earth; it makes it possible for us, in imitation of our Lord, to "surrender ourselves to death with absolute love and self-abandonment." (M of M 145).

Thus Teilhard would have us see our death and that of others we love in the context of the great process of "creative union" going on in the universe, by which a body is being formed for the risen and glorified Christ. "To die normally means to sink back into the multiple; but it can also be for it the re-shaping of what is indispensable to its entry under the dominion of a higher soul. The bread we eat appears to be decomposed within us, but it nevertheless becomes our flesh. ... In every union the dominated term becomes one with the dominant only by first ceasing to be itself. In the case of the definitive union with God in omega, we can see that if the world is to be divinized it must, in each one of us and in its totality, lose its visible form. ... From the Christian point of view, that, in virtue of the death of Christ, is the life-giving function of human death." (S & C 63) Without death there can be no life; and life, as the resurrection of Christ assures all is what this whole business is about, life eternal in ecstatic union with the Lord and Giver of all life.

And yet, not the least part of the sting of death, both our

own and that of others, is the prospect of separation from earth and all that has been loved on earth. Since to Teilhard the work of God in Christ is uniting, he is sure that the specter of loss is just that — only one of those many deceiving appearances through which we have to learn to trust the loving power of God. "Even when . . . " he writes, ". . ., it is gathered up again into Christ, the soul is not lost to the earth that nourished it. Borne up by the cosmic power of Christ and united henceforth to the ultimate principle of created life, its radiating influence is most vigorously and profoundly active in beings that have still to be made holy. Thus the two phases of the soul's development meet together in a common peak, and the soul finds itself *in possession, at the same time, both of Christ and of the universe.*" (WTW 264)

These words bring to mind both the picture the writer of Hebrews gives of the "great cloud of witnesses" cheering us on in the Christian life (Hebrews 12:1), and Jesus' statement that "the meek shall inherit the earth." (Matthew 5:5).

The Problems of Sin and Evil

There is one more power for diminishment with which I have not dealt in this consideration of the Christian life — that of evil. There are many who would expect this since this is the area in which most people fault Teilhard, not least of all those who blocked his publication. However, I am convinced that they do not do him justice, perhaps from a careless reading of his work.

Too often the charge is made that he sees evil simply as an "evolutionary lag" which, therefore, will be overcome simply by letting things take their course. This, of course, would eliminate any suggestion of the need for the Saviour or for the need of forgiveness for the past or faith for the future.

Although I have already dealt with the work of Christ at some length, perhaps all this needs to be set into the context here of the Christian life. If Teilhard's idea of the "multiple" as the warp on which all material things are woven, and therefore the basis even of the spiritual, be a sort of "evolutionary lag," then this is indeed his idea of evil. But he sees it as much more dynamic than that — a force to be reckoned with. The pull on all things, that makes them fly apart, is indeed very real and strong. It is the power which God has put to his own use in the evolution of the world, and indeed, Scripture assures us he can make use of all to his good purpose. Now that God has entrusted to humanity the continuance of his work on earth, they must battle the evil. This can only be done by the power of God, drawn on by faith. The supreme victory over evil was won by Jesus, as man, for humanity. Without that victory the whole scheme could not move forward, as that victory had to be won within the system. Faith in Jesus gives both the motive — in love of his person — for further integrated effort, and the advantage of placing them within the "field" of his attractive power uniting them in themselves, with others, and drawing them to himself, into the new life which is his.

But Christ's victory was won for all. Those who cannot know him because they have not yet heard of him, or those who, because of the failure of his followers properly to present him, may yet share this victory through their devotion to those things for which Christ died. Those who, as Teilhard called his "gentiles" to do, are true to the finest and highest in themselves and in the world, are being drawn by him. When, at the moment God chooses to reveal that the finest and highest which has drawn them on, and the risen Saviour and Lord, are one, they will then have to make their final judgment as to whether their allegiance will be to themselves or to God. At that time, as our Lord's own parable of the Great Assizes suggests, there will be revealed to them what service of God consists in, and the final invitation will be issued to "enter into the joy of the Lord." (Matthew 25:31 ff). As Teilhard suggested he did even with his own work, it is well that we leave to God the sorting out of the tares and the wheat since he alone is able to see the whole and has the wisdom to "know good and evil."

The great danger that besets people, not least the Christian, is the danger of forgetting that we are not God and that therefore, however right and full of knowledge and power we may feel ourselves to be, it is always possible that we are wrong. Because we have been both entrusted and therefore equipped by God to be God's co-worker, there is much we can and must do, often much more than we are ready to undertake. There are many, many times when we must make very weighty decisions and undertake very serious risks. Because we are still in the process of being integrated by God, our greatest difficulty probably lies in making the relation between what we are capable of and our limitations. Because it appears that we are alone in our dilemma, our temptation is even greater; therefore, our worst state comes when, often out of sheer terror, we succeed in assuring ourselves that there is no limit beyond what we, as an individual, or part of a group, have reached.

What are the dreadful consequences of this spirit in man was movingly and horrifyingly recalled by the commentator in the last episode of the BBC television series, THE ASCENT OF MAN, shown during the 1973-74 season. Standing in the mud of one of the infamous concentration camps in Germany in which the ashes of his family had been mingled, he reflected for us all that what had been done there had been done, not by inhuman monsters, but by people like ourselves, who had been so sure that they were right that they could do what they had done.

Both the parable of Genesis 3 and the word from the Cross, "They know not what they do," are warnings to us of our need, a need not smaller but greater when we also realize how great is the trust God has put in people in choosing to make them his co-workers. As they come to realize, as Teilhard reminds them, that they too are still part of that work which is being done and therefore is still unfinished, they will be able to keep themselves open to new knowledge, new growth, new insight, new revelation which can come to them, as all they are and have come to them, from the very poorest and least of God's creation, the dust itself. As they realize their debt to all these, and the presence within them of that which is akin to what is within themselves, there is hope that they will walk with the reverence and the meek pride which will allow them to live and work with others and with God in the glorious work of creation-redemption-incarnation.

This is the message God has spoken unmistakably in Jesus Christ — from the openness of Mary to the incredible thing asked of her, through Jesus' first sermon about his mission in which he proclaims the "openness" which is God's plan for all, to the discovery of the women on Easter morning when even death itself was revealed not to be a dead end. In God's world all stones are rolled away provided we act in faith that they will be, and by the energy of love, do what we can to move them. Our task is to press on in faith, knowing ourselves to be fallible but in the service of one who knows our frame, yet trusts, enables, and loves us.

Holiness According to Teilhard

To accept that we are part of a whole, still in the process of making, but a part so important and so trusted that the fate of the whole depends on the faithfulness and humility with which we use every opportunity for advancing the whole; to accept that we are part of a whole of which the love of God, and therefore unity, is the beginning and the ending and the milieu in which we live; this is Teilhard's view of the Christian life. It is the life lived by Jesus of Nazareth; it is the life through which he was glorified to take his place as Omega, the Cosmic Christ; it is the life he makes possible to every one who, loving what he loved, lives by faith in Life, or the Lord of Life. It is the life which, ending in joyous self-abandon to God, is life eternal.

At the time he took his final vows as priest, Teilhard wrote the following words about the commitment he was making: "As far as my strength will allow me, *because I am a priest* I would henceforth be the first to become aware of what the world loves, pursues, suffers. I would be the first to seek, to sympathize, to toil: the first in selffulfillment, the first in self-denial — would be more widely human in my sympathies and more nobly terrestrial in my ambitions than any of the world's servants... I want to plunge into the midst of created things... [to] disengage from them all they contain of life eternal... to hallow, through chastity, poverty, obedience, the power enclosed in love, in gold, in independence. That is why I have taken my vows and my priesthood." (WTW 222).

I realize that time has robbed these words of the revolutionary sound they would have borne when he conceived them in the early years of the twentieth century. The idea that the church and all its members should serve the world has become almost a cliche in these days. Nevertheless, I believe that there is here such a profound and subtle blend of commitment to God and to God's work that I commend it to any who would lead the Christian life. How better, in this second half of the twentieth century, could one commit oneself to the task which belongs to all who make their vows of loyalty to Jesus Christ — the priesthood of all believers?

NOTES

1. Mortier and Aboux, *Album*, p. 128.
2. Henri de Lubac, *The Faith of Teilhard de Chardin*, Tr.R. Hague (London: Burns & Oates, 1965) p. 87.
3. Robert Speight, *Teilhard de Chardin, A Biography* (London: Collins 1967), p. 331.
4. Arthur Peacocke, *Science and the Christian Experiment* (New York and Toronto: Oxford University Press 1971), p. 138.
5. Rollo May, *Psychology and the Human Dilemma*, p. 179.
6. May, 178.
7. May, 179.
8. C.S. Lewis, *A Grief Observed* (London: Faber & Faber, 1961) p. 41.

Chapter 9
"A VIEWPOINT FROM WHICH EVERYTHING IS BATHED IN LIGHT"

PART I
LOOKING AT THEOLOGY

"We all need a new face of God to worship." (LTF 112)
"With Teilhard things seem to make sense again."[1]
"Theology is certainly anything but a mummified structure of thought. I can create openings for adventures of the mind and of the heart, if we have the courage to embark upon them and both the courage and humility to retrace our steps as soon as we become aware of having erred."[2]

". . . the time-boundedness of theological statements is . . . given by their universality. Any understanding of reality as a whole is always approximative and is constantly changing basically, with the addition of every new piece of knowledge, since this has consequences for the whole. Dogmatics must participate in such change since it may not allow itself to deteriorate into the spirit of a given age but must be 'timely' in the sense of confirming the deity of the God of Israel revealed in Jesus Christ in relation to the experience of reality in every successive present age. It is a matter not of establishing a basis but of providing subsequent confirmation of the deity of God revealed in Jesus, insofar as he is essentially the God of all men and all times."[3]

"Whatever may be said, our century is religious — probably more religious than any other . . . only it has not yet the God it can adore."[4]

"A closed society is the opposite of a Christian community. Its very deadness declares that the winds of the spirit cannot blow there any more, new truths from God are not expected nor wanted."[5]

"No generation can merely reproduce its ancestors. You may preserve life in a flux of form, or preserve form amid an ebb of life, but you cannot permanently enclose the same life in the same mould."[6]

"Without science religion is blind,"[7] wrote Albert Einstein at the turning point of the twentieth century. More than thirty years before that, in the suffering, the mud, and the comradeship of First World War trenches, Teilhard de Chardin had discovered that "with science" the vision revealed to his religion was filled with vistas so glorious and thrilling that he had spent the rest of his life, not only sharpening his own eyesight, but calling out to those behind him, in every way left open to him, "Come and see!"

A Call To Re-think Religion In Teilhard's Terms

Move from your fixed position, your calcified opinions, your petrified dogmas, and realize the marvel of the universe in which God brought you forth. However lame science may be because she sees you as her enemy, let her show you the wonders your God has done, and is doing, in His universe. And to those who have learned to look with eyes sharpened by her insight, speak in terms with which they are familiar, using models that have become meaningful to them, claiming for your sovereign Lord what you profess to be his — all truth! Learn the lesson of the Three Wise Men, that if you will find the God who incarnated Himself in human flesh, you must not only be true to the highest and finest truth you know, but follow that truth wherever it leads you. This you must do at risk, constant risk, ready to leave behind at every step all that is familiar and comfortable. For He is to be found most fully, not where you are, but where you are meant to be — at the end of a long and arduous journey, whose mark is the daily Cross. Never forget that endless risk and faithful journeying are the marks of those who at length find the Lord of Life — for it is only "he who would save his life who loses it." Therefore, on that journey you will have many companions who, journeying only because they love life and truth, may not know or care that at the end of such journeying they will find the Lord. But, as one of the great travellers, once Saul of Tarsus, changed on a journey to Paul in Christ, has said in essence, it matters not whether those who commend the way do it out of love of Christ or from any other motive, as long as God is glorified by our working with Him in the great enterprise of creation. Whether we know or will such an end, that end will be a universe drawn by Christ to its fulfillment in Him; then God's purpose will be satisfied and He will be glorified — the end and goal of all.

Because theology has for too long been thought out on the lines, not of the new science but of the old philosophy, while the generation born within the late twentieth century thinks, speaks, and hears in a world moulded by science, Teilhard has said, "In order to convert the world, we Christians must . . . *with all that is human in us*, re-think our religion." (S & C p. 126).

In these latter years his plea is being echoed by a great host of theologians, following the visions Teilhard had during the first quarter of this century. Indeed, I believe that to appreciate fully what many of the theologians of the late twentieth century are saying and doing, one needs a background of Teilhard's thought, so much do they take what he has worked out as their standpoint, consciously or not. For instance, the term "The Cosmic Christ," has become almost a cliche in our day; yet, without following the careful working out of this idea in Teilhard, with all its scientific assumptions, how can anyone grasp the full content of that name so it will act as Teilhard knew it must — to give zest and hope to Christian travellers; so it will fulfill the role Teilhard saw for it, stir them up enough to make him leave where they are so rigidly settled to "come and see" how much there is to inspire them to greater effort and adoration?

By all means, use the phrase "Cosmic Christ" — even better, the concept — but there needs to be a deeper re-thinking of our religion than this. From my study of Teilhard, inevitably a limited and personal point of view, I see at least the following directions needing to be taken.

First, last, and always, to be on our guard to keep our minds open, aware, as Tyndale once asserted about the Bible: "God has new truths to break forth from his Word;" and that word, as he has made clear in Jesus of Nazareth, is not limited to the Bible, but is to be found in every truth. But should we begin only with the Bible, Teilhard promises that to read the Gospels with an open mind is to see beyond all possibility of doubt that Jesus came to bring us new truth concerning our destiny. He brought not only new truth, but a new life superior to that we are conscious of, and also — in a very real sense — a new physical power of acting upon our *temporal* world; therefore we must not allow timidity or modesty to turn us into poor craftsmen. If it is true that the development of the world can be influenced by our faith in Christ, then to let this power lie dormant within us would be unpardonable.

Let me, therefore, be bold enough to suggest how I now think some basic religious terms can be defined from the viewpoint found by following, even limitedly, Teilhard's journey.

Basic Religious Terms From Teilhard's Point of View

The world . . . is that which shapes us and has shaped us, with whose every part we are intimately related and with whose welfare and ultimate success is inextricably linked our own. Beloved of God, the object of his great enterprise, it must be loved by us — not for our sake, but for God's sake. He wills to clothe himself in the seamless robe of its perfection when at last its complexity-in-unity has extended to its farthest limit and prepared all for the final breakthrough into his likeness, spirit, "prepared as a bride adorned for her husband." (Revelation 21:2). For this end it was created.

Creation . . . is primarily an act of love, empowered by love, and still going on all around and in us. Its beginning, therefore, was, and always will continue to consist in, the self-giving of God. Even, therefore, the tendency to return to "death" — the pull to multiplicity against God, works in his will to unite and is part of the love, since love continually spreads out from itself to give itself away. The creative act is essentially the splitting up into multiplicity, the uniting into more complex forms. It is a very slow, gradual process. It does not move in a straight line, but by "groping." There are more abortive attempts than "successes." Nevertheless, these are as essential to the progress as the "successes;" without them there is no chance of any success. All experience is necessary. The continuous movement in creation takes place in answer to the magnetic pull of God to himself.

Up to humanity the response of "matter" was unconscious. The pull to the multiple was always there, against which the pull of God's love constantly strove. He suffered with all that was lost to it, as any worker suffers from material loss. However, with the great breakthrough of consciousness in the advent of humans, not only was the physical sphere of creation over, but the unconscious phase was also over. A new era had arrived. Humans being conscious of both "pulls," could respond to either one. It then became their choice which was determinative as to whether creation continued or continues. They can respond to the pull towards entropy that is death, and this being the "dust" from which they are made, this pull is basic; or they can respond to the upward pull of God. Whenever there is loss now, however, the suffering of God is that of a loving father who loses a dear child. Our power to hurt God is placarded on the Cross.

Moreover, whether creation reaches its fulfillment in the final completion of God's unity with a creation raised to its highest level that it may enter into full relationship with him who is perfect depends, from then onwards, on our choice — whether we will, in union in love with all things, all people yield all in love to God, or not, is vital. When this happens, and only then, will creation be complete.

Incarnation . . . therefore, is the completion of creation, the end towards which the whole process is oriented and to which it moves. Creation is a mighty act of incarnation, the clothing of God, the great Father, Creator, Lover, in the seamless robe of the creation of his love.

The historic "incarnation," in which, during the lifetime of Jesus of Nazareth, people were aware of having come into immediate touch with God, was God's message to humanity, in a form which it could understand. It was about what God was doing, what is involved, and how it is to be done. It is also an appeal for our cooperation. Because of "the thinking layer" the "historic" incarnation became necessary, for we must know and must consent — indeed, must will — to give loving cooperation. Therefore the revelaton had to be personal to win our love; it had to be personal because the goal is personality at its highest, and only love preserves and heightens what is subject to it and therefore united with the object of its love. In Jesus Christ God reveals to us what is going on in the whole mighty process in which we are involved — that is, the process of Incarnation. As it takes every step of the process up to Jesus to bring him into existence, so the final Incarnation will involve all before it. The steps by which Jesus yielded all to the will of the Father and thus made plain the presence of the Kingdom in creation's midst, will be the course to be followed in the final Incarnation, needing — as did that one — the deliberate God-oriented choices — of the renunciation of self and the pull to pleasure, and the acceptance of rejection. In the historic Incarnation, the perfection of the human Jesus, we have focused both the magnetic power of God that transforms that which yields to it, and the power which destroys that which rejects it.

Christ . . . As Peter, with his openness to the Holy Spirit, was to say — more wisely than he knew at the time — that in Jesus he saw the Christ, the purpose and the power for which and through which Creation was begun and proceeds to its final end. As Teilhard expresses it, "If God wished to have Christ, to launch a whole universe and scatter life with a lavish hand was no more than he was obliged to do." (C & E 32). Christ is the great magnetic goal towards which, by God's sovereign choice and love, the whole creation is being drawn. He is the only end, the only foundation, on which all is built. He is the Alpha, but he is also the Omega. And as he is the end for which the beginning was made, all things exist for him, and he will be completed only by the union with him of all things. He is the Cosmic Christ. He is the goal; and since all things must be drawn to the goal, through him is focused the energy that moves the whole creation. That energy is the love of God. *Because it is love,* it must be responded to. In the unconscious part of Creation, this response was unconscious. In the conscious part, it must be voluntarily and lovingly given.

Sin . . . is our refusal to give the response of love and trust. It is our yielding to the strong pull of the "multiple," which is the raw material out of which all things emerge. It makes itself felt in us, in the drive to autonomy, to independence, to separateness, to selfishness and exploitation, in the passion to seize and keep control in our hands. It is "original" in that it is basic to our very being, the "dust" of which we and all things are made. In truth, at our very core, we are all "sinners." It is our native state and, as it is, we must humbly accept that this is what we are. But we must also recognize that it is the opposite of what we are called and empowered by God to be. Therefore, with all the power at our disposal, we must resist it and rise above it. That the power to do so is available to us, and in us, is made plain in Jesus Christ. We see this proof, not only in his manhood, but also in his triumph over every pull to trust himself instead of God, to anything which would break or foil the unity of humankind, and they with God — the perfection of all things.

To yield to sin is to yield to the pull to immobility, to refuse to move higher and closer to God and to all things in love. Since it is, therefore, capitulation to the pull of the "multiple," of separation from God and all of his creation, its end is death. . Sin is a constituent part of all created things, including humans. It is the basis of "matter;" on it God poured his love — the power to unite and therefore create. Out of it he brought spirit, "Consciousness," in its supreme form in Jesus Christ, whose efforts and responding love once for all broke the power to destroy, possessed by sin in everyone.

Jesus . . A man, the product of the highest and most responsive branch of the human race, by a human life lived in willed openness and responsiveness to the love of God, achieved for all Creation this breakthrough from the power of the "multiple" — of sin — to destroy. His human life was absolutely essential to the achievement of this breakthrough. He did it for all humanity. But how does it affect humankind?

Let us look again at the process of evolution from Teilhard's point of view. With the emergence of *Homo Sapiens*, the end of the "physical" phase of evolution was reached. No further twigs of more physically sophisticated creatures grew on the bush of life, or on the hominid stem. Thus, Teilhard concluded that the emergence of "complexity — consciousness" — personality — revealed the direction towards which the whole process had been tending. Now the new stage had been reached, the spiritual one; all development from then on would be not physical, but spiritual. Consciousness becoming greater consciousness would result in increased spirituality. This would come about, in accord with the principle of "complexity-consciousness," through complexity created by the development of a new social order — "Mankind" — a new organic unity.

For this to come about there needed to be injected into the human race the power to overcome the pull of the "multiple" which causes us to be hostile to each other and to God. Where was that power to come from? How could self-willed humanity be changed in spirit and thought? At exactly the right time (Galatians 4:4), says Paul, a child was born to a branch of humanity long prepared for this change, who would win the victory over sin. This Jesus grew up to do. His life of perfect love for man, and trust in and obedience to God, crowned supremely by his death on the Cross, maintained his fellowship with both others and God unbroken despite every conceivable pull against unity.

But Jesus' victory was not to be for himself only. He is, as the writer of Hebrews so triumphantly declares, "the pioneer and perfecter of our faith." (Hebrews 12:2). Because his achievement was in accordance with the plan and purpose of God, it was to be incorporated into the onward march of creation. Previously all contributions to progress, being physical, had been physically transmitted, without the recipient playing any part in accepting or rejecting it. Such an inheritance came, "not by the will of man but by God." With the appearance of humans their will was involved. Though Jesus Christ, as Paul triumphantly declares, began a new order of creation (II Cor. 5:17), to be a part of that new order all must be "in Christ." This is not a physical blood-relationship but a new psycho-social relationship of loving trust and commitment. All who accept for themselves the victory of Jesus for them and desire the power of Christ in their life become, through that new relationship of trust and commitment, members of the new order of creation. They will still be, of course, in process of being; but they now have new equipment, which is spiritual, and which will therefore require them to march to a new tune and to obey altogether new laws. This new relationship, as Jesus made plain in the Gospels, relates them even more fundamentally than does blood or genes to all others who are in the same relationship as they to Christ Jesus. This new power is one which will express itself not only in raising them closer to Christ, but also in bringing them closer to all humankind in love and service, and closer to all creation. Because they are people and not "things" they must will with all their power to respond to all in love. Because they are flesh and not pure spirit, the pull of the "multiple" is still there. They must fight against it. But they can, if they will, know that its power to destroy and overcome them has already been destroyed by the power available to them, indeed now in them. It is their relationship with Christ, for they are by faith "in Christ." They are in the family "in Christ," as they were before in humanity. Jesus, by his complete yielding of his humanity to God throughout his life, and supremely in his death, thus raised humanity, and therefore all creation — of which humanity is the crown — to the height God willed for it from the beginning. In himself he provided the focus and the power whereby all the rest of creation might become one with God. In Jesus we see the irrefutable evidence of God's power to perfect what he had begun by the means he chose to use. Jesus is the justification of all faith in God. Jesus, as Father Yarnold stated in a lecture given in the Oxford Examination Schools in the spring of 1973, "is not so much a model to be copied as a revelation and embodiment of the same grace of God that would work in us."

The Atonement . . . The life and death of Jesus Christ is therefore, above all, a great victory — for humanity, for God. True, it was a sacrifice — the supreme sacrifice and the type of all the sacrifices which have been made and must yet be made that God's great purpose may be fulfilled. It is the revelation of what it costs God, and humanity, to complete the creation. But above all, it is a victory — God's victory — and the pledge of the At-one-ment of his purpose and its fulfillment. Of this, of course, the resurrection is the evidence. The power of God to unite had at the beginning pitted itself against the pull to divide, which ends in "nothingness," in death. Death's defeat in its home in the foremost phase of matter, humanity, is a decisive defeat indeed. This victory all are invited to share. Even as Jesus Christ, through absolute trust in God's power to unite all things, was drawn beyond the pull of the multiple that destroys, so all who trust in Christ open themselves to that power which will draw them into that great one-in-himself for which God began creation.

The Church . . . is, as it were, that completion in prospect. It is incomplete and therefore sinful — far from finished, very much in process. However, the Church consists in a unity of those who, through faith, have been lifted into "A New Creation," where they are in closer unity with others in that same creation. It is organic unity, since these share the same inheritance through faith, which unites more than blood. This unity, Teilhard insists, is not just metaphorical but biological. It is a unity which not only makes them one "body," but in this greater complexity of which each is, as it were, a cell, the Christ lives more fully. As Jesus himself said, "Where two or three are gathered in my name, I am in their midst." The power to unite, transform, and raise the whole creation is therefore potently present here. The more consciously and obviously the Church makes it her sole purpose, to create for God the seamless robe with which he will be clothed when his plan is completed, the more perfectly that church fulfills her function.

The marks of the church, therefore, will be oneness in love and devotion to the ends and purposes of God in all creation, through openness to the power of God as experienced in Jesus Christ. The presence of the church in the world must be to be both a witness to his power to overcome all that separates and therefore destroys, and a catalyst — to focus the living power of God on all creation that it may respond to his love.

Faith . . . is the conscious response to the pull of the

power and love of God. It involves not only intellectual acceptance but also total commitment to the ends and purposes of God as seen in Jesus Christ. In Jesus Christ Christians see the ends and purposes of God most clearly, focused most powerfully. Thus they have a reason for their faith and a greater responsibility for responding to, and furthering, the purposes of God's love. However, God has offered other appeals and revelations — less focused than in Jesus — which have awakened the response of faith. Without any acceptance of, or commitment to, the man Jesus, people have committed themselves to the great forward movement which is the response of creation to the love of God. Therefore, all drawn by Christ and all who know God in other ways will come to him, providing they choose, at every step of the way, adoration of God rather than themselves.

The Last Things . . . Because there is choice, therefore judgment and "Last Judgment" are all really of the same kind — the choice of staying where one is, yielding to the pull of the "multiple," closing one's life to the pull of God; or renouncing that which is for that which lies ahead — oneness with God. The last and final choice, the great choice, is this: having reached the peak of development, will one use the power won for oneself or for *the* goal — the glory and completeness of God. To choose to go forward is to enjoy God in all his completeness and ours, in the bliss of face to face communion forever. Our moments of fleeting closeness to him become unending; our split seconds of being our best go on forever. However, to choose ourselves is to be drawn backward through all the stages by which we have come to endless dissociation — to dust. This is not a threat but an inevitability.

The Glory of God . . . becomes something real, in which one can see oneself playing a part. The exhortation, "to live to the Glory of God," given by the saints of the past, begins to make sense in the light of Teilhard's thought. It means that, whatever we do, we must do it to the very peak of our present ability. At the same time we will realize that, whatever we accomplish does not merit either our worship or our defence against its being improved or changed by someone else, or ourselves, further along in the great pilgrimage of life. Whatever we do, if we do it as best we can, faithfully, humbly, reverently, with faith, hope, and love, we may trust will make its contribution to the purpose of God in creation, and thus "to the glory of God."

Hope . . . is that without which the whole process will grind to a halt. Now that humans has been given "dominion over all things," responsible for forwarding the movement, unless they have hope to continue, all will fly back to primeval dust and nothingness. Cynicism or despair, which tempts us to relax our effort or close our life to the pull of God's magnetic love, will short circuit that power. Because the power is invisible; because the rate of progress is on a Cosmic scale(see Chapter 2); because God has ordered this progress to be made, not in a direct line but in the "groping" that involves both great suffering and sacrifice, and makes possible the variety necessary for the complexity out of which new things develop; because the pull to disintegration — to the "multiple" — being basic and essential, is so powerful, growing with the opposing power, the temptation to cynicism and despair are very strong indeed. Especially is this so for humans, who know themselves at once so responsible, so powerful, and yet also so limited and fallible because their very "stuff" consists in this multiple. It is inevitable that they alternate between hope and despair, between arrogant self-confidence and limp humiliation. If it were not for Jesus Christ, in whom they have proof of the reasonableness of their hope and their power to fight the enemy, they would be an easy prey. In Jesus Christ they have truly "the way, the truth, and the life." Therefore Christians have both the responsibility and the privilege of making hope possible to the world. They must look for signs of it in all that God does and is doing in his creation. They must point this evidence out, cherish it, and work to perfect every part of it. In Jesus Christ they have the clues as to what the nature of this evidence will be — the perfection of humanity, the drawing together of all in love, and all offered in adoration, love, trust, and response to unity with God. Whenever they see a crumb of these marks present they will point it out to all, knowing that, without hope, people will not pay the price of responding to God's love, and so the mighty work of God will never be completed.

Love . . . is, first of all, the energy and the power of God in which, by which, and through which, all things consist and are being drawn to their fulness of life in union with him. There is, strictly speaking, nothing but the love of God. We know it in human form in many guises and modes, and express it with equal variety, depending where we are on our own private "spiral staircase" of development to the perfection God wills for us, and where we are on the great cosmic "spiral staircase." No doubt, the coming together of the particles of "dust" in the nuclear furnace of the star to form the first elements is the primitive expression of that love. Indeed, the initial flying apart may have been the great self-giving of a love that willed the beginning of creation. This may have been the first "supreme sacrifice" of which the self-giving of Jesus on the Cross is both the Word made flesh and the pattern for that final self-giving of the completed cosmos to Christ, and "all in all" to God. Wherever we see it, it is clear that the marks of love are at least two — abandonment of self for the greater glory of God, and unity. It will express itself in the willingness to leave all behind, however precious it may be or however painfully bought, to be united with what is above and beyond.

Thus, as Paul says, "Abide faith, hope, and love." All three are essential in us, who must both will and love both God and creation, "but the greatest of these is love."

No doubt this is an incomplete and perhaps mutilating summary of "re-thought" religious terms in the light of Teilhard's massive thinking. Each reader will, I hope, have gathered and thought through much more from the previous exposition or from reading Teilhard himself. My hope is not that I have produced a definitive work, but rather have opened up new avenues of thought and exploration and invented an open-ended state of mind and faith. This, of course, was Teilhard's aim. He never expected or desired people to preach him and his ideas; he hoped rather to lure them to the openness with which he himself was convinced God can work.

NOTES

1. Bernard Towers, *Concerning Teilhard and Other Writings on Science and Religion* (London: Lutterworth Press,

1966), p. 235.

2. Karl Rahner, *Inspiration in the Bible* (Edinburg: Nelson 1961) p. 8.

3. Wolfhart Pannenberg, *Basic Questions in Theology*, Tr. George H. Kehm (London: SCM Press, 1970) p. 202.

4. Claude Cuenot, *Teilhard de Chardin*, Tr. V. Colinare and R. Hague (London: Helicon Press, 1965) p. 368.

5. Editorial, *Reform*, November 1972.

6. Arthur N. Whitehead, *Science and the Modern World* Cambridge: (Cambridge University Press, 1927) p. 233.

7. Albert Einstein, *Out of My Later Years*, (Tottawa, N.J.: Littlefield Adams 1962).

Chapter 10
"A VIEWPOINT FROM WHICH EVERYTHING IS BATHED IN LIGHT"

PART II:

LOOKING AT THE CHURCH

"Many things can be hated and fought against, in this world. And yet, there is only one foe against whom I should fully like to give my life: immobility." (LTF 136).

"Perhaps Teilhard is the answer to Marx, and the only form of Christianity that may prove acceptable to modern man is perhaps 'the gospel according to Teilhard.' "[1]

"You can convert only what you love." (S & C 127).

* * * * * * * * *

What does all this mean to the life of the church?

First, I believe it calls for . . . "a new type of worship (based on adventure and discovery)," to use Teilhard's own words quoted by Lucille Swan from a 1936 letter.[2]

Need Of Experiment

What form this will take will have to be worked out by the church through those very avenues suggested, adventure and discovery. If we really have the Teilhardian cast of thought, we will realize that in a dynamic universe *movement forward* is that "which was at the beginning, is now, and ever shall be." Reverence will make it not only possible but necessary both to adapt and to change. This attitude may even include the abandonment of rites and ceremonies once held sacred, when they no longer express the truth as we have come to know it or lift our hearts closer to God. This has been the fate of so much of what we are using now in worship. This material no doubt was right and good in the past; but it is no longer the past, so it is now wrong. Experiment and adventure will undoubtedly produce a great deal that is not good, that is ugly, even crude, because it is a new beginning and therefore patently imperfect and immature. This should not deflect or deter us. We must remember that it is only by "groping" that any progress is made, and much that the groping produces comes to nothing and must and will be set aside. But groping is also necessary in our efforts to find a way to help people open themselves and their lives to the love of God. This has been what groping has done in the process that brought humankind into being and will eventually bring the glory, the Kingdom, the end of all things in God.

Accentuating The Positive

Some "newnesses" I can suggest for this worship are these. First, that it be positive, not negative. Perhaps the past needed the grovelling of the "beseeching" and "miserable sinner-ing" of earlier services. We were not there to know and cannot therefore judge. Of course we are "sinners" and to forget this is more deadly dangerous than the worst disaster we can imagine. We certainly always need a real and powerful "humility," but away with humiliation. Let us by all means be conscious that we must wear our "L" plate. (These are signs which are required to be carried with the license plates on cars in England by those who are still learning to drive, whether they have received their driver's license or not.) But let us also be aware that we have an incredibly wonderful teacher. The God who calls us is the one who continually says to the prophet

Ezekiel, "Son of man, stand upon your feet and I will speak to you." This is because he calls us to be his sons and daughters and (praise be to him) offers us freely, in infinite love, the power so to be. Therefore the dominant note of our worship must surely be praise and rejoicing. Of the importance of praise C.S. Lewis writes, "Praise is the mode of love which has always some element of joy in it. Praise in due order; of Him as the giver ... Don't we in praise somehow enjoy what we praise, however far we are from it?"[3] Another note must certainly be hope; indeed, let there above all be hope. Every Sunday we celebrate the resurrection, God's definitive proof that what he is doing in the universe and the way he is doing it are certain to succeed, and we are both part of that enterprise and, incredibly, offered a share in its accomplishment.

All that makes for a sense of joy, of hope, of uplift, and also of comradeship, should be expressed in, and awakened by, our worship. How far we are from this was revealed to me by a very perceptive student in a confirmation class one time. After I had explained to her the meaning of Holy Communion, she asked in wonder, "But why, then, are you always so sad?" Why indeed? Somehow we have muddled reverence and solemnity with grief and stuffiness, and the truth is no longer in us. She who had been spectator at many a communion service had seen in that great celebration of God's love, victory, and triumph, only sorrow and defeat.

We must somehow also (and for this we must always be willing to "grope") express the unity and the sense of brotherliness which is the essence of the church whose business is worship. How can Christ be among us when the two or three are really *gathered together* as one, feeling one with each other, incomplete without each other, without all the rest, while sitting carefully insulated from each other in our stiff pews, carefully bunched so that we will not touch, not dare to exchange glances or smiles, let alone physical contact, joining only to sing hymns that carefully nourish the blasphemous idea that salvation is a matter of only *God and Me.* Yes, I say "blasphemous," for nothing in Scripture allows us to believe that any "I" can reach fulness of life in God without all the rest. Why else do we think Jesus, the risen Christ, immediately sent his followers out to gather in "all the world and preach the gospel to every creature?"

Our services of worship must therefore have a positive, an accepting, indeed a loving, attitude and spirit towards all creation. Perhaps in the past there was needed the negative, rejecting attitude to God's creation, to the world "God so loved" as to label it a "vale of tears," "a barren wilderness," and decry every effort and aspiration of the human heart. However, that day is gone. Without the love of the world, the ardent wish leading to dedicated action that will further the work of God in perfecting his creation, we now know God's will never will be done, however often we patter the petition. Let us, therefore, stop thinking, saying, praying, preaching, singing, *against* the world and the changes in it. Certainly many things in it are wrong, many must be so imbued with the spirit of God that all that is destructive and divisive and deadly in them will be defeated. But let us remember it was the powerful pull of God which caused any change. It is our task as God's co-workers, to bend the strength of our heart — soul, mind, and body always kept open toward God for his direction and his contribution of power, to make those changes which will bring forth greater humanity in humankind, greater unity with each other and with God in his world.

Let us then sing songs of joy, of faith, and of hope, of praise for what God has done, and is doing, and has proven he will do; songs offering ourselves to him in all the marvel of life and power he has given and offers to us, that we may become what we say we want to be. Let us read psalms and hear scripture, reading with minds open to hear and learn new truths, new directions, new points of view. Only thus will we ever be ready for the necessary "repentance," the readiness to undertake entirely new directions as God shall call us.

"Christianity," says Teilhard, "has to take a constructive standpoint *now*, based on a rejuvenated presentation of God, Christ, and charity." (LTF 150).

If we catch even a glimpse of the marvels of "Evolution," or whatever else science can or will show to us of the way in which creation has moved to this point, we surely cannot stay off our knees in reverence and awe. We will not be able to refrain from echoing the marvellings of the psalmist, or singing old or new hymns of praise to God. If we glimpse the marvel of Christ — not just in the Jesus of Nazareth, adorable and marvellous though he is — but as the begining and ending of that mighty process; if we catch a glimpse of the exalted and glorious role to which God has called us as his co-workers, the destiny he has for us at length, worthy to be part of his glorified body united with himself, surely our worship, our service, our faith, our life will come radiantly alive.

Her Task In The World

Surely, too, the church would be enabled to become what Christ called her to be, the custodian and the herald of the most wonderful and heartening news ever given the world, the good news of Jesus Christ, of God's power and purpose for all and his ability to fulfill it. This is the task she can know is so essential in God's plan that to fail to do it would mean that the whole enterprise would grind to a halt; for faith, hope, love, are the only conditions in which we can either progress to the next stage, or live and grow, once he has stepped into it through faith in Christ. No congregation, however depleted, is therefore dispensable or unimportant if it is attempting with all its might and its faith to do this. Neither numbers, nor "success" by material standards is required, but faithfulness, hope, and love.

It is essential, therefore, that the attitude and spirit of the church be marked by love — love of the world — not primarily for what it is but for what the church knows it to be, the object of God's love and prepared by him for completion with himself. This love will express itself most of all in dedication to the ends and purposes of God in everyone and everything; in acceptance rather than rejection. Such love must also mark the relation between the members of the church and the churches. Acceptance means a looking always for the positive, or a readiness to learn from each other; a search for and a cherishing of all that can be felt to be good; a growth in understanding and positive appreciation; a realization before the world of the fact that we are inexplicably related through the love of Christ, for the church must be both the truth that God can make a unity out of the great variety of humanity, and the catalyst of the wider unity God is working for in his universe. In order to carry out this task Teilhard believed the church must keep "the sense of *Someone Alive*," by being open towards society that it may not be alienated; and loving the world. So to love and to do her work the church needs to look at, as well as to use, for her understanding and teaching, the insights of science; not least of all when the going gets rough. Then she will learn that the old framework resists hardest when it is at the breaking point, and she will persist in faithfulness.

For her encouragement, let her hear Teilhard's version, written in Flanders fields, of a metaphor of Jesus: "You are the leaven spread by providence throughout this battlefield so that, by your mere presence, the huge mass of our toil and agony may be transformed." (W.T.W., p. 223).

Her Moral Teaching

Of morality, Teilhard would teach us that here too, we are inevitably involved in movement. Whether we like change or not, we are in the position of the woman who was reported as having said to Carlyle that she accepted the universe. The aged philosopher's reply was definite, "By God, she'd better!" We have no more choice about change — movement is the very nature of the universe.

Christian morality, therefore, must be the morality of movement. To say this is risky is to say that it is part and parcel of life. As early in the Bible as the second chapter of Genesis (verse 17), the Bible assures us risk is of the essence in living. Jesus was crucified because the Jewish Church saw him introducing too much risk into morality. All he required was trust in the love of God, the power of the action in which we are involved. For too long we Christians have exhibited the spirit I heard a teenager very astutely, though not too correctly, attribute to the Old Testament . . . "Tut-tut" . . . to almost everything. No doubt some things need to be warned against. This, I believe, is one of the chief functions of Old Testament history. But questing spirit is so strong and so universal I agree with Teilhard that it must be part of the spirit of God.

Certainly we will make mistakes. We cannot escape the character of universal movement, "groping." As Christians, if we see the movement to be of God, we will know that "groping" also to be his. Mistakes we will make; tragedies we will perpetrate; sufferings we will initiate, cause, and have to undergo — because we are creatures not God. But we will not be afraid or be immobilized by guilt. We have learned through Jesus Christ that God is a loving Father who forgives. And the wonder of forgiveness is not that it wipes out what is done — nothing can do that — but it does rob it of its power to do harm, to break relationships in creation, and makes it instead a power for good, both mending relationships and enabling progress. Thus God deals with all groping. When it is human groping we must both agree with God about the evil it produces, and surrender the result to his transforming power in trust and humble acceptance. Thus Teilhard can write, "Whatever Christians may say in the last resort about . . . any of the new theories which attract the modern mind, let us never give the impression of being timid about anything that can bring fresh light and greater breadth to our ideas concerning the universe. The world would never be vast enough, nor humanity powerful enough, to be worthy of him who created them and is incarnate in them." (H. of U., p. 97). If we feel that such morality is too insecure for us, too frighteningly like walking in complete darkness, then we are scarcely followers of him who, when anyone asked him a question seeking to be given moral direction, asked another in return, expecting the seeker to work out his/her own answer. All he offered was a personal relationship with himself. Thus he called, "Follow me," and "Come and see." Unless we will rise from where we are at any given moment, and go towards, and with him, we will never, never see, "the glory that is to be revealed to us." (Romans 8:18).

To our fear, Teilhard speaks both explanation of our longing for old security, and our need to move for the sake of the future.

"For all the claims implicit in its expression, my faith does not produce in me as much real charity, as much calm trust, as the catechism still taught to children produces in the humble worshipper kneeling beside me. Nevertheless, I know too that the sophisticated faith, of which I make such poor use, is the only faith I can tolerate, the only faith that can satisfy me — and even (of this I am certain) the only one that can meet the needs of the simple, souls, the good folk, of tomorrow." (L.M.E., p. 157).

So ends my exposition of the contribution I see Teilhard de Chardin making to "blind" religion in these last years of the twentieth century — a time of great change, and therefore not of decay.

Final Call To Move And See Teilhard's Vision

I am quite certain that there is more, much more, to be learned and seen from the Teilhardian point of view. It has been part of the agony of this task to find the huge ideas he presents so much bigger than my power to grasp and express.

However, all I had hoped to do was to lure working Christian pastors, faithful believers, and perhaps even seekers who, in this last part of the twentieth century may be finding themselves disheartened and tempted to give up on the Christian faith, to respond to Teilhard's call, "Come and see." Come and see, from the eminence to which Teilhard climbed, the wonders that are the Christian's to know and proclaim in word and life, and seeing, take fresh courage. Then, like the wise men who saw a new revelation of truth in the Christ Child, return to your place by another way.

About that way I would let Teilhard himself speak: "If I have faith in life, I believe that the world records everything good and useful that is done in it; it notes and assimilates to itself every movement and every impulse that is fitted to harmonize with its own becoming, of whose real goodness there can be no doubt. My life may be unknown, monotonous, commonplace, boring, hidden from all men's eyes but I shall carry out its duties in the consciousness that I am effectively collaborating in the absolute evolution of Being." (W.T.W. p. 43).

As for what I have done or failed to do here, I would dare to echo the words of him whose thought I have tried to present. Because his influence on my thinking has been so very great, I present this volume — limited and incomplete as I realize it to be — sharing his faith:

"What my lips fail to convey to my brother or sister, he will tell them better than I. What my heart desires for them with anxious, helpless ardour, he will grant them if it be good. What men cannot hear for the feebleness of my voice, what they shut their ears against so as not to hear it, this I can confide to Christ who will one day tell it again, to their hearts. And if all this is so, I can indeed die with my ideal, I can be buried with the vision I wanted to share with others. Christ gathers up for the life of tomorrow our stifled ambitions, our inadequate understandings, our uncompleted or clumsy but sincere endeavours. 'Lord, now lettest thou thy servant depart in peace.' " (HU 109)

NOTES

1. R.C. Zaehner, *Concordant Discord*, (Oxford: Clarendon Press, 1970) p. 423.

2. Neville Braybrooke, *Teilhard de Chardin, Pilgrim of the Future* (New York: Seabury Press, 1964) p. 44.

3. C.S. Lewis, *A Grief Observed*, (London: Faber & Faber Ltd., 1961) p. 49.

APPENDIX
Chapter 11
THE SMILING SCIENTIST

"Teilhard, like every newcomer to China, was given a Chinese name. . . . When naming foreigners, an effort is made to find some three-word combination which vaguely suggests to Chinese ears the sound of the person's name as pronounced in his own tongue. . . . Unconventional though Teilhard's name was, to the Chinese it stood for the man, and was more prophetic than his unknown donor guessed — 'Father Daybreak Virtue.' "[1]

Teilhard's Credentials

Teilhard was a French Jesuit priest who was also a brilliant, learned and respected scientist. His special fields were geology, paleontology (the study of extinct organisms) and paleo-anthropology (the study of fossil humans).

He died in April, 1955 in his seventy-fifth year in New York City — a virtual exile because of conflict with his church and order over some of the views he had arrived at in making a whole out of his two faiths — science and religion. This conflict had resulted in the total banning of the publication of all but his purely scientific writings. He had written, and sought permission to publish, two books — *The Phenomenon of Man*, the fruit of thinking on science and religion, and *The Divine Milieu*, concentrated on the devotional life — but neither was approved.

His Writings

There were in existence at his death, however, a great number of papers which had been circulated among friends in mimeographed form, and other writings in notebooks. All these had been left to his secretary and literary executrix, Mlle. Jeanne Mortier, of Paris.

Within months of his death she, with the backing of a group of friends and admirers in the fields of science and other disciplines (including such eminent people as Arnold Toynbee, Julian Huxley, Robert Oppenheimer, and Andre Malraux), had made arrangements for the publication of *The Phenomenon of Man.* Even before Teilhard's death Mlle. Mortier had secured a publisher who was ready to agree that he would not alter the text in any way, no matter what presure was put on him to do so.

When *The Phenomenon of Man* appeared in Paris in 1955 the first edition sold seven thousand copies. An English translation came out in 1959 with a foreword by Sir Julian Huxley which begins, *"The Phenomenon of Man* is a very remarkable work by a very remarkable human being."[2] By 1957 four collections of Teilhard's work had been published in France, the fourth being *The Divine Milieu,* which appeared in English in 1959.

This was the beginning of a great flood of material in which even the most minor and personal letters have been and are still being, placed on the market, not only in France but around the world. On July 23, 1970, *The Evening Standard* reported that, with twenty-four of his works translated, Teilhard was among the top six of France's translated authors, tying with the fifth. The fifteen languages I saw on the shelves of the mother centre in Paris in the summer of 1973 were English, Catalon, Spanish, Greek, Portuguese, Italian, Chinese, Japanese, Vietnamese, Korean, Danish, Finlandish, Norwegian, Dutch, and German. Those did not include Russian, into which *The Future of Man* was translated and published unexpurgated in Moscow in 1967. By the fifteenth anniversary of his death over two million copies of his works had been sold.

By 1964 Antony Leguine reported that twelve hundred

books and articles had been written on him, and this number steadily increases. I myself counted, in the new bibliography in the early 70's issued before 1955, 115; in 1955, 116, with five special numbers of publications dedicated to him; to 1959, 377; to 1966, 234; and to 1970, 111. By 1972 there were twenty theses being written on him in France, South Africa, Germany, Australia, Brazil, Spain, the United States, Italy, and Switzerland.

Evidences Of His Appeal

On May 21st, 1965, La Fondation de Teilhard de Chardin was brought into existence largely through the efforts of Mlle. Mortier. M. Jean Piveteau, a French scientist and personal friend of Teilhard, was its first president. Three rooms set aside in the Museum of Natural History to house records, manuscripts, and memorabilia of Teilhard, became the home of this association. It was the first of fifteen associations across the world. The Teilhard Association of Great Britain and Ireland, founded the following year, had a membership in 1973 of 1,287, including people from every continent, sixty of whom were from Canada. Other Associations are located — two in the United States, Germany, Italy, and Belgium, and one each in Austria, Denmark, Australia, and Canada. The associations exist to foster the ideas of Teilhard and work closely with groups interested in future studies. In addition, there are study groups in local areas; for instance, there are thirty-eight in England, and groups are reported also from places as far away from France as the Philippines and Ceylon.

The British Association, of which I have been a member since 1965, has held annual conferences since 1966, with outstanding speakers from various areas of the sciences and other disciplines, and publishes a magazine, *The Teilhard Review*, which has a fine record of scholarship. Of the conference in 1966 a writer in the *Irish Times* of August 4th wrote, "The founding of national associations has gone forward speedily, perhaps a unique phenomenon in the case of one man's thought."

What struck me personally at the first of these conferences I was able to attend was the incredibly wide variety of people in the over 850 in attendance. There were old and young, "hippies," and the most conservatively dressed clergymen, trim business people, obviously intellectual middle-aged women, and young emancipated girls, one of whom breast-fed her baby during the speeches. There were those who wanted to emphasize only the religious side of Teilhard's work, and those who would have none of this. I have never, except on the streets of London, seen a crowd covering such a wide variety of people.

Such has been the appetite for his work that two long-playing records of readings of two of his works, with music especially written for the background, have been released. Another, consisting of folk songs "in the spirit" of Teilhard de Chardin, is also on the market.

In the British Archives of press cuttings are quotations from him, or references to him, from every possible type of publication. These range all the way from an entry in the *Russian Philosophical Journal, Harlequin* (a leisure magazine), *The Methodist Record, Chemistry and Industry, La Figaro, The South China Post, The Ottawa Citizen*. They appear in articles dealing with the ecology and oceans, to Lady Astor's account of her conversion, to Britain's entry into the Common Market, to astronautics as a creative art. Perhaps, most notably, considering what happened to him and his work during his lifetime, articles on him or quotations from him are most numerous in Roman Catholic publications published after 1967.

The date, of course, is not without significance. Not a few Roman Catholics acknowledge that what was stated by Pieter Smulders, Dutch Jesuit in a Pax Romano Journal article (THE OPTIMISM OF TEILHARD DE CHARDIN AND VATICAN II), "Without the message of Teilhard (re hope for the world), the constitution of the church for the Modern World would probably never have been possible."[3]

Those who quote him or make reference to him and his influence range as widely in variety as do the publications containing them. Leopold S. Senghor, French-educated Catholic president of Senegal, paid tribute to Teilhard's influence on the form taken by his newly liberated country; that Teilhard's thought had enabled them to dispense with Marxism and leave that stage behind . . . to transcend the paradox of materialism and spirituality. He led us out of a dead end.[4] Marshall McLuhan refers to him, and so too do writers on economics, psychosynthesis, modern science and eastern religions, information processes and church unity. Over and over newspapers report that extension courses offering lectures on Teilhard have drawn large crowds, whether they are offered to professional clergy or the ordinary public. The works and influence of Teilhard have enabled dialogues to take place between Marxists and Christians. His work is also having tremendous impact on the thinking of people engaged in future's research, a development which would have particularly pleased Teilhard. Although almost the whole of his working life was devoted to studying the very distant past, during his last years he thought of nothing but the future.

Although he was in official disfavour with his Church, we read of many evidences of his influence even on this body. In the Vatican Pavilion at the Brussels World's Fair Teilhard's portrait appeared in a gallery of the century's greatest men. An Italian expert on the Vatican Council went so far as to predict that the outcome of the Council (re-convened by Pope Paul) would either reflect the spirit of Teilhard or would accomplish nothing significant, and that Teilhard's insistence that the insights given by material science cannot extinguish the light of revelation "as light does not extinguish light" was a principle implicitly approved by Vatican II. Another reporter points out that a dialogue being carried on in New Zealand between Roman Catholics and Baptists shows the influence of Teilhard.

In articles in the files of the British Association Teilhard is compared with the most widely diverse people. John Donne, Marx, Darwin, Marshall McLuhan, Einstein, Duns Scotus, Gerard Manley Hopkins, St. Francis of Assisi, and Martin Luther King are some of these. A book on humility compares him with Pope John XXIII. Another writer sees him to be "of the same mind" as Kagawa. Still another speaks of him as in the global tradition of H.G. Wells. His influence on the twentieth century is said by another to be as great as that of Blaise Pascal. Another writer finds him comparable with Friedrich von Hugel in spiritual greatness, while someone else finds a similarity in his views to those of Schweitzer. A writer on mysticism compares him with the Indian mystic Sri Aurobindo, while another states that his theology is worthy of a place beside those of Tillich and Bultmann. In an amazing way people of widely differing outlooks see Teilhard as the man for them.

His devotional book, *The Divine Milieu*, has been compared with the classic, *The Imitation of Christ*, and has even been predicted as likely to supplant this and *The Spiritual Exercises* for devotional reading.

Despite widespread approbation for him in Roman Catholic publications, hostility to him and his work is far from dead. In the August 2nd edition , 1973, *L'Osservatore Romano*, a widely read paper, there is a violent attack on him entitled "Teilhard de Chardin, a False Prophet." Moreover, the official monitum still bars his works from open shelves in Catholic seminaries and from being used in courses in such institutions "to protect the minds, especially of the young, against the dangers of the works of Pierre Teilhard de Chardin and his disciples."

Tributes to him from the field of science are many. Perhaps the greatest of these is the housing of La Fondation in two rooms especially set aside for Teilhard's memorabilia by the Paris Museum of Natural History. Just after his death his nation recognized him by striking a medallion in his honour which bore his profile and mystic axiom, "Everything that rises converges." Among the many tributes paid to him by his fellow scientists at his death, that of A.T. Habgood, head of the Mammalian Section of the London Museum of Natural Science, is perhaps the most balanced and moving. He speaks first of Teilhard's work in science, especially that of greatest interest to the body he is addressing, and then concludes, "Theologian and savant, mystic and poet, he towered above his fellows as a giant. Teilhard was a man of great charm, one of the kindest and most humble of men. Himself the soul of honour, incapable of an unworthy thought or deed, he gave freely of the fund of his experience in many fields of knowledge and asked for nothing but complete intellectual honesty in return. He could never understand the influence he had on others, an influence that he often found embarrassing, but when the history of his time comes to be written it may well be found that he did more to influence the development of French thought and hence of European thought than any other man of his generation. As one looks back over the whole life and work of this loyal son of his church and tries to realize how much richer the world is for his endeavours, there comes to mind the petition that runs like a refrain through the Vespers for the dead, 'Eternal rest grant to him, O Lord. And let light perpetual shine on him.' "[5]

Criticism Of His Work

There were the other English voices raised as well. When *The Phenomenon of Man* came out a research scientist very much in the public eye at the time, wrote a highly critical review of the book and its author. Because of the reviewer's prominence his opinions prejudiced many against Teilhard and his work. Indeed, when a friend of mine, Dr. Norman Whitney, now of the University of New Brunswick, but then in his second year of theology at McGill, requested that he might write his Philosophy of Religion essay on Teilhard, he was flatly refused. His professor said that he would not be able to make a critical appraisal of the essay because he had not read any of Teilhard's books, deeming them not worthwhile. When Norman asked on what he based his decision about Teilhard he replied that it was on the basis of a "bad" review (the one above.) Norman then discovered that this decision against Teilhard was made by the faculty "because Teilhard's work was not worthy of attention." Norman decided to investigate further and found that there were none of Teilhard's books on the library shelves even though he was being widely read in Canada at the time.

When he visited McGill again in 1966, Norman found that minds had been changed. Teilhard was well represented in the library, and the professor who hadn't wanted Norman to do his work on Teilhard confessed to him that his own reading of the books Norman had pretty well forced him to read had so proved to him that Teilhard was not a fraud that he had recommended the placing of his books in the library.

Many English and English-speaking people, for the same reason as that faculty at McGill, summarily dismissed Teilhard and his ideas, on the basis of one book review.

But other English voices had been raised in Teilhard's defence. Bernard Towers, a British anatomist of high distinction, pointed out in his broadcast reply to Medawar, March 8th, 1965, that both Piveteau in France and Dobzhansky in America regarded Teilhard as a seminal force of great significance in science. Joseph Needham of Cambridge, in an early appreciation of Teilhard in *The New Statesman,* speaks of *The Phenomenon of Man* as "the work of a first rate evolutionary biologist who knew his facts." Desmond Clark, a British anthropologist, speaks of Teilhard's death as the loss of a very great paleontologist. And Canon Raven notes in a radio script by Braybrooke that his severest critic who had caused others to discount Teilhard's competency, in his Herbert Spencer lectures given in 1963," puts forward as his own, an evolutionary process in three phases, chemical, organic and psycho social, which was set out in great detail in 1927 by Teilhard and his friend . . . LeRoy."[6]

Canon Raven had been one of the first in the English-speaking world to appreciate Teilhard's genius. He had been long in the battle for the reconciliation of science and religion himself; therefore he welcomed one whom he saw as a powerful ally. His last published work was a very warm and perceptive volume about Teilhard's life, work, and influence. In 1967, during a discussion of Teilhard on the BBC, asked about the "unsympathetic reaction" to Teilhard's views existing in Britain, his biographer-in-chief, Cuenot, remarked, that he felt that Teilhard was not, [as perhaps the English thought he ought to be] "quite French." He may have been influenced by Anglo-Saxon pragmatism until he was "something of an Anglo-Saxon." *The Phenomenon of Man,* Cuenot sees, as the continuation of an effort, theological and scientific to "reconcile Darwin and the Christian faith." Because of all these Cuenot felt you could say, "Teilhard belongs to English thought."

On the theological side he has been criticized, and continues to be criticized, by both Roman Catholic and Protestant theologians for neglecting the significance of the Cross, being insensible to the enormities of sin and evil in the world, and especially in human life, and misrepresenting the role and person of Christ. Another charges that the whole Teilhardian system does not develop Catholic dogma but perverts and warps it so that what is left is impure. In a lighter vein, I still remember the remark of a hitch-hiker I picked up in Oxford who, hearing the subject of my research, remarked, "He's a bit rosy, isn't he?"

Others have charged him with being "a pseudo-scientist, a pseudo-philosopher." No doubt this is because, as the distinguished geneticist Dobzhansky puts it, his work is "a curious spiritual compound that was hitherto unknown." (LTF 227).

The Newsletter issued by a group in Manila, the Phillipines, speaks of Teilhard as one of the most controversial men of the century, a man whose vision has influenced not only the evolution of the contemporary world but, almost imperceptibly the consciousness of the whole western world. During my two years of research at Oxford and Cambridge I noted, often with considerable amusement, that those who professed to have little regard for his views, nevertheless in their lectures sounded amazingly Teilhardian in the development of their own thoughts. I think, in all fairness, it might be said, as does H. A. Blair in *Teilhard Re-assessed*, "Like other great thinkers, the originality of Teilhard consists not in saying things never said before, but in making old things acceptable in a new age."[8]

His Influence As A Priest

Perhaps for readers of this book and the purposes for which it is written, the most telling of all are statements about Teilhard's power to do what Blair says he is able to do with the "old things" of the Christian faith. A friend from New Zealand told me recently that her lawyer sister had turned her back completely on the Christian faith and the church, but when she read some of the works of Teilhard she had been able to return to her earlier beliefs. A young post-graduate student of biology whom I met at Oxford confessed that, after he had been alienated from his faith by the teachings he received in a confirmation class, he had found life singularly empty and meaningless without any spiritual basis. This had been restored to him through his acquaintance with the writings of Teilhard. Indeed, it would seem that what his writings have been able to do is simply an extension of what he himself did among those whom he affectionately called "the gentiles", to whom he saw himself an apostle. One of his scientific friends, Max Begouin, has said that what Teilhard explained to him restored his faith. Of that experience he writes that he was brought to life "like Lazarus coming out of the tomb at the Lord's command, 'Come forth!' . . . a dazzling experience which soon changed my life from top to bottom."[9]

And in a symposium on Teilhard as reported by Braybrooke D. Poulain said, "The . . . number of persons brought into, or back into, the church because of Teilhard's sympathetic understanding of their difficulties and his success in dissipating these would seem to speak for his more novel approach."[10] Of this approach Father Corbishly says, "Teilhard in the twentieth century drew on a vast wealth of scientific lore to open men's minds to the majesty of God and the appeal of Christ."[11]

I believe that the man who said of Teilhard that he was "his own worst enemy" was perhaps nearest the truth. It is his insistence all the way through *The Phenomenon of Man* that what he has written is all science and nothing but science that got him into trouble with scientists, for there is no doubt that while all admit there is indeed science here — and no one who knew Teilhard doubts his integrity — there is much more. The "much more" gets him into trouble with the theologians. Because all his works have been published after his death, and none but *The Phenomenon of Man* and *The Divine Milieu* were prepared by him for publication (the rest being collected papers, letters, articles, notes, and speeches), they can be found repetitive — sometimes boringly so — sometimes obscure, and very often difficult. Yet his enthusiasm for them survives all this, for they have a tremendous power to lift the heart.

Teilhard's Life: Early Years

Marie-Joseph Pierre Teilhard de Chardin was born at Sarcenat, his family's country estate on one of the hills overlooking the industrial city of Clermont-Ferrand, in the district of Auvergne, almost directly in the center of France.

The house is a little chateau, set idyllically at the end of a tree-lined roadway, facing directly down into the city and looking just like the traditional fairy-tale castle. The day I visited it was one of light, shadow, and sudden rain, when dramatic clouds crossed and re-crossed the sun. At times the great round hills surrounding the city of Clermont-Ferrand on the plain below were lit up, while the city was in darkness; at other times the hills became black and foreboding while the city sprang alive. In the sunlight it seemed to be made up of white houses centered around the black cathedral. Behind, not far from Sarcenat, the dominating feature of the whole landscape is Puy de Dome, the volcanic hill which has at its peak both a geological exhibit and also, inevitably in 1973, a television tower. Both of them I believe Teilhard would have approved.

Teilhard's father, according to his cousin, Marguerite Teilhard-Chambon, was a gentleman farmer actively engaged in running several farms, "a humanist with a strong cultural bent"[12] — his interest in natural objects certainly conveyed itself to his fourth child, Pierre, who even at the age of eleven, was writing to his parents about "my passion for stones'."[13]

His mother was the great-niece of Voltaire, whose "mischievousness" someone has attributed to Teilhard. She was a cultured and deeply religious woman of whom her son once wrote, "I owe her my soul." She was a frequent worshipper at the parish church of Orcine in the tiny village across the fields. It has heavy, rather gloomy walls and sturdy pillars, on one of which is to be seen a plaque commemorating the fact that Pierre Teilhard de Chardin was baptized there. On the Honour Roll for the First World War, pathetically long for such a little community, as yellowing and fly-specked as such documents now are in similar places all over the western world, are the names and photographs of the two Teilhards who were killed, Olivier and Gonzagues. On the walls are small stations of the Cross, dedicated to those same Teilhards, as to the rest of their comrades on that Roll.

Although the picture of the church in the beautiful Teilhard de Chardin *Album* issued in 1966 makes it look very attractive, the building is really of rather heavy, Romanesque architecture. Here are no soaring Gothic arches, but perhaps the very solidity is more fitting to that area where one is always conscious of the overhanging grandeur and weight of the surrounding volcanic hills.

That such a countryside and such parents should have produced Teilhard de Chardin seems exactly right. Even the history of his tragic conflict with the church is foreshadowed in the loving devotions of his mother in that oppressively heavy sanctuary. For her, despite its unattractiveness, the church was the bearer of a light without which life would be unbearable. For her son, who found its ecclesiastical structures equally heavy and immovable, the church was still an institution without which he would not live.

Teilhard received his first formal education in Clermont-Ferrand, where the family spent their winters. He was an excellent student in everything except religious studies. His independence of spirit and perhaps his inheritance from Voltaire inspired the statement attributed to him, "I didn't care for the way they put religion across. All that nonsense about God blessing Jesus and those goody-goody romances about saints and martyrs . . . What normal child would ever want to spend everlasting life in such company!"[14]

However, "a desire for the most perfect" led him to enter the Jesuit Order, the most disciplined and learned of the Orders of the Roman Catholic Church. It was a course which would last thirteen years, most of which, because of anti-clerical feeling in France at the time, was to be spent outside his own country. First he was in Jersey, where the good sense of the novice master kept him from giving up his interest in petrology for 'supernatural activities'. (His own tribute in *Heart of the Matter*). Then he was sent to Cairo where he spent his required three years as a teacher, responsible for physics and chemistry. Finally, in Hastings, he did his theological training.

During these years he was constantly busy with his scientific work. In both Egypt and Hastings he made notable finds; in Egypt, fossilized teeth which came to bear his name, and in Hastings, fossilized plants, both genus and species of which now bear the name "Teilhard." It was at Hastings that Teilhard was introduced to the concept of evolution which, for him, was like a conversion experience. He himself says of it, "What an intellectual revolution!" Certainly it was to shape all his life and thinking from then on as he wrestled with all his sensitive powers to make a unity of his world of religion and of science.

It was at Hastings too, although at a later period, that Teilhard became connected with the infamous Piltdown Man case. A skull, a jawbone, and a tooth — the last found by Teilhard — were put forward by a Mr. Dawson as evidence that one of the many links in the history of human development had been found in England. They were later proved to be a hoax. This association has been cited as proof of Teilhard's disqualification to be called a scientist. As a matter of fact, he wrote as early as August 15th, 1913, shortly after his discovery of the controversial tooth, that he wasn't entirely satisfied with the skull. When, in 1953 the whole thing was found to be a fraud, Teilhard wrote at once congratulating the man who had proved it so.

Two months before he was ordained a priest, in 1911, his sister, Francoise, died tending the poor in Shanghai. This event, along with the earlier deaths of a brother and a sister, that of the two brothers killed in the war, and the permanent invalidism of his favourite sister, Marguerite-Marie, led him to ponder deeply on the meaning and place of suffering and death. Of these he was to see much more in the next four years, as his course in paleontology at the Natural History Museum in Paris was interrupted by the war of 1914-18.

Life During The Great War And Following

Almost immediately after the outbreak of hostilities he enlisted in the ranks as a stretcher-bearer. Perhaps this choice had been commended to him by the devotion of the stretcher-bearers he had seen at Lourdes, about whom he had written to his parents. At any rate he did spend the war years as a stretcher-bearer in spite of considerable pressure to take a commission and become a chaplain. At this time he seems to have begun to feel his mission to those he was to call fondly, "the gentiles," those outside the church. He felt he could reach them better if he remained in the ranks. The value of his services there is attested to by his war record. In 1915 he was mentioned in despatches; in 1916, mentioned in Orders and awarded the Croix de Guerre; in 1917 promoted to honorary stretcher-bearer and awarded the Medaille Militaire; and in 1921, at the request of his regiment, made a chevalier of the Legion d'Honneur.

There is little doubt in my mind but that in the earthiness and action of war the basis of Teilhard's thought was laid. The development of this thought he shared in correspondence with trusted friends and relatives, and later this correspondence appeared under the title, *Writings In Time Of War*. Through this work we come to realize that, though he himself insisted that the basis of his thought with regard to creative union was in his scientific observations, the real root was much more personal. The creative union which determined his thinking and his life was his own deep mystical union with God in Christ, deepened and strengthened in the agony and the ecstasy of those years of humble and dedicated service.

After demobilization Teilhard returned to his interrupted studies. He took his doctorate in geology at the Institut Catholique in Paris with great distinction. At that time the distinguished scientist, Marcellin Boule, remarked on his gift for synthesis and his careful work, and predicted a brilliant future for him. He began lecturing as an assistant professor of geology at the Institut.

In 1923 he was sent by the Museum to China to take part in a French Paleontological Mission directed by Pere

Licent. China was to be the site of most of his life from then until the end of the Second World War, except for occasional visits to Paris and professional expeditions to other parts of the world.

When he returned from China in 1924 and resumed his lectures, he became extremely popular with the students. So enthusiastically were his advanced and unorthodox ideas received and spread that in May, 1925 he was posted back to China at the express orders of his religious superiors. Thus began a long and sad conflict between the church and one of her most brilliant and devoted sons, one of whom a superior could write after his death, that from the point of view of obedience, Teilhard was the perfect subject.

Teilhard's Conflict With The Church

If I write at greater length on this aspect of his life, it is not the old business of a triumphant Protestant pulling out the hairs of the Roman Church's beard. Rather it is because I believe that, in Teilhard's relations with his church, we learn perhaps more than from any other area of his life. Moreover, the ban on publication of his work robbed Teilhard of the opportunity to prune it for publishing and to expose it to the criticism of his peers in the scientific field. Nevertheless, the conflict played a large part in the shaping of his thought.

In this conflict the preliminary skirmish would appear to have occurred when, according to De Lubac in his introduction to *Letters To Leontine Zanta* — the first woman in France to receive a Ph.D. — in 1924 writings done for a colleague "mysteriously turned up in Rome." (LTF 29) It was not until 1967 that the reason for the ban on the publication of the Divine Milieu, of 1942, was disclosed by the ecclesiastical reviewer at that time. The charge was that Teilhard did not properly present the Dogma of Original Sin, the doctrine of Redemption and the sacramental character of the church. Altogether his judges had felt he had made no place in his theology for the problem of the mystery of evil. So Teilhard had to write in the last paper sent home by him before his death, "Go quietly ahead with your scientific work without getting involved in philosophy or theology.' Throughout my whole life, that is the advice (and the warning) that authority will be found repeatedly to have given me." [S & C 214] But Teilhard could no more do this than the prophet Jeremiah could cease from his preaching because "it seemed like a fire burning in my heart, imprisoned in my bosom." (Jeremiah 20:9).

Indeed, I cannot help feeling that there is a very strong parallel between the great seventh century prophet, Jeremiah, and the priest-scientist, Teilhard de Chardin. Both were in conflict with the authority under which they lived; both were shut up in one way or another to prevent them from getting their message abroad. Both were indebted to faithful friends who preserved their works and made them known in spite of official ban; for both the message was "to tear down" and "to build up." Both spoke and lived in a love-hate relationship for the body which they sought to save, because their overwhelming loyalty was to God and the word they felt he had given them to speak. Both shared honestly the ups and downs of their inner lives — Jeremiah we know not how, and Teilhard in his letters to friends. Both died in exile, Jeremiah in Egypt and Teilhard in the United States.

Indeed, the words of Major William Clark about Jeremiah in the devotional booklet, *The Soldier's Armoury*, could very well have been written also of Teilhard, at least from the point of view of his church: "From first to last it appears that Jeremiah was a failure. No one listened to his message; he was regarded as a traitor; he died a reluctant exile . . . yet Jeremiah never gave up; he went on to the end working in God's name on behalf of the very people who had rejected him."[15]

The blow which fell on Teilhard in 1924, bringing with it abandonment of the professorship which he had been offered at the Institut, and exile from Paris, was just the first of many his church was to deal him.

Perhaps the conflict had begun even earlier, as early as that boyish abhorrence of "all that nonsense about God blessing Jesus." Certainly there are warnings of it in a letter written to his parents, February 5th, 1913, "I am expecting

Father Alphonse to be here tomorrow . . . I really think he will sound me out on the subject of divine grace and freedom; if that's the case he'll find I am singularly cold to such scholarly questions."[16]

The ground of the conflict was laid in Hastings where he was introduced to the theology of evolution. Of this period he writes, "All that I can remember from that time (apart from the magic word 'evolution' that continually comes back to my mind like a refrain, like something desired, like a promise, like a summons) . . . all I can remember is the extraordinary solidity and intensity I saw in the English countryside about that time — at sunset in particular — when the Sussex woods seemed to be charged with all the 'fossil' life I was then looking for, from cliffs to quarries, and in the clays of the Weald. Sometimes it really seemed to me as though suddenly some sort of universal being was about to take on shape in nature before my very eyes."[17]

The position which he took, and continued to take all his life despite the conflict which caused him so much grief and frustration, was won out of a deep struggle to bring integrity to his own inner life. This is obvious from many passages in his writings, of which this from the war years is typical, "The real problem of my interior life . . . is how to reconcile progress and detachment, a passionate and legitimate love of earth's highest development, and the exclusive quest for the Kingdom of God. How can one be as much a Christian as no other man and yet more a man than anyone?"[18]

In 1927, probably after another of the "warnings" he was repeatedly given, he writes: "One thing is certain — they will have trouble confining me to pure science. For me geology is like a root that pushes me with its sap toward the human questions: unification, prospection, and organization (especially psychological) of the human stratum. I cannot live outside of this realm." (LTF 66).

It may well be, as De Lubac suggests, that at least at first he did not realize "how bold some of his own ideas could seem."[19] Teilhard's passion for both science and religion was an unusual one and anything unusual is, in the annals of human history, invariably suspect. He was committed with all his soul to a universal truth and, as Polanyi says in *Personal*

Knowledge, universal validity is not an observed fact. Unfortunately, the church, despite its insistence that people must walk by faith and not by sight, is far too often as distrustful as any other human institution about the things she herself does not see.

At first it seems he had hopes of finding acceptance for his ideas and of being able to be at peace with his Order. So he writes to Leontine Zanta regarding one of the two works he prepared for publication, *The Divine Milieu*, "I am writing a little spiritual treatise ... which I hope will be orthodox." (P. 76). From a note in a letter written to a friend, it seems the work was unanimously accepted by the theologians of Louvaine in 1930 and read extensively and used "by a lot of priests and religious people of all feathers." However, it must have been circulating in the form in which all his work was read before his death — in mimeographed copies — for, in February 1949, he writes that the printing of this book had been definitely forbidden.

In his reaction to these frustrations Teilhard was wholly human, as all his friends attest. Although we find him writing when the blow fell in 1924, "Basically I am perfectly tranquil. Even this is only one more manifestation of our Lord; it is another example of his operation, so why should I worry?" (WTW 244 foot note 19). We learn from other later letters that his struggle within himself still goes on. In 1930 (LLZ 101) he writes, "I now find myself 'beyond revolt.' " Again in 1933 he writes, "I want to get hold of myself intellectually and spiritually, and if I don't do it immediately I never will." (LTF 80) When the last struggle to get his books approved for publication was going on, Teilhard tells his correspondent that he has become almost indifferent as to whether permission is granted or not. However, when Rome vetoes an important field trip in 1949, he writes, (LTF 174), "I still feel sore about the African trip, which apparently was so exactly the next step for me." And when he does get final clearance for the African trip in 1950 he writes its value will be that it will "allow things cool off in Rome." (LTF 114)

It was not just being unable to get his ideas circulated officially that troubled Teilhard during his exile in China; it was the exile itself. Over and over he speaks of his longing to get back to France, to Paris, which he says is his "own native milieu." "I am born to speak in French to Europeans," he says again. (LTF 65). And although he valued the wonderful experience of being in an international community such as Peking, he never really appreciated the Chinese "milieu." Nor did he feel any bond with the Chinese people, with the exception of those intellectuals among whom he worked and "one marvellous one who has long been the 'boy' of a prospector of the mine. I would love to take him away with me some day." (LTF 61). In China he felt stifled, cut off from the intellectual mainstream where he longed — with the yearning of a thirsty man for water — for the stimulation and sympathy of his circle in Paris. Only the infrequent visits home kept him going.

Nevertheless, he would not compromise his integrity by confining himself to pure science as he had many times been ordered. In 1927 he was given permission for one of these brief visits on condition that he do no teaching. However, at this time he notes that his Order is not dismissing the idea that he might eventually be allowed to re-locate permanently in Paris, restricted to pure science. That he does not intend to accept this is clear when he goes on to refer to his future as a "traveller."

But this is not the only battle he had to fight. As was to be expected, his friends — especially those who were not of the church — were continually urging him to quit his Order and defy the authorities. Because of his "apostleship to the gentiles" and the nature of his work, not a few of his friends, and certainly many of his associates, were agnostics, atheists, and even anti-clericals. To these his clinging to the body which stifled his work made no sense at all. The intimate correspondence contained in *Letters To Two Friends* and to *Leontine Zanta* was with people of this sort. It is in these volumes that we are allowed to see the extent of the struggle that went on in Teilhard's mind and life. Here we see his reasoning about which he quite frankly writes on one occasion, "To tell the truth, all this is not as absolutely clear in my mind as it is on paper," (LTF 62), a very human situation and also a delightfully honest and humble admission of that humanity.

Of the winter of 1926-7 he admits, "I went through a

rather bad crisis of anti-clericalism, not to say, anti-Christianity." (LZ 91). At the same time he refused to entertain the idea of a break. "I am held fast in the Church by the very views which help me see her insufficiencies." (LTF 58).

Of these "insufficiencies" he writes very perceptively, "One sometimes gets the impression that our little churches hide the earth from us . . . There are some who want to identify Christian orthodoxy with . . . respect for the tiniest wheels of a little microcosm constructed centuries ago . . . it implicitly excludes from God's Kingdom (or denies on principle) the huge potentialities whirling around us in social and moral questions, in philosophy, in science, etc. That is why I have declared war on it to the death . . . I don't quite know how I'll set about waging this war, now that my possibilities of outside action have become more and more restricted." (LLZ 79). He was under no illusion as to how determined the forces were against him. "I am fully aware," he writes to another friend, "of the savage beast that sleeps within the instinct to preserve 'established orders.' " (LTF 70).

However, over and over he was to repeat in one form or the other the final sentence of the above paragraph to Leontine Zanta, "I think that the best way of making an attitude triumph is to live it as faithfully as possible." (79). "Would it be logical," he writes to the other friends, "for me by breaking with my Church impatiently to force the growth of the Christian stem in which, I am persuaded, the sap of the religion of tomorrow is forming?" (LTF 58).

Even under the most extreme provocation Teilhard remained true to this position to the very end, and the provocation was often extreme.

In 1933 he writes that he had been warned by his Order not to accept any position offered him in Paris. This was a condition which must have been very hard to take as life was becoming increasingly more restricted in China with the growth of nationalism and the consequent anti-foreign feeling. In 1939, after the visit of a superior, he writes about plans to have his articles circulated, a warning he must often have had to give his friends, "Make what use you please of these reflections. But don't print them." (SC 223).

During the Japanese occupation of China, when he was

cut off almost completely from Paris and the world which stimulated him, and from physical activity in the field, the ever-hopeful Teilhard wrote what he felt would be the definitive expression of his thought, *The Phenomenon Of Man*. Perhaps he still hoped the authorities would come to realize, as Buber puts it, that "the apparent turning away of the man who is fulfilling his mission belongs in truth to the universal movement towards the primal source."[20] Indeed, his doing this work was in accord with the conviction he had expressed about the Chinese awakening in the Boxer Rebellion: "Nothing stops ideas; outward restraint only lends them force." (LTF, p. 69). Moreover, he was impelled by a stronger motive than this — his love for the church. "I cannot fight against Christianity," he wrote in 1941. "I can only work inside it by trying to transform and convert it . . . I know that the tide is rising which supports me." (LTF, p. 155). Much as he had said two years before, "I am probably feeling closer to my Church and my Order just now than I was a year ago. *Not at all*, I sincerely think, that I am slackening in my line of progress . . . I have got, recently, so many evidences that people (outside as well as inside what they call the Church) expect me to be . . . another type of Christian *in* Christianity." (LTF, p. 129-130).

He was haunted by the fear that the authorities in Rome would, by their stubbornness and failure to entertain any new ideas, take the church out of the main stream by detaching it from the world in motion. He compared this situation to that existing at the time of Galileo. He kept hoping, however, that the church, by acting differently this time, would give such an example that people "four centuries ahead, being faced with some new parting of the ways we cannot yet foresee will look back and say, 'In the twentieth century they saw clearly. Let us seek to follow their example.' " (FM 270).

However, we find him writing in 1941 about "the growing feeling that personal projects are just now rather futile." (Participation in a Congress in New York had not been approved.) But . . . They agree that I should send to Rome the manuscript of my book for sympathetic (?) revision . . . it is not so bad as I could fear." (LTF p. 155) That was the beginning of a long period in which Teilhard tried, without yielding on any major point, to modify *The Phenomenon Of Man* to meet official objection. But in vain. In 1948 he even went to Rome itself to try to get a hearing for his ideas. But, as Raven notes, "He was given no access to any competent theologians and went away convinced that Rome was still living as if Galileo had never been born . . . "[21]

In the same year he was asked to let his name stand for a chair in the College de France, assured that it would be unanimously offered to him. Rome again refused permission, even as the previous year it had forbidden him "to publish two carefully edited papers on Le Comte du Nouy, a personal friend!" (LTF, p. 101). Vainly he had attempted to make his superiors understand "what seemed to me to be the real source of modern man's restlessness;" . . . the answer from Rome was "that my diagnosis did not coincide with the ideas currently accepted in the Eternal City." (C & E pp. 212-3).

By 1949 he ws having to write, "I am thinking of writing to Weindenreich, [Scientist in Teilhard's field at the American Museum of Natural History] to ask him (just in case) for a letter of invitation that will enable me to obtain a visa of entry into America if necessary." (LTF 101). It did become necessary. In 1951 his second and final exile began when he accepted a post in anthropological research with the Wenner-Gren Foundation in New York City.

In the Jesuit house in that city Teilhard did find some relief, for he could write of his relations with the head that it was "the first time a superior has invited me to think freely and constructively with him . . . "[22] How tragic that he could not have found such response in Rome. If only it could have been with such a person, rather than an agnostic friend, he could have shared his wry observation that in ennunciating the 1950 dogma of the assumption of the Virgin Mary in a series of statements which seem to fall on our modern earth from a long-disappeared world, the church had, by its mere affirmation . . . "expressed (ed) the view that the dogma is still *evolving* (since there is not a word of it in Scriptures), they are becoming evolutionist in spite of themselves." (LTF 216). Yet of this dogma he also wrote, "I believe I see what is in the minds of the Roman theologians, and I agree with them. But their views are expressed in the most impossible language." (LTF 216).

Here is the sad part of this whole situation. Teilhard was *not* an extremist in theology. Indeed, what he found as he struggled to reconcile his faith and his science confirmed for him the basic teachings of classical Christianity. It was not just that he saw in the church the guardians of what he felt to be "the religion of the future," the hope of the world, and that which guaranteed the continuation of evolution to its glorious and divine climax; the deeper he went into his science the more firmly he believed in the teachings of the Bible and the principal doctrines of the church. The difficulty lay in the refusal of the church to re-think them in the thought-forms of a century in which the greatest scientific explosion of all times has been taking place. It was reluctant to express the eternal truth in language which has any connection with life in a time when people have to live with the realization that the power that holds the universe together is in their hands and that it is their decision whether the universe will flower to its appointed end or explode into a million fragments.

He himself realized in his lifetime that the hostility and shackling he received from the church helped to make both him and his ideas. They prevented him, as he once put it, "from throwing out the baby with the bath water." However, the church was much slower to see his value to itself.

If there were many precious souls the church did not lose during that period because of the faults of which Teilhard tried so hard to rid it, it could have been thankful that through the "spreading everywhere of my clandestine papers" and his own personal influence, many were brought to faith.

As I have shown earlier, the tide has turned somewhat. In the New Catholic Encyclopedia, published in 1967 (just twelve years after Teilhard's death), we find this entry, "Teilhard has been characterized as one of the great minds of the contemporary world, and eminent churchmen have invited scholars to continue to elaborate what Cardinal Feltin has called his marvellous and seductive 'global vision' of the universe wherein matter and spirit, body and soul, nature and supernature, science and faith, find their unity in Christ."[23]

A late awakening it is true, and sad for that noble soul who was so harassed by the very body he loved so well; but still the awakening came, as Teilhard had felt it would, for he had written in his later years, "What distresses me is not that I am shackled by Christianity but that Christianity at the moment should be shackled by those who are its official guardians — the same problem that Jesus had to face two thousand years ago."[26]

If, as many feel, the Roman Catholic Church, so long immobilized in the Middle Ages, now appears to have leapt forward in many areas, even ahead of the Protestant Church, could it not be that those are right who see in Teilhard one through whom blind eyes were opened?

During the years of conflict with his Church and Order, Teilhard led a very full and active life making a prominent place for himself in the world of science to which the church had tried in vain to confine him.

Teilhard As A Scientist

Fellow scientists who worked with him are unstinting in their praise of the integrity, the thoroughness, and the accuracy of his work. Counselling young scientists, he himself insisted on accuracy, observation, and material facts rather than personal interpretation. Certainly the many scientists who have written about their work with him — and he worked with men of many countries during his lifetime — attest that he carefully folowed his own advice. But there was more than just "accuracy and observation" from the start of his career. Marcellin Boule, Professor of Palaeontology at the Paris Museum, to which Teilhard had returned after the War, to complete his interrupted studies, a man "rarely wrong in his judgement about men"... summed up Teilhard's prospects as a naturalist and pronounced him well equipped for a brilliant future. But he also detected another quality, 'valuable as it is rare, a combination of minute analysis, a gift of wide synthesis, and great independence of mind."[25]

Later the noted German anthropologist, Helmut de Terra, was to write, "It was always hard to wrest Teilhard away from a promising geological discovery before he had exhausted all its possible interpretations. In so doing he invariably devised certain criteria of whose validity he had to be thoroughly convinced. Only then would his thoughts turn to wider implications, and, before one knew it he had given his listeners an entirely new view of things. He had a brilliant capacity for proceeding straight to a synthesis from carefully sifted details."[26] And again, "when scrutinizing fossils or artefacts he gave the impression that he could grasp their underlying significance by means of a kind of inner eye. This unusual gift may account for his dislike for expert classification . . . a characteristic he shared with other scientists . . . the salient experience to be gained from working with Teilhard was of his ability to invest the most inaminate objects with life and ply one with a constant stream of ideas, thereby assuring one of the existence of a spiritual domain in which it somehow became urgently necessary to believe."[27]

Yet one must not, from this, see Teilhard as an evangelist posing as a scientist and using his science as a vehicle for making converts. De Terra makes it plain, as do others, that he *was the last person to behave in an arrogant or sermonizing way* . . . "rather, he took his place among us with a humility that put us all to shame." A member of one of his expeditions remarked on Teilhard's unconditional respect for the individual conscience which kept him from saying grace at their meals. And Andre George, noted French critic, essayist, and physicist, writes in the preface to the Teilhard Album, "His priestly character expressed itself not in any religiosity but in a contagious ardour, and yet few religious have helped so many souls in the hidden places of their hearts."

Long before it became common for priests to lay aside their distinctive dress on non-religious occasions, Teilhard dressed like his companions in the field. Indeed, he writes from a retreat, during one of his brief visits to France, "Just now I am stranded . . . in the monastery . . . of my Order . . . I am dressed in a long black gown . . . and I feel completely unnatural to myself." (LTF 128).

It seems that the words written of him as a novice remained true of him all his life: "modest and apparently shy . . . simple and unassuming, anxious not to appear in any way different from others, gay and lively and a great walker, . . . a big fellow, very friendly and affable, . . . well set up on his long legs firmly planted on big feet which were very turned out as he walked . . . an agreeable companion."[24] However, the years added something more, something that shines out of the picture in *The Teilhard Album* where, turning the pages, one can watch his face being honed into real beauty. It is the quality that impressed a man who met him and later remarked to a friend of mine, "I was prepared for a brilliant mind, but the overwhelming impression I got was of sheer goodness."

This good man, who was determined to be both theologian and scientist, was a scientist of international renown. His bibliography lists five hundred titles of writings on geology, palaeontology, and palaeoanthropology, with one hundred and thirty-nine of these being major works. Dobzhansky, a biologist of international repute puts it, "His studies on the geology of China stand out as a fundamental contribution to the understanding of the geological history of the heartland of Asia . . . A whole generation of Chinese geologists and palaeontologists had him as one of their mentors and leaders." (LTF 223).

Life In China

The largest part of his professional life, as was noted, was spent in China where he was based almost continuously from 1925-46. During this time in China he worked with scientists, not only of China and France, but also of Sweden, the United States, Canada, Germany, Australia, Scotland, New Zealand, Russia, and The Netherlands. It seems odd and a little sad that, despite all his years in China, he never learned the language. The inevitable result of this was that one person who knows China well from long residence there could remark to me that Teilhard never seemed to appreciate the quality of ordinary Chinese people. Perhaps it is not surprising. His work was in a very specialized field that brought him into direct contact almost exclusively with Chinese intellectuals. His only contact with ordinary people would be with the workers on the "digs." And it would seem likely that he was carefully excluded from much contact with the young Chinese of his Order, as he writes, "I heard that the new Peking superior of my Order did not like to see me so close to his youngsters

... Tientsien wants me back on the contrary" (LTF 130)

His scientific stature, in the eyes of the Chinese scientific community, was so great that in a period when Chinese nationalism was making it difficult for Westerners to work with them, Teilhard was made general supervisor of all research and scientific work on fossil mammals ". . . by agreement among all the Chinese, Americans and Swedes . . ."[28]

In places in his writing Teilhard seems to have depreciated the Chinese and to have felt that their culture had come to such a dead end that he even speaks of them as "Neolithic." Nevertheless, he also writes, that he believes that the "heavy sap" running through Chinese veins might well enrich the western spirit while being enlivened by it. As early as 1926 he is writing, "I am beginning to think that their (i.e., Bolshevist) success would be the signal for the reorganization of China — but at the expense of the Europeans." (LLZ 73). Earlier he had expressed his sympathies with the Communists as he writes, "What distresses me is to see Communism resisted by Fascism, that is to say, the brutal and retrogressive negation of what has been dimly foreseen and desired by many *good* elements in the Communist *awakening*." (LLZ 80).

Attitude To Some Controversial Topics

There are those who are distressed by what seems, as they read some of Teilhard's writings, a callous and even fiendish delight in such horrors as the Fascist movement and the explosion of the atomic bomb. One needs to read more than one article to understand his views on these.

It is obvious from the quotation above that he was fully aware of, and horrified at, the excesses of the Fascist movement. Nevertheless, he saw the values of such a society in which human energy was so stirred up and organized. He also knew very well that this organization done, as it was, by force, could never succeed in really unifying human beings. He dreamed of this same oneness being attained voluntarily and gladly through mutual love. He therefore saw the Fascist experiment as one of those "gropings" in human evolution similar to those by which, on the biological level, nature "tries everything."

As far as the atomic bomb was concerned, Teilhard's reactions were equally mixed. He did not condone the destruction and savagery of its use. Nevertheless, he knew humans from this time forward possessed a fearful and wonderful knowledge. They have now in their possession control over the powers that hold the universe together. Thus they had reached a new stage in their maturity, bringing with it awesome potentialities and therefore awesome responsibilities. Henceforth they are obviously in possession of the key to the forces that shaped the world.

The fact that Teilhard did not believe in, or champion, the equality of races has distressed many people, not least of all the young. Cuenot defends him thus, Theilhard recognized not the equality but the complementarity of races . . . he was not a racist in that he believed there were no higher or lower races . . . but he also believed that some races act as spearheads in evolution and others have reached a dead end . . . he felt there was a particular role for every race . . . and that every state of humanity needs the others in order to attain maturity.[29] He was convinced that the line of advance for mankind was running through the West. Because at times he expressed the opinion that the Chinese seemed to be among those who had reached "a dead end," I asked Mlle. Mortier, [who had been instrumental both in having Teilhard published and in the founding of La Fondation Teilhard de Chardin in Paris,] in October, 1973, if she thought Teilhard would have been surprised at the great Chinese leap forward in these recent years, or have seen it as a contradiction of his conviction about the West. Very quickly she leapt to his defence, pointing out that the seed of this advance *had* come from the West, from Russia. It does seem that what has happened and may well go on happening as China makes her contribution to the development of humankind, is something very Teilhardian, a synthesis of East and West. It may well be another evidence of the convergence he sees as one of the fundamental movements in evolution.

His Wide Interests And Contacts

Teilhard's field work, which was as necessary to him as

breathing, took him into the most difficult of terrains and climates, in China, Central Asia, India, Burma, Java, and several parts of Africa. He was constantly undergoing the wear of transoceanic travel to attend conferences, largely before air travel became common. During his "holiday" visits to Paris he was beseiged by requests to speak, counsel, present papers and, also less ardous affairs such as perform marriages and baptize babies. Here we have just a glimpse of the many-sidedness of this man. Though he was a famous scientist and a thinker of enormous religious ideas, he was stranger to the aloofness of those whose thoughts are always on the abstract formula or the theological concept. To many, many people he was a very warm, understanding, and marvellous spiritual director, pointing them to the faith they never had had, or gently but clearly bringing them back to that which they had lost. A Jewish friend who had long since deserted the faith of her fathers found her place among her own again through his influence, and she was only one among a great multitude. He was especially attractive and helpful to the young. Cuenot notes that a group of students, in trouble with the authorities, turned to Teilhard for understanding, mediation, and direction.[30] Behind all this activity was the constant strain of the hostility of his Order. In 1946 he writes, "I am surprised [and just a little scared] to discover how widely my small papers have spread, and impressed people of every kind . . ." (LTF 165).

    The people to whom in his lifetime he appealed did indeed embrace "every kind." He was invited to address or counsel with worker priests, a group of psychoanalysts, Marxists, people designing modern tapestries, a symposium on the sociology of animals, a group of artists, sculptors, painters, and musicians; the World Congress of Faiths, the head of the C.I.A., the New York Congress on Science and Religion; college students in the United States and France. He was consulted about, and very active in, the setting up of UNESCO, and in its early stages had had hopes that it would be the body which would do the work he felt so needed to be done — the study and control of the human forces of self-evolution. However, he soon discovered that he had to look elsewhere for that support. He visited Canada and South

America, and made two trips to South Africa during which he evolved a theory of human descent which finds made later showed to be true. For his theory he had no proof at the time. He arrived at it through what he had observed in Africa and the things he had seen in other parts of the world where he had been working.[31] Ardrey, an anthropologist connected with Africa, paid tribute to Teilhard because he accepted the evidence of the African site as birthplace of the human group despite the fact that he had done all his work in Asia. No one who knew Teilhard or knows his work would have expected anything different from one of his integrity.

Last Years: Sickness, Honour, Death

With such a rigorous program it is no wonder that in 1947 he suffered a severe heart attack which caused postponement of a planned trip to South Africa. However, his great physical stamina and the loving care of his many friends enabled him to make a successful recovery and finally take up his work again.

In recognition of his scientific work he was offered, in 1946, a professorship at the College de France which, as Dobzhansky points out, is "one of the most prestigious positions to which a scientist can aspire in that country (i.e., France)." (LTF 224). He had been assured that, if he let his name go forward, he would be the unanimous choice. However, as we noted earlier, this was the time when he was also seeking publication of *The Phenomenon of Man*, and both were vetoed by Rome.

The church was not able to prevent his being honoured by his nation and by independent academic bodies. In June, 1947, at the instance of the Ministry of Foreign Affairs, he was promoted to the rank of Officer in the Legion d'Honneur "for outstanding services to the intellectual and scientific influence of France, through a body of work mostly written and published in China, which has established him as a leading authority in international, and particularly in English-speaking, scientific circles. He may now be regarded, in the field of palaeontology and geology, as one of the chief ornaments of French science, whose international standing he has done much, by his personal contacts with foreign scientists, to maintain and exalt."[32] In 1950 he was elected to membership in the Academie des Science (Institut de France).

During his last years, as he says of himself, he developed a "kind of nausea for the past" and became more and more interested in the future. In 1950 he wrote to a friend, "for some time now the principal interest of my life is no longer fossil man but the man of tomorrow or, more exactly, 'the God of tomorrow'." (LTF 114). The most modern advance in science interested him. He looked into cybernetics and made sure that he saw the cyclatron on his visit to Berkley, California, for in 1951, after his tour of South Africa and a visit to England, he had been exiled to the United States, as he had foreseen. Here he held a post in anthropological research with the Wenner-Gren Foundation in New York.

From here he went abroad again a number of times, but New York became his final home. After expressing a wish, a little more than a year before at a dinner, (noted by one of his nephews) to die on the day of Resurrection, he died on Easter evening, April 10, 1955. There were few present at his funeral, Cuenot reports, "It was a very quiet, simple ceremony, even poor: Low mass, with no singing ... It was raining."[33] He was buried in the Jesuit Cemetery at St. Andrews on the Hudson. When they heard of his death, the elevator boy in his building and the woman who looked after his rooms were in tears. "He was a good man," they said.

Some of his critics have diagnosed his insistence that the human spirit is indestructible as evidence that he couldn't face his own death. They based their claim on a childhood incident which he himself tells, when he cried at seeing a lock of his hair burned in the fire, because he realized his own destructibility. However, the adult Teilhard has written, "In itself the problem of personal survival does not worry me greatly. ... It is enough for me that ... what is best in me should pass, there to remain forever, into one who is greater and finer than I." (C & E 115). Of his ideas, he said shortly before his death, "If I have had a mission to fulfill it will be possible to judge whether I did so only by the extent to which I am superceded."[34]

Such was the humility and faith of the famous man his Chinese colleagues named, "The Smiling Scientist," who has written of his life and work, "It seems to me a whole lifetime of effort would be nothing if I could reveal for one instant what I see." (LTF 40).

NOTES

1. George B. Barbour, *In the Field with Teilhard de Chardin* (New York: Herder and Herder, 1965) pp 222-23.

2. Sir Julian Huxley, *Introduction to The Phenomenon of Man* Teilhard de Chardin, tr. B. Wall (London: Fontana, Collins 1955) p. 11.

3. Pieter Smulders, "The Optimism of Teilhard de Chardin and Vatican II." *Pax Romana Journal.*

4. Leopold S. Senghor, assembled from *Pere Pierre Teilhard de Chardin et le Politique — Africaine* and the letter he wrote with it to the author.

5. Proceedings of the Linnaean Society of London, Vol. 167 pt. I pp 1141-2.

6. Neville Braybrook, *Teilhard de Chardin, Pilgrim of the Future* (New York: Seabury Press, Ltd. 1964) p. 123.

7. "A Radio Discussion, Vernon Sproxton in the Chair" *Evolution, Marxism and Christianity, Studies in the Teilhardian Synthesis,* Various Contributors (London: The Garnstone Press Limited, 1967) p. 102.

8. Blair, in *Teilhard Reassessed,* 82.

9. Editorial, Frontier. 3 (Autumn 1960): p. 167.

10. Braybrooke, p. 104.

11. Thomas Corbishly, *The Spirituality of Teilhard de Chardin* (London: Collins, Fontana, 1971) p. 126.

12. Album, p. 9.

13. Album, p. 18.

14. Braybrooke, p. 113.
15. William Clark, *The Soldiers Armoury,* June 30, (1973).
16. Teilhard de Chardin, *Letters from Paris*, tr. Mazzarese (New York: Herder & Herder, 1967) p. 57.
17. Album, p. 41.
18. Album, p. 54.
19. DeLubac, in *Letters to Leontine Zanta*, p. 31.
20. Buber, *I and Thou,* p. 116.
21. Charles Raven, *Teilhard de Chardin, Scientist and Seer* (London: Collins, 1962). p. 171.
22. Cuenot, 364
23. E. L. Boné. "Teilhard de Chardin," *New Catholic Encyclopedia,* (1967) 13, p. 177-8.
24. Album 25
25. Cuenot, 367, 177-8.
26. Vernon Sproxton, *Teilhard de Chardin,* (London: SCM Press Ltd., 1971) p 34.
27. de Terra, *Memories of Teilhard de Chardin,* p 24.
28. de Terra 67
29. Cuenot, 30 (summary).
30. Cuenot 88
31. Cuenot 323 (footnote)
32. Album 176.
33. Cuenot 387
34. Emile Rideau, *Teilhard de Chardin, A Guide to His Thought* (London: Collins, 1967) p 658.

BIBLIOGRAPHY

Books by Teilhard with Symbols Used for Reference in the Text

(AE) *Activation of Energy*. tr. Rene Hague, London: Collins, 1970.

(CE) *Christianity and Evolution*. tr. Rene Hague, London: Collins, 1971.

(COR) *Correspondence*, ed. Henri de Lubac, tr. W. Whitman, New York: Herder and Herder, 1967.

(HE) *Human Energy*, tr. J.M. Cohen, London: Collins, 1969.

(HU) *Hymn of the Universe*. tr. G. Vann: London, Collins Fontana, 1970.

(DM) *The Divine Milieu*, tr. B. Wall, London: Collins Fontana, 1967.

(LME) *Let Me Explain*. tr. R. Hague and others, London: Collins, 1970.

(LT) *Letters from a Traveller*, tr. R. Hague and others, London: Collins Fontana, 1967.

(LTP) *Letters from Paris*, 1912-1914. tr. Henri de Lubac, New York: Herder and Herder, 1967.

(LZ) *Letters to Leontine Zanta*. tr. B. Wall, London: Collins, 1969.

(LTF) *Letters to Two Friends*. tr. R. D'Ounce, London: Collins, 1968.

(MPN) *Man's Place in Nature*. tr. R. Hague, London: Collins, 1971.

(SC) *Science and Christ* tr. R. Hague, London: Collins, 1965.

(AM) *The Appearance of Man*. tr. J.M. Cohen, London: Collins, 1965.

(FM) *The Future of Man*, tr. N. Denny, London: Collins, Fontana, 1970.

(MM) *The Making of a Mind*. tr. R. Hague, London: Collins, Fontana, 1965.

(PM) *The Phenomenon of Man.* tr. B. Wall, London: Collins, Fontana, 1970.

(VP) *The Vision of the Past.* tr. J.M. Cohen, London: Collins, Fontana, 1966.

(WTW) *Writing In Time of War.* tr. R. Hague, London: Collins, 1968.

Also containing a considerable body of writings of Teilhard not found in other sources:

(A) *Teilhard Album.* edited by Jeanne Mortier and Marie-Louise Aboux, London: Collins, 1966.

OTHER BOOKS OF REFERENCE

Barbour, George, *In the Field with Teilhard de Chardin.* New York: Herder and Herder, 1965.

Barth, Karl, *The Humanity of God.* London: Collins, Fontana, 1967.

Boulding, Kenneth, *The Meaning of the Twentieth Century.* London: Allen & Unwin, 1965.

Braybrooke, Neville, *Teilhard de Chardin, Pilgrim of the Future.* (Ed.) New York: Seabury Press, 1964.

Buber, Martin, *I and Thou.* tr. R.G. Smith, Edinburgh: T. & T. Clark, 1958.

Corbishley, Thomas, *The Spirituality of Teilhard de Chardin.* London: Collins Fontana, 1971.

Coulson, C.A., *Science and Christian Belief.* London: Oxford Press, 1955.

Cuenot, Claude, *Teilhard de Chardin.* tr. V. Colinare and R. Hague, London: Helicon Press and Burns & Oates, 1965.

Cuenot, Claude and Others, *Evolution, Marxism and Christianity.* Teilhard Study Library, London: Garnstone Press, 1967.

Dobzhansky, Theodosius. *The Biology of Ultimate Concern.* London: Collins Fontana, 1967.

Dobzhansky, Theodosius, *Mankind Evolving.* New Haven

and London: Yale University Press, 1967.

Eddington, Thomas, *The Nature of the Physical World.* Cambridge University Press, 1948.

Einstein, Albert, *Out of My Later Years.* London: Thames & Hudson, 1950.

Eliot, T.S., *The Confidential Clerk.* London: Faber & Faber, 1954.

Fisher, R.A., *Creative Aspects of Natural Law*, Eddington Memorial Lectures, Cambridge University Press, 1950.

Hanson, Anthony, *Teilhard Reassessed.* London: Darlan, Longman, Todd, 1970.

Harris, Errol, *The Foundations of Metaphysics in Science.* London: Allen & Unwin, 1965.

Heinsenberg, Werner, *Physics and Beyond.* London: Allen & Unwin, 1971.

Heywood, Rosalind, *The Sixth Sense.* London: Chatto & Windus, 1966.

Hick, John, *Biology and the Soul.* Cambridge University Press, 1972.

Koestler, Arthur, *The Roots of Coincidence.* London: Hutchison, 1972.

Jeans, James, *The Mysterious Universe.* Cambridge: University Press, 1930.

Lewis, C.S., *George MacDonald, An Anthology.* London: Geoffrey Bles, 1955.

Lewis, C.S., *A Grief Observed.* London: Faber, 1961.

de Lubac, Henri, *The Faith of Teilhard de Chardin.* tr. R. Hague, Burns & Oats, 1965.

May, Rollo, *Psychology and the Human Dilemma.* Princeton, Van Nostrand, 1967.

Medawar, Peter, *The Future of Man.* London: Methuen & Co. Ltd., 1960.

Oxenham, John, "The Sacrament of Fire," in *Poems of the English Race*, pg. 395, New York: Charles Scribner's Sons, 1921.

Pannenberg, Wolfhart, *Basic Questions in Theology.* tr. G.

Kehm, London: SCM Press, 1970.

Partridge, Basil, *Chaplet of Grace*. Philadelphia: Westminster, 1956.

Peacocke, Arthur, *Science and the Christian Experiment*. New York and Toronto: Oxford Press, 1971.

Polanyi, Michael, *Personal Knowledge*. London: Routledge and Kegan Paul, 1958.

Rahner, Karl, *Inspiration in the Bible*. London: Burns & Oates, 1964.

Raven, Charles, *Teilhard de Chardin, Scientist and Seer*. London: Collins, 1962.

Rideau, Emile, *Teilhard de Chardin, A Guide to His Thought*. London: Collins, 1967.

Speight, Robert, *Teilhard de Chardin, A Biography*. London: Collins, 1967.

Sproxton, Vernon, *Teilhard de Chardin*. London: SCM Press, 1971.

Terra, Helmut de, *Memories of Teilhard de Chardin*. tr. J.M. Brownjohn, London: Collins, 1964.

Thorpe, W.H., *Science, Men and Morals*. London: Methuen & Co. Ltd., 1965.

Towers, Bernard, *Teilhard de Chardin*. London: Lutterworth Press, 1966.

Towers, Bernard, *Concerning Teilhard de Chardin, Essays in Science and Religion*. London: Lutterworth Press, 1966.

White, T.H., *The Sword in the Stone*. New York: G.H. Putnam's Sons, 1939.

White, V. *God and the Unconscious*. London: Collins, Fontana, 1960.

Whitehead, A.N., *Science and the Modern World*. Cambridge: University Press, 1927.

Zaehner, R.C., *Concordant Discord*. Oxford: Clarendon Press, 1970.

ENCYCLOPEDIAS

Bone, E.L., "Teilhard de Chardin," *New Catholic Encyclopedia* (1972) 13, 177-8.

"Geology," *Encyclopedia Britanica*. (14th ed.) 10.

PERIODICALS

Dobzhansky, Theodosius, "Teilhard and Monot." *The Teilhard Review* 8 (June 1973): 36-40.

Elliott, F.G., "The World Vision of Teilhard de Chardin." *The Teilhard Review*. 1:1 (summer 66), 5-14.

Myers, Arthur J., from J.L. Kulp, *Oklahoma Geology Notes*. Oklahoma Servey, 1963.

Habgood, John, "They Changed our Thinking," I: Darwin (1809-82) *The Expository Times*. 84 (Jan. 1973): 100, 105.

Hindmarsh, W. Russel, "They Changed Out Thinking: Albert Einstein" *The Expository Times*. 84 (April 1973): 199.

Schmitz-Moorman, Karl, "Theological Methods in an Evolutionary World." *The Teilhard Review*. 9 (Oct. 1974): 66-72.

Editorial, *Reform* (November 1972).

Editorial, *Frontier*. 3, (Autumn, 1960) 167.

Needham, Joseph, "Book Review of The Phenomenon of Man" *New Statesman*.

Clark, William, "June 30th Meditation." *The Soldier's Armoury* Jan-June, 1973.

OTHER

The Proceedings of the Linnaean Society of London, 1955, Tribute to Teilhard at his death, by Habgood. 167 Pt. I. 1141-2.

BACKGROUND READING

Adair, John, E., (Unpublished B. Litt. thesis) "A Theology of Work in an Industrial Society," The Bodleian Library, Oxford.

Anderson, David, *Simone Weil.* London: SCM Press, 1967.

Barbour, Ian G. *Issues in Science and Religion.* London: SCM Press, 1966.

Bennett, John C., *Christianity and Communism Today.* New York: Grand Reflexion Books Association Press, 1948-62.

Brown, Margaret, *The Manager's Guide to the Behavioural Sciences.* London: An Industrial Society Publication, Robert Hyde House, 1969.

Cadman, W.H., *The Open Heaven*, ed. G.B. Caird, Oxford, Basil Blackwell, 1969.

Cannon, H. Graham, *The Evolution of Living Things.* Manchester: Manchester Press, 1958.

Cousins, Ewart, Ed. *Hope and the Future of Man.* London: Teilhard Center for the Future of Man, 1973.

Davidman, Joy, *Smoke on the Mountain*, New York: Hodder and Stoughton, 1963.

Dobinson, C.H., *The Use and Effects of Nuclear Energy.* London: Harrap, 1964.

Gilkie, Langdon, *Religion and the Scientific Future.* London: SCM Press, 1970.

Good, Irving, Ed. *The Scientist Speculates.* Cambridge: University Press, 1950.

Grenet, Charles, *Teilhard de Chardin.* London: Souvenir Press, 1965.

Hartshorne, Charles, *Process and Divinity.* La Salle, Ind.: Open Court Division of Carus Corp., 1964.

Hardy, Alister. *The Living Stream.* London: Collins, 1965.
The Divine Flame. London: Collins, 1966.

Hering, Jean, *Epistle to the Hebrews.* London: Epworth Press, 1970.

Jenkins, David, *What is Man?* London: SCM Press, 1970.

Johnston, George, *Phillipians, Colossians and Philemon.* The New Century Bible. London, Nelson, 1967.

Jones, Gareth, *Teilhard de Chardin, An Analysis and Assessment.* London: The Tyndale Press, 1969.

Koestler, Arthur, *The Case of the Midwife Toad.* London: Hutchinson, 1971.

Jung, C. G., *Modern Man in Search of a Soul.* London: Pagan, Paul, Trench, Truber, 1933.

Lassky, Vladamir, *The Vision of God.* London: The Faith Press, 1963.

Lewis, C. S., *The Great Divorce.* London: Geoffrey Bles, 1946.

────── *Mere Christianity.* London: Collins, Fontana, 1967.

Lifton, R. J., *Thought Reform and the Psychology of Totalism.* London: Victor Gollancz Ltd., 1961.

Lindars, Barnabas, *The Gospel of John,* The New Century Bible. London: Oliphants, 1972.

Lohse, Bernhard, *Colossians and Philemon.* Philadelphia: Fortress Press, 1968.

Lorenz, K. *King Solomon's Ring.* New York: Thomas Y. Crowell & Co., 1952.

Mascall, E. R., *The Openness of Being.* London: Darton, Longman & Todd, 1971.

Milne, E. A., *Modern Cosmology and the Christian.* Oxford: Clarendon Press, 1952.

Minear, Paul, *The Command of Christ.* Edinburgh: St. Andrew's Press, 1972.

Mooney, C. F., *Teilhard de Chardin and the Mystery of Christ.* Westminster, Md.: Christian Classics, 1965.

Mortier, J. M., Avec Teilhard de Chardin, "Vues ardentes". Paris: aux Editions du Seul, 1967.

Polanyi, Michael, *The Tacit Dimension.* London: Routledge and Kegan Paul Ltd., 1966.

Ramsay, I. J., *Religion and Science; Conflict and Synthesis* London: SPCK, 1964.

Reynolds, J. H. R., *Gospel of John*, Pulpit Commentary, London: Funk & Wagnall's 1906.

Richardson, Alan, *Genesis I - XI*. London: SCM Press Ltd., 1953.

Smith, Maynard, "Agnostic View of Evolution," in *Biology and Personality*. ed. I. J. Ramsay, Oxford: Basil Blackwell, 1965.

Steera, D. V., *Spiritual Counsels and Letters of Baron Friedrich von Hugel*. London: Darton, Longman & Todd, 1964.

Tremonta, *Pierre Teilhard de Chardin*. Baltimore: Helicon Press, 1965.

Weil, Simone, *Gravity and Grace*. London: Routledge & Kegan Paul, 1952.

Wickenham, E. C., *Hebrews,* Westminster Commentary. London: Methuen, 1910.

Wiseman, P. J., *Creation Revealed in Seven Days*. London: Marshall, Morgan and Scott, Ltd. 1957.

PERIODICALS

Ackland, R. "The Next Stop" II. *The Teilhard Review* 8 (June 1973) 40-42.

Buchan, V. "ESP's Everywhere." *Healthways* 27 (March 1973).

Dobzhanski, T. "Teilhard de Chardin and the Orientation of Evolution." *Zygon* 3 (Sept. 1968): 242-258.

Dunn, James. "The Rediscovery of the Spirit." *The Expository Times* 84: Pt. I, 7-12, Pt. II 40-44.

Goldsmith, E. "Blueprint for Survival." *The Teilhard Review* 7 (June 1973): 3-4.

Hick, John. "The Christian View of Other Faiths." *The Expository Times* 84 (Nov. 1972) : 36-39.

Jones, Bernard. "They Changed our Thinking: Sigmund Freud (1859-1939) Captivator and Liberator." *The Expository Times* 84 (March 1973): 168-171.

Kee, Alistair. "Learning from Other Faiths: Neo-Marxism."

The Expository Times 4:19.

North, R. "Teilhard de Chardin and the Problem of Creation." *Theological Studies* 24: 577-601.

Scott, W. T. "A Bridge from Science to Religion Based on Polanyi's Theory of Knowledge." *Zygon* 5 (March, 1970): 41-61.

Thomas, I. ed. "Word for the World." *Bible Reading Fellowship 1970.*

Thorpe, W. "Reductionism: Its Powers and Limits." *The Teilhard Review* 8 (June 1973): 34-36.